Approaching (Almost) Any Machine Learning Problem

It would not have been possible for me to write this book without the support of my family and friends. I would also like to thank the reviewers who selflessly devoted their time in reviewing this book (names in alphabetical order).

Aakash Nain
Aditya Soni
Andreas Müller
Andrey Lukyanenko
Ayon Roy
Bojan Tunguz
Gilberto Titericz Jr.
Konrad Banachewicz
Luca Massaron
Nabajeet Barman
Parul Pandey
Ram Ramrakhya
Sanyam Bhutani
Sudalai Rajkumar
Tanishq Abraham
Walter Reade
Yuval Reina

I hope I did not miss anyone.

Before you start, there are a few things that you must be aware of while going through this book.

This is **not** a traditional book.

The book expects you to have basic knowledge of machine learning and deep learning.

Important terms are **bold**.

Variable names and function/class names are *italic*.

All the code is between these two lines

Most of the times, the output is provided right after the code blocks.

Figures are locally defined. For example, figure 1 is the first figure

Code is very important in this book and there is a lot of it. You must go through the code carefully and implement it on your own if you want to understand what's going on.

Comments in Python begin with a hash (#). All the code in this book is explained line-by-line only using comments. Thus, these comments must not be ignored.

Bash commands start with $ or ⟩.

If you find a pirated copy of this book (print or e-book or pdf), contact me directly with the details so that I can take necessary actions.

If you didn't code, you didn't learn.

Table of Contents

Setting up your working environment 5

Supervised vs unsupervised learning 7

Cross-validation 14

Evaluation metrics 30

Arranging machine learning projects 73

Approaching categorical variables 85

Feature engineering 142

Feature selection 155

Hyperparameter optimization 167

Approaching image classification & segmentation 185

Approaching text classification/regression 225

Approaching ensembling and stacking 272

Approaching reproducible code & model serving 283

Setting up your working environment

Before we begin with coding, it's essential to get everything set-up on your machine. Throughout this book, we will be using **Ubuntu 18.04** and **Python 3.7.6**. If you are a Windows user, you can install Ubuntu in multiple ways. On a virtual machine, for example, Virtual Box which is provided by Oracle and is free software. Alongside Windows as a dual boot system. I prefer dual boot as it is native. If you are not an Ubuntu user, you might face problems with some of the bash scripts in this book. To circumvent that you can install Ubuntu in a VM or go for Linux shell on Windows.

Setting up Python on any machine is quite easy with Anaconda. I particularly like **Miniconda**, which is a minimal installer for conda. It is available for Linux, OSX and Windows. Since Python 2 support ended at the end of 2019, we will be using the Python 3 distribution. You should keep in mind that miniconda does not come with all the packages as regular Anaconda. We will, thus, be installing packages as we go. Installing miniconda is quite easy.

The first thing that you need to do is download **Miniconda3** to your system.

```
$ cd ~/Downloads
$ wget https://repo.anaconda.com/miniconda/...
```

where the URL after wget command is the URL from miniconda3 webpage. For 64-bit Linux systems, the URL at the time of writing this book was:

```
https://repo.anaconda.com/miniconda/Miniconda3-latest-Linux-x86_64.sh
```

Once you have downloaded miniconda3, you can run the following command:

```
$ sh Miniconda3-latest-Linux-x86_64.sh
```

Next, please read and follow the instructions on your screen. If you installed everything correctly, you should be able to start the conda environment by typing *conda init* the terminal. We will create a conda environment that we will be using throughout this book. To create a conda environment, you can type:

```
$ conda create -n environment_name python=3.7.6
```

This command will create a conda environment named *environment_name* which can be activated using:

```
$ conda activate environment_name
```

And we are all set-up with the environment. Now it's time to install some packages that we would be using. A package can be installed in two different ways when you are in a conda environment. You can either install the package from conda repository or the official PyPi repository.

```
$ conda/pip install package_name
```

Note: It might be possible that some packages are not available in the conda repo. Thus, installing using pip would be the most preferred way in this book. I have already created a list of packages used while writing this book which is saved in the *environment.yml*. You can find it in extra material available in my GitHub repository. You can create the environment using the following command:

```
$ conda env create -f environment.yml
```

This command will create an environment called *ml*. To activate this environment and start using it, you should run:

```
$ conda activate ml
```

And we are all set and ready to do some applied machine learning!

Always remember to be in the "ml" environment when coding along with this book.

Let's start with our real first chapter now.

Supervised vs unsupervised learning

When dealing with machine learning problems, there are generally two types of data (and machine learning models):

- Supervised data: always has one or multiple targets associated with it.
- Unsupervised data: does not have any target variable.

A supervised problem is considerably easier to tackle than an unsupervised one. A problem in which we are required to predict a value is known as a **supervised problem**. For example, if the problem is to predict house prices given historical house prices, with features like presence of a hospital, school or supermarket, distance to nearest public transport, etc. is a supervised problem. Similarly, when we are provided with images of cats and dogs, and we know beforehand which ones are cats and which ones are dogs, and if the task is to create a model which predicts whether a provided image is of a cat or a dog, the problem is considered to be supervised.

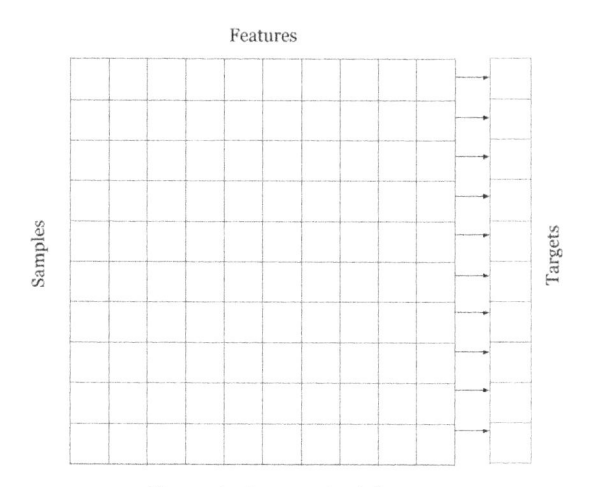

Figure 1: A supervised dataset.

As we see in figure 1, every row of the data is associated with a target or label. The columns are different features and rows represent different data points which are usually called samples. The example shows ten samples with ten features and a target variable which can be either a number or a category. If the target is categorical, the problem becomes a classification problem. And if the target is a real number, the problem is defined as a regression problem. Thus, supervised problems can be divided into two sub-classes:

- **Classification**: predicting a category, e.g. dog or cat.
- **Regression**: predicting a value, e.g. house prices.

It must be noted that sometimes we might use regression in a classification setting depending on the metric used for evaluation. But we will come to that later.

Another type of machine learning problem is the **unsupervised** type. Unsupervised datasets do not have a target associated with them and in general, are more challenging to deal with when compared to supervised problems.

Let's say you work in a financial firm which deals with credit card transactions. There is a lot of data that comes in every second. The only problem is that it is difficult to find humans who will mark each and every transaction either as a valid or genuine transaction or a fraud. When we do not have any information about a transaction being fraud or genuine, the problem becomes an unsupervised problem. To tackle these kinds of problems we have to think about how many clusters can data be divided into. **Clustering** is one of the approaches that you can use for problems like this, but it must be noted that there are several other approaches available that can be applied to unsupervised problems. For a fraud detection problem, we can say that data can be divided into two classes (fraud or genuine).

When we know the number of clusters, we can use a clustering algorithm for unsupervised problems. In figure 2, the data is assumed to have two classes, dark colour represents fraud, and light colour represents genuine transactions. These classes, however, are not known to us before the clustering approach. After a clustering algorithm is applied, we should be able to distinguish between the two assumed targets. To make sense of unsupervised problems, we can also use numerous decomposition techniques such as **Principal Component Analysis (PCA), t-distributed Stochastic Neighbour Embedding (t-SNE)** etc.

Supervised problems are easier to tackle in the sense that they can be evaluated easily. We will read more about evaluation techniques in the following chapters. However, it is challenging to assess the results of unsupervised algorithms and a lot of human interference or heuristics are required. In this book, we will majorly be focusing on supervised data and models, but it does not mean that we will be ignoring the unsupervised data problems.

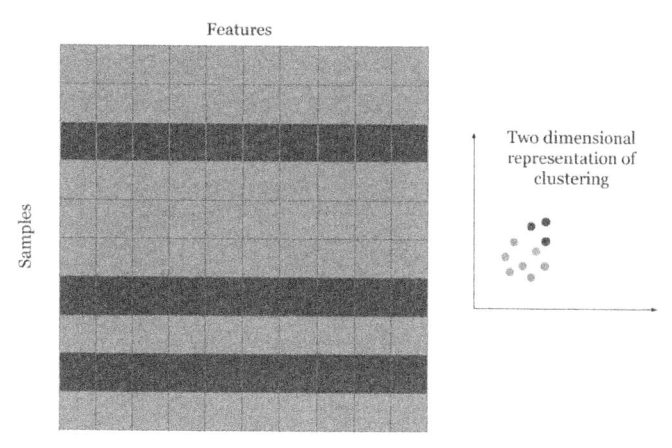

Figure 2: An unsupervised dataset.

Most of the time, when people start with data science or machine learning, they begin with very well-known datasets, for example, Titanic dataset, or Iris dataset which are supervised problems. In the Titanic dataset, you have to predict the survival of people aboard Titanic based on factors like their ticket class, gender, age, etc. Similarly, in the iris dataset, you have to predict the species of flower based on factors like sepal width, petal length, sepal length and petal width.

Unsupervised datasets may include datasets for customer segmentation. For example, you have data for the customers visiting your e-commerce website or the data for customers visiting a store or a mall, and you would like to segment them or cluster them in different categories. Another example of unsupervised datasets may include things like credit card fraud detection or just clustering several images.

Most of the time, it's also possible to convert a supervised dataset to unsupervised to see how they look like when plotted.

For example, let's take a look at the dataset in figure 3. Figure 3 shows **MNIST** dataset which is a very popular dataset of handwritten digits, and it is a supervised problem in which you are given the images of the numbers and the correct label associated with them. You have to build a model that can identify which digit is it when provided only with the image.

This dataset can easily be converted to an unsupervised setting for basic visualization.

Figure 3: MNIST dataset[1]

If we do a t-Distributed Stochastic Neighbour Embedding (t-SNE) decomposition of this dataset, we can see that we can separate the images to some extent just by doing with two components on the image pixels. This is shown in figure 4.

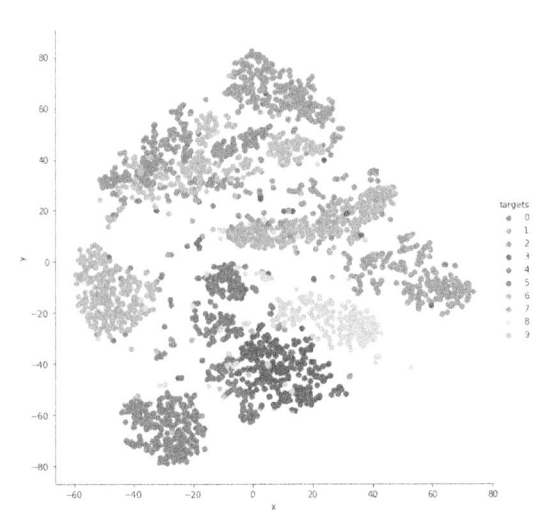

Figure 4: t-SNE visualization of the MNIST dataset. 3000 images were used.

Let's take a look at how this was done. First and foremost is importing all the required libraries.

---

[1] Image source: By Josef Steppan - Own work, CC BY-SA 4.0, https://commons.wikimedia.org/w/index.php?curid=64810040

```
import matplotlib.pyplot as plt
import numpy as np
import pandas as pd
import seaborn as sns

from sklearn import datasets
from sklearn import manifold

%matplotlib inline
```

We use matplotlib and seaborn for plotting, numpy to handle the numerical arrays, pandas to create dataframes from the numerical arrays and scikit-learn (sklearn) to get the data and perform t-SNE.

After the imports, we need to either download the data and read it separately or use sklearn's built-in function that provides us with the MNIST dataset.

```
data = datasets.fetch_openml(
            'mnist_784',
            version=1,
            return_X_y=True
)
pixel_values, targets = data
targets = targets.astype(int)
```

In this part of the code, we have fetched the data using sklearn datasets, and we have an array of pixel values and another array of targets. Since the targets are of string type, we convert them to integers.

pixel_values is a 2-dimensional array of shape 70000x784. There are 70000 different images, each of size 28x28 pixels. Flattening 28x28 gives 784 data points.

We can visualize the samples in this dataset by reshaping them to their original shape and then plotting them using matplotlib.

```
single_image = pixel_values[1, :].reshape(28, 28)

plt.imshow(single_image, cmap='gray')
```

This code will plot an image like the following:

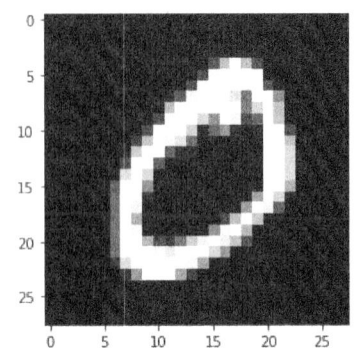

Figure 5: Plotting a single image from MNIST dataset.

The most important step comes after we have grabbed the data.

```
tsne = manifold.TSNE(n_components=2, random_state=42)

transformed_data = tsne.fit_transform(pixel_values[:3000, :])
```

This step creates the t-SNE transformation of the data. We use only two components as we can visualize them well in a two-dimensional setting. The *transformed_data*, in this case, is an array of shape 3000x2 (3000 rows and 2 columns). A data like this can be converted to a pandas dataframe by calling *pd.DataFrame* on the array.

```
tsne_df = pd.DataFrame(
    np.column_stack((transformed_data, targets[:3000])),
    columns=["x", "y", "targets"]
)

tsne_df.loc[:, "targets"] = tsne_df.targets.astype(int)
```

Here we are creating a pandas dataframe from a numpy array. There are three columns: *x*, *y* and *targets*. x and y are the two components from t-SNE decomposition and targets is the actual number. This gives us a dataframe which looks like the one shown in figure 6.

	x	y	targets
0	-5.281551	-28.952768	5
1	-26.105896	-68.069321	0
2	-42.503582	35.580391	4
3	38.893967	26.663395	1
4	-14.770573	35.433247	9
5	63.997231	-1.102326	2
6	-6.551701	9.943600	1
7	20.086042	-44.003902	3
8	-0.806248	12.682267	1
9	-1.481194	45.506077	4

Figure 6: First 10 rows of pandas dataframe with t-SNE components and targets.

And finally, we can plot it using seaborn and matplotlib.

```
grid = sns.FacetGrid(tsne_df, hue="targets", size=8)
grid.map(plt.scatter, "x", "y").add_legend()
```

This is one way of visualizing unsupervised datasets. We can also do **k-means clustering** on the same dataset and see how it performs in an unsupervised setting. One question that arises all the time is how to find the optimal number of clusters in k-means clustering. Well, there is no right answer. You have to find the number by cross-validation. Cross-validation will be discussed later in this book. Please note that the above code was run in a jupyter notebook.

In this book, we will use jupyter for simple things like the example above and for plotting. For most of the stuff in this book, we will be using python scripts. You can choose what you want to use since the results are going to be the same.

MNIST is a supervised classification problem, and we converted it to an unsupervised problem only to check if it gives any kind of good results and it is apparent that we do get good results with decomposition with t-SNE. The results would be even better if we use classification algorithms. What are they and how to use them? Let's look at them in the next chapters.

Cross-validation

We did not build any models in the previous chapter. The reason for that is simple. Before creating any kind of machine learning model, we must know what cross-validation is and how to choose the best cross-validation depending on your datasets.

So, **what is cross-validation**, and why should we care about it?

We can find multiple definitions as to what cross-validation is. Mine is a one-liner: *cross-validation is a step in the process of building a machine learning model which helps us ensure that our models fit the data accurately and also ensures that we do not overfit*. But this leads to another term: **overfitting**.

To explain overfitting, I think it's best if we look at a dataset. There is a **red wine-quality dataset**[2] which is quite famous. This dataset has 11 different attributes that decide the quality of red wine.

These attributes include:
- fixed acidity
- volatile acidity
- citric acid
- residual sugar
- chlorides
- free sulfur dioxide
- total sulfur dioxide
- density
- pH
- sulphates
- alcohol

Based on these different attributes, we are required to predict the quality of red wine which is a value between 0 and 10.

---

[2] P. Cortez, A. Cerdeira, F. Almeida, T. Matos and J. Reis; Modeling wine preferences by data mining from physicochemical properties. In Decision Support Systems, Elsevier, 47(4):547-553, 2009.

Let's see how this data looks like.

```
import pandas as pd
df = pd.read_csv("winequality-red.csv")
```

This dataset looks something like this:

fixed acidity	volatile acidity	citric acid	residual sugar	chlorides	free sulfur dioxide	total sulfur dioxide	density	pH	sulphates	alcohol	quality
6.8	0.67	0.00	1.9	0.080	22.0	39.0	0.99701	3.40	0.74	9.7	5
7.2	0.63	0.00	1.9	0.097	14.0	38.0	0.99675	3.37	0.58	9.0	6
8.0	0.31	0.45	2.1	0.216	5.0	16.0	0.99358	3.15	0.81	12.5	7
7.9	0.72	0.17	2.6	0.096	20.0	38.0	0.99780	3.40	0.53	9.5	5
7.6	0.52	0.12	3.0	0.067	12.0	53.0	0.99710	3.36	0.57	9.1	5
...	...	...	...	...	...	...	...	...	...	...	...
10.4	0.41	0.55	3.2	0.076	22.0	54.0	0.99960	3.15	0.89	9.9	6
9.2	0.59	0.24	3.3	0.101	20.0	47.0	0.99880	3.26	0.67	9.6	5
10.2	0.67	0.39	1.9	0.054	6.0	17.0	0.99760	3.17	0.47	10.0	5
8.1	0.78	0.10	3.3	0.090	4.0	13.0	0.99855	3.36	0.49	9.5	5
7.8	0.52	0.25	1.9	0.081	14.0	38.0	0.99840	3.43	0.65	9.0	6

Figure 1: A snapshot of the red wine quality dataset.

We can treat this problem either as a classification problem or as a regression problem since wine quality is nothing but a real number between 0 and 10. For simplicity, let's choose classification. This dataset, however, consists of only six types of quality values. We will thus map all quality values from 0 to 5.

```
# a mapping dictionary that maps the quality values from 0 to 5
quality_mapping = {
    3: 0,
    4: 1,
    5: 2,
    6: 3,
    7: 4,
    8: 5
}

# you can use the map function of pandas with
# any dictionary to convert the values in a given
# column to values in the dictionary
df.loc[:, "quality"] = df.quality.map(quality_mapping)
```

When we look at this data and consider it a classification problem, a lot of algorithms come to our mind that we can apply to it, probably, we can use neural networks. But it would be a bit of a stretch if we dive into neural networks from the beginning. So, let's start with something simple that we can visualize too: **decision trees**.

Before we begin to understand what overfitting is, let's divide the data into two parts. This dataset has 1599 samples. We keep 1000 samples for training and 599 as a separate set.

Splitting can be done easily by the following chunk of code:

```
# use sample with frac=1 to shuffle the dataframe
# we reset the indices since they change after
# shuffling the dataframe
df = df.sample(frac=1).reset_index(drop=True)

# top 1000 rows are selected
# for training
df_train = df.head(1000)

# bottom 599 values are selected
# for testing/validation
df_test = df.tail(599)
```

We will now train a decision tree model on the training set. For the decision tree model, I am going to use scikit-learn.

```
# import from scikit-learn
from sklearn import tree
from sklearn import metrics

# initialize decision tree classifier class
# with a max_depth of 3
clf = tree.DecisionTreeClassifier(max_depth=3)

# choose the columns you want to train on
# these are the features for the model
cols = ['fixed acidity',
        'volatile acidity',
        'citric acid',
```

```
            'residual sugar',
            'chlorides',
            'free sulfur dioxide',
            'total sulfur dioxide',
            'density',
            'pH',
            'sulphates',
            'alcohol']

# train the model on the provided features
# and mapped quality from before
clf.fit(df_train[cols], df_train.quality)
```

Note that I have used a *max_depth* of 3 for the decision tree classifier. I have left all other parameters of this model to its default value.

Now, we test the accuracy of this model on the training set and the test set:

```
# generate predictions on the training set
train_predictions = clf.predict(df_train[cols])

# generate predictions on the test set
test_predictions = clf.predict(df_test[cols])

# calculate the accuracy of predictions on
# training data set
train_accuracy = metrics.accuracy_score(
    df_train.quality, train_predictions
)

# calculate the accuracy of predictions on
# test data set
test_accuracy = metrics.accuracy_score(
    df_test.quality, test_predictions
)
```

The training and test accuracies are found to be 58.9% and 54.25%. Now we increase the *max_depth* to 7 and repeat the process. This gives training accuracy of 76.6% and test accuracy of 57.3%. Here, we have used accuracy, mainly because it is the most straightforward metric. It might not be the best metric for this problem. What about we calculate these accuracies for different values of *max_depth* and make a plot?

```python
# NOTE: this code is written in a jupyter notebook

# import scikit-learn tree and metrics
from sklearn import tree
from sklearn import metrics

# import matplotlib and seaborn
# for plotting
import matplotlib
import matplotlib.pyplot as plt
import seaborn as sns

# this is our global size of label text
# on the plots
matplotlib.rc('xtick', labelsize=20)
matplotlib.rc('ytick', labelsize=20)

# This line ensures that the plot is displayed
# inside the notebook
%matplotlib inline

# initialize lists to store accuracies
# for training and test data
# we start with 50% accuracy
train_accuracies = [0.5]
test_accuracies = [0.5]

# iterate over a few depth values
for depth in range(1, 25):
    # init the model
    clf = tree.DecisionTreeClassifier(max_depth=depth)

    # columns/features for training
    # note that, this can be done outside
    # the loop
    cols = [
        'fixed acidity',
        'volatile acidity',
        'citric acid',
        'residual sugar',
        'chlorides',
        'free sulfur dioxide',
        'total sulfur dioxide',
        'density',
        'pH',
        'sulphates',
```

```
        'alcohol'
    ]

    # fit the model on given features
    clf.fit(df_train[cols], df_train.quality)

    # create training & test predictions
    train_predictions = clf.predict(df_train[cols])
    test_predictions = clf.predict(df_test[cols])

    # calculate training & test accuracies
    train_accuracy = metrics.accuracy_score(
        df_train.quality, train_predictions
    )
    test_accuracy = metrics.accuracy_score(
        df_test.quality, test_predictions
    )

    # append accuracies
    train_accuracies.append(train_accuracy)
    test_accuracies.append(test_accuracy)

# create two plots using matplotlib
# and seaborn
plt.figure(figsize=(10, 5))
sns.set_style("whitegrid")
plt.plot(train_accuracies, label="train accuracy")
plt.plot(test_accuracies, label="test accuracy")
plt.legend(loc="upper left", prop={'size': 15})
plt.xticks(range(0, 26, 5))
plt.xlabel("max_depth", size=20)
plt.ylabel("accuracy", size=20)
plt.show()
```

This generates a plot, as shown in figure 2.

We see that the best score for test data is obtained when *max_depth* has a value of 14. As we keep increasing the value of this parameter, test accuracy remains the same or gets worse, but the training accuracy keeps increasing. It means that our simple decision tree model keeps learning about the training data better and better with an increase in *max_depth,* but the performance on test data does not improve at all.

This is called overfitting.

The model fits perfectly on the training set and performs poorly when it comes to the test set. This means that the model will learn the training data well but will not generalize on unseen samples. In the dataset above, one can build a model with very high *max_depth* which will have outstanding results on training data, but that kind of model is not useful as it will not provide a similar result on the real-world samples or live data.

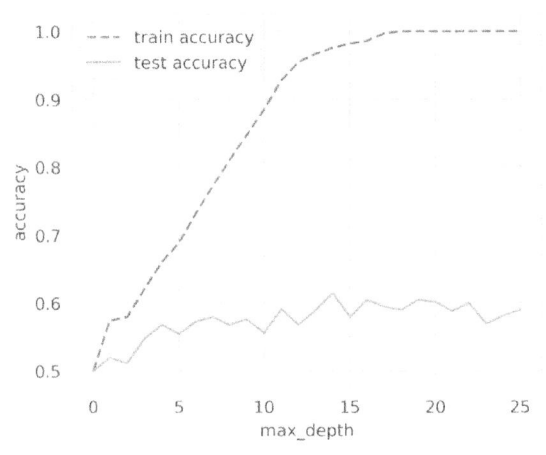

Figure 2: Training and test accuracies for different values of max_depth.

One might argue that this approach isn't overfitting as the accuracy of the test set more or less remains the same. *Another definition of overfitting would be when the test loss increases as we keep improving training loss.* This is very common when it comes to neural networks.

Whenever we train a neural network, we must monitor loss during the training time for both training and test set. If we have a very large network for a dataset which is quite small (i.e. very less number of samples), we will observe that the loss for both training and test set will decrease as we keep training. However, at some point, test loss will reach its minima, and after that, it will start increasing even though training loss decreases further. We must stop training where the validation loss reaches its minimum value.

This is the most common explanation of overfitting.

Occam's razor in simple words states that one should not try to complicate things that can be solved in a much simpler manner. In other words, the simplest solutions are the most generalizable solutions. In general, whenever your model does not obey Occam's razor, it is *probably* overfitting.

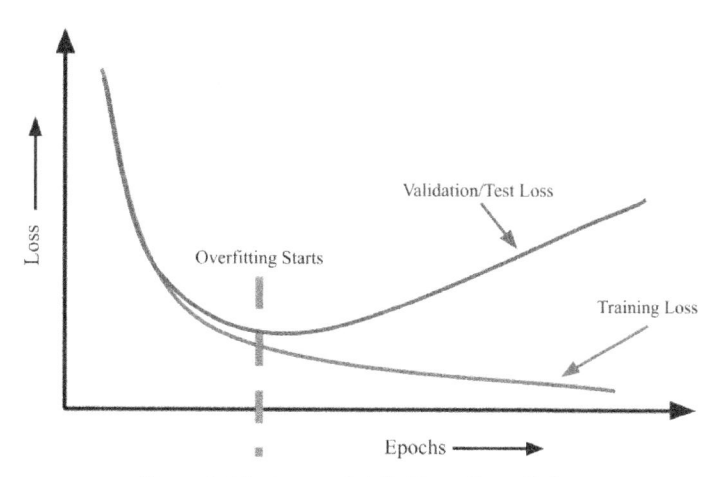

Figure 3: Most general definition of overfitting.

Now we can go back to cross-validation.

While explaining about overfitting, I decided to divide the data into two parts. I trained the model on one part and checked its performance on the other part. Well, this is also a kind of cross-validation commonly known as a **hold-out set**. We use this kind of (cross-) validation when we have a large amount of data and model inference is a time-consuming process.

There are many different ways one can do cross-validation, and it is the most critical step when it comes to building a good machine learning model which is generalizable when it comes to unseen data. **Choosing the right cross-validation** depends on the dataset you are dealing with, and one's choice of cross-validation on one dataset may or may not apply to other datasets. However, there are a few types of cross-validation techniques which are the most popular and widely used.

These include:

- k-fold cross-validation
- stratified k-fold cross-validation

- hold-out based validation
- leave-one-out cross-validation
- group k-fold cross-validation

Cross-validation is dividing training data into a few parts. We train the model on some of these parts and test on the remaining parts. Take a look at figure 4.

Figure 4: Splitting a dataset into training and validation sets

Figure 4 & 5 say that when you get a dataset to build machine learning models, you separate them into **two different sets: training and validation**. Many people also split it into a third set and call it a **test set**. We will, however, be using only two sets. As you can see, we divide the samples and the targets associated with them. We can divide the data into k different sets which are exclusive of each other. This is known as **k-fold cross-validation**.

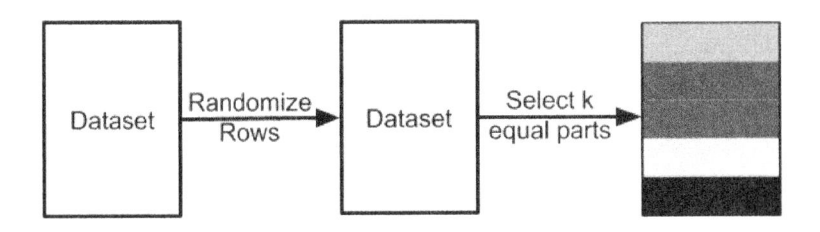

Figure 5: K-fold cross-validation

We can split any data into k-equal parts using *KFold* from scikit-learn. Each sample is assigned a value from 0 to k-1 when using k-fold cross validation.

```python
# import pandas and model_selection module of scikit-learn
import pandas as pd
from sklearn import model_selection


if __name__ == "__main__":
    # Training data is in a CSV file called train.csv
    df = pd.read_csv("train.csv")

    # we create a new column called kfold and fill it with -1
    df["kfold"] = -1

    # the next step is to randomize the rows of the data
    df = df.sample(frac=1).reset_index(drop=True)

    # initiate the kfold class from model_selection module
    kf = model_selection.KFold(n_splits=5)

    # fill the new kfold column
    for fold, (trn_, val_) in enumerate(kf.split(X=df)):
        df.loc[val_, 'kfold'] = fold

    # save the new csv with kfold column
    df.to_csv("train_folds.csv", index=False)
```

You can use this process with almost all kinds of datasets. For example, when you have images, you can create a CSV with image id, image location and image label and use the process above.

The next important type of cross-validation is **stratified k-fold**. If you have a skewed dataset for binary classification with 90% positive samples and only 10% negative samples, you don't want to use random k-fold cross-validation. Using simple k-fold cross-validation for a dataset like this can result in folds with all negative samples. In these cases, we prefer using stratified k-fold cross-validation. Stratified k-fold cross-validation keeps the ratio of labels in each fold constant. So, in each fold, you will have the same 90% positive and 10% negative samples. Thus, whatever metric you choose to evaluate, it will give similar results across all folds.

It's easy to modify the code for creating k-fold cross-validation to create stratified k-folds. We are only changing from *model_selection.KFold* to *model_selection.StratifiedKFold* and in the *kf.split(...)* function, we specify the target column on which we want to stratify. We assume that our CSV dataset has a column called "target" and it is a classification problem!

```python
# import pandas and model_selection module of scikit-learn
import pandas as pd
from sklearn import model_selection

if __name__ == "__main__":
    # Training data is in a csv file called train.csv
    df = pd.read_csv("train.csv")

    # we create a new column called kfold and fill it with -1
    df["kfold"] = -1

    # the next step is to randomize the rows of the data
    df = df.sample(frac=1).reset_index(drop=True)

    # fetch targets
    y = df.target.values

    # initiate the kfold class from model_selection module
    kf = model_selection.StratifiedKFold(n_splits=5)

    # fill the new kfold column
    for f, (t_, v_) in enumerate(kf.split(X=df, y=y)):
        df.loc[v_, 'kfold'] = f

    # save the new csv with kfold column
    df.to_csv("train_folds.csv", index=False)
```

For the wine dataset, let's look at the distribution of labels.

```python
b = sns.countplot(x='quality', data=df)
b.set_xlabel("quality", fontsize=20)
b.set_ylabel("count", fontsize=20)
```

Note that we continue on the code above. So, we have converted the target values. Looking at figure 6 we can say that the quality is very much skewed. Some classes have a lot of samples, and some don't have that many. If we do a simple k-fold, we won't have an equal distribution of targets in every fold. Thus, we choose stratified k-fold in this case.

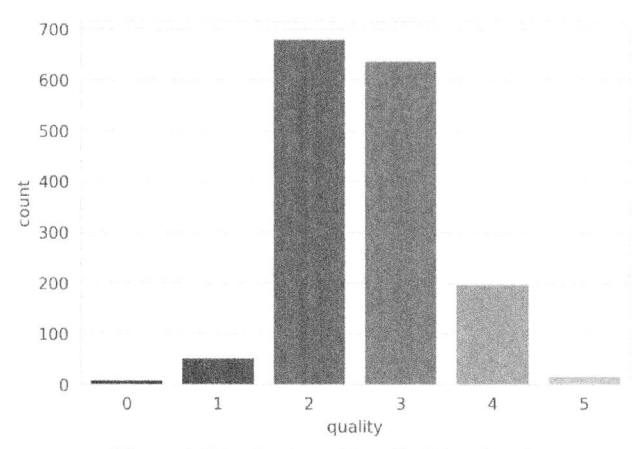

Figure 6: Distribution of "quality" in wine dataset

The rule is simple. If it's a *standard* classification problem, choose stratified k-fold blindly.

But what should we do if we have a large amount of data? Suppose we have 1 million samples. A 5 fold cross-validation would mean training on 800k samples and validating on 200k. Depending on which algorithm we choose, training and even validation can be very expensive for a dataset which is of this size. In these cases, we can opt for a **hold-out based validation**.

The process for creating the hold-out remains the same as stratified k-fold. For a dataset which has 1 million samples, we can create ten folds instead of 5 and keep one of those folds as hold-out. This means we will have 100k samples in the hold-out, and we will always calculate loss, accuracy and other metrics on this set and train on 900k samples.

Hold-out is also used very frequently with **time-series data**. Let's assume the problem we are provided with is predicting sales of a store for 2020, and you are provided all the data from 2015-2019. In this case, you can select all the data for 2019 as a hold-out and train your model on all the data from 2015 to 2018.

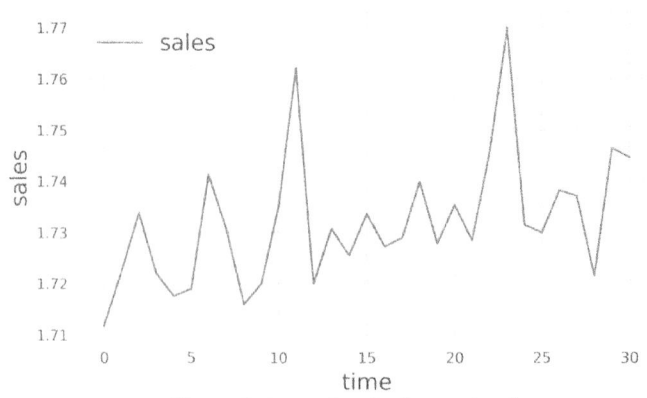

Figure 7: Example of a time-series data

In the example presented in figure 7, let's say our job is to predict the sales from time step 31 to 40. We can then keep 21 to 30 as hold-out and train our model from step 0 to step 20. You should note that when you are predicting from 31 to 40, you should include the data from 21 to 30 in your model; otherwise, performance will be sub-par.

In many cases, we have to deal with small datasets and creating big validation sets means losing a lot of data for the model to learn. In those cases, we can opt for a type of k-fold cross-validation where k=N, where N is the number of samples in the dataset. This means that in all folds of training, we will be training on all data samples except 1. The number of folds for this type of cross-validation is the same as the number of samples that we have in the dataset.

One should note that this type of cross-validation can be costly in terms of the time it takes if the model is not fast enough, but since it's only preferable to use this cross-validation for small datasets, it doesn't matter much.

Now we can move to regression. The good thing about regression problems is that we can use all the cross-validation techniques mentioned above for regression problems except for stratified k-fold. That is we cannot use stratified k-fold directly, but there are ways to change the problem a bit so that we can use stratified k-fold for regression problems. Mostly, simple k-fold cross-validation works for any regression problem. However, if you see that the distribution of targets is not consistent, you can use stratified k-fold.

To use **stratified k-fold for a regression problem**, we have first to divide the target into bins, and then we can use stratified k-fold in the same way as for classification problems. There are several choices for selecting the appropriate number of bins. If you have a lot of samples(> 10k, > 100k), then you don't need to care about the number of bins. Just divide the data into 10 or 20 bins. If you do not have a lot of samples, you can use a simple rule like **Sturge's Rule** to calculate the appropriate number of bins.

Sturge's rule:
$$Number\ of\ Bins = 1 + log_2(N)$$

Where N is the number of samples you have in your dataset. This function is plotted in Figure 8.

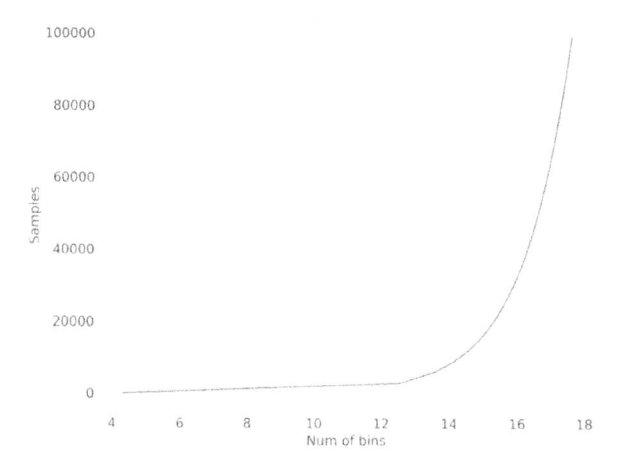

Figure 8: Plotting samples vs the number of bins by Sturge's Rule

Let's make a sample regression dataset and try to apply stratified k-fold as shown in the following python snippet.

```
# stratified-kfold for regression
import numpy as np
import pandas as pd

from sklearn import datasets
from sklearn import model_selection
```

```python
def create_folds(data):
    # we create a new column called kfold and fill it with -1
    data["kfold"] = -1

    # the next step is to randomize the rows of the data
    data = data.sample(frac=1).reset_index(drop=True)

    # calculate the number of bins by Sturge's rule
    # I take the floor of the value, you can also
    # just round it
    num_bins = int(np.floor(1 + np.log2(len(data))))

    # bin targets
    data.loc[:, "bins"] = pd.cut(
        data["target"], bins=num_bins, labels=False
    )

    # initiate the kfold class from model_selection module
    kf = model_selection.StratifiedKFold(n_splits=5)

    # fill the new kfold column
    # note that, instead of targets, we use bins!
    for f, (t_, v_) in enumerate(kf.split(X=data, y=data.bins.values)):
        data.loc[v_, 'kfold'] = f

    # drop the bins column
    data = data.drop("bins", axis=1)
    # return dataframe with folds
    return data

if __name__ == "__main__":
    # we create a sample dataset with 15000 samples
    # and 100 features and 1 target
    X, y = datasets.make_regression(
        n_samples=15000, n_features=100, n_targets=1
    )

    # create a dataframe out of our numpy arrays
    df = pd.DataFrame(
        X,
        columns=[f"f_{i}" for i in range(X.shape[1])]
    )
    df.loc[:, "target"] = y

    # create folds
    df = create_folds(df)
```

Cross-validation is the first and most essential step when it comes to building machine learning models. If you want to do feature engineering, split your data first. If you're going to build models, split your data first. If you have *a good cross-validation scheme in which validation data is representative of training and real-world data*, you will be able to build a good machine learning model which is highly generalizable.

The types of cross-validation presented in this chapter can be applied to almost any machine learning problem. Still, you must keep in mind that cross-validation also depends a lot on the data and you might need to adopt new forms of cross-validation depending on your problem and data.

For example, let's say we have a problem in which we would like to build a model to detect skin cancer from skin images of patients. Our task is to build a binary classifier which takes an input image and predicts the probability for it being benign or malignant.

In these kinds of datasets, you might have multiple images for the same patient in the training dataset. So, to build a good cross-validation system here, you must have stratified k-folds, but you must also make sure that patients in training data do not appear in validation data. Fortunately, scikit-learn offers a type of cross-validation known as *GroupKFold*. Here the patients can be considered as groups. But unfortunately, there is no way to combine *GroupKFold* with *StratifiedKFold* in scikit-learn. So you need to do that yourself. I'll leave it as an exercise for the reader.

Evaluation metrics

When it comes to machine learning problems, you will encounter a lot of different types of metrics in the real world. Sometimes, people even end up creating metrics that suit the business problem. It's out of the scope of this book to introduce and explain each and every type of metric. Instead, we will see some of the most common metrics that you can use when starting with your very first few projects.

At the start of the book, we introduced supervised and unsupervised learning. Although there are some kinds of metrics that you can use for unsupervised learning, we will only focus on supervised. The reason for this is because supervised problems are in abundance compared to un-supervised, and evaluation of unsupervised methods is quite subjective.

If we talk about classification problems, the most common metrics used are:
- Accuracy
- Precision (P)
- Recall (R)
- F1 score (F1)
- Area under the ROC (Receiver Operating Characteristic) curve or simply AUC (AUC)
- Log loss
- Precision at k (P@k)
- Average precision at k (AP@k)
- Mean average precision at k (MAP@k)

When it comes to regression, the most commonly used evaluation metrics are:
- Mean absolute error (MAE)
- Mean squared error (MSE)
- Root mean squared error (RMSE)
- Root mean squared logarithmic error (RMSLE)
- Mean percentage error (MPE)
- Mean absolute percentage error (MAPE)
- R^2

Knowing about how the aforementioned metrics work is not the only thing we have to understand. We must also know when to use which metrics, and that depends on what kind of data and targets you have. I think it's more about the targets and less about the data.

To learn more about these metrics, let's start with a simple problem. Suppose we have a **binary classification problem**, i.e. a problem in which there are only two targets. Let's suppose it's a problem of classifying chest x-ray images. There are chest x-ray images with no problem, and some of the chest x-ray images have collapsed lung which is also known as pneumothorax. So, our task is to build a classifier that given a chest x-ray image can detect if it has pneumothorax.

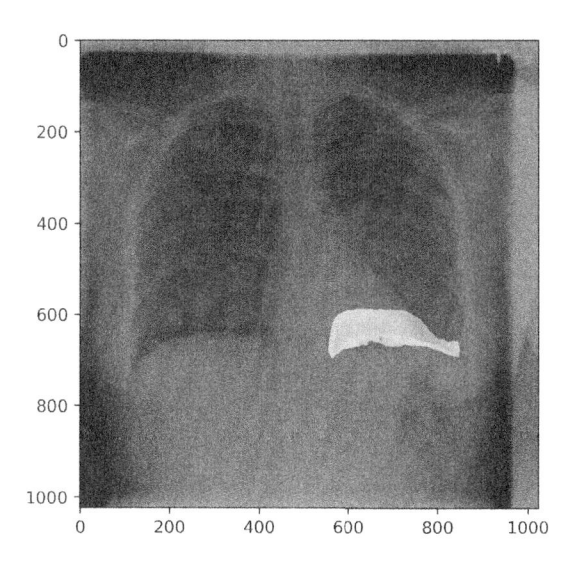

Figure 1: A lung image showing pneumothorax. Image is taken from SIIM-ACR Pneumothorax Segmentation Competition[3]

We also assume that we have an equal number of pneumothorax and non-pneumothorax chest x-ray images; let's say 100 each. Thus, we have 100 positive samples and 100 negative samples with a total of 200 images.

The first step is to divide the data described above into two equal sets of 100 images each, i.e. training and validation set. In both the sets, we have 50 positive and 50 negative samples.

---

[3] https://www.kaggle.com/c/siim-acr-pneumothorax-segmentation

When we have an equal number of positive and negative samples in a binary classification metric, we generally use accuracy, precision, recall and f1.

Accuracy: It is one of the most straightforward metrics used in machine learning. It defines how accurate your model is. For the problem described above, if you build a model that classifies 90 images accurately, your accuracy is 90% or 0.90. If only 83 images are classified correctly, the accuracy of your model is 83% or 0.83. Simple.

Python code for calculating accuracy is also quite simple.

```python
def accuracy(y_true, y_pred):
    """
    Function to calculate accuracy
    :param y_true: list of true values
    :param y_pred: list of predicted values
    :return: accuracy score
    """
    # initialize a simple counter for correct predictions
    correct_counter = 0
    # loop over all elements of y_true
    # and y_pred "together"
    for yt, yp in zip(y_true, y_pred):
        if yt == yp:
            # if prediction is equal to truth, increase the counter
            correct_counter += 1
    
    # return accuracy
    # which is correct predictions over the number of samples
    return correct_counter / len(y_true)
```

We can also calculate accuracy using scikit-learn.

```
In [X]: from sklearn import metrics
   ...: l1 = [0,1,1,1,0,0,0,1]
   ...: l2 = [0,1,0,1,0,1,0,0]
   ...: metrics.accuracy_score(l1, l2)
Out[X]: 0.625
```

Now, let's say we change the dataset a bit such that there are 180 chest x-ray images which do not have pneumothorax and only 20 with pneumothorax. Even in this case, we will create the training and validation sets with the same ratio of positive to negative (pneumothorax to non- pneumothorax) targets. In each set, we have 90 non- pneumothorax and 10 pneumothorax images. If you say that all images in the validation set are non-pneumothorax, what would your accuracy be? Let's see; you classified 90% of the images correctly. So, your accuracy is 90%.

But look at it one more time.

You didn't even build a model and got an accuracy of 90%. That seems kind of useless. If we look carefully, we will see that the dataset is skewed, i.e., the number of samples in one class outnumber the number of samples in other class by a lot. In these kinds of cases, it is not advisable to use accuracy as an evaluation metric as it is not representative of the data. So, you might get high accuracy, but your model will probably not perform that well when it comes to real-world samples, and you won't be able to explain to your managers why.

In these cases, it's better to look at other metrics such as **precision**.

Before learning about precision, we need to know a few terms. Here we have assumed that chest x-ray images with pneumothorax are positive class (1) and without pneumothorax are negative class (0).

True positive *(TP)*: Given an image, if your model predicts the image has pneumothorax, and the actual target for that image has pneumothorax, it is considered a true positive.

True negative *(TN)*: Given an image, if your model predicts that the image does not have pneumothorax and the actual target says that it is a non-pneumothorax image, it is considered a true negative.

In simple words, *if your model correctly predicts positive class, it is true positive, and if your model accurately predicts negative class, it is a true negative.*

False positive *(FP)*: Given an image, if your model predicts pneumothorax and the actual target for that image is non- pneumothorax, it a false positive.

False negative *(FN)*: Given an image, if your model predicts non-pneumothorax and the actual target for that image is pneumothorax, it is a false negative.

In simple words, *if your model incorrectly (or falsely) predicts positive class, it is a false positive. If your model incorrectly (or falsely) predicts negative class, it is a false negative.*

Let's look at implementations of these, one at a time.

```
def true_positive(y_true, y_pred):
    """
    Function to calculate True Positives
    :param y_true: list of true values
    :param y_pred: list of predicted values
    :return: number of true positives
    """
    # initialize
    tp = 0
    for yt, yp in zip(y_true, y_pred):
        if yt == 1 and yp == 1:
            tp += 1
    return tp

def true_negative(y_true, y_pred):
    """
    Function to calculate True Negatives
    :param y_true: list of true values
    :param y_pred: list of predicted values
    :return: number of true negatives
    """
    # initialize
    tn = 0
    for yt, yp in zip(y_true, y_pred):
        if yt == 0 and yp == 0:
            tn += 1
    return tn

def false_positive(y_true, y_pred):
    """
    Function to calculate False Positives
    :param y_true: list of true values
    :param y_pred: list of predicted values
    :return: number of false positives
    """
    # initialize
```

```
        fp = 0
        for yt, yp in zip(y_true, y_pred):
            if yt == 0 and yp == 1:
                fp += 1
        return fp

def false_negative(y_true, y_pred):
    """
    Function to calculate False Negatives
    :param y_true: list of true values
    :param y_pred: list of predicted values
    :return: number of false negatives
    """
    # initialize
    fn = 0
    for yt, yp in zip(y_true, y_pred):
        if yt == 1 and yp == 0:
            fn += 1
    return fn
```

The way I have implemented these here is quite simple and works only for binary classification. Let's check these functions.

```
In [X]: l1 = [0,1,1,1,0,0,0,1]
   ...: l2 = [0,1,0,1,0,1,0,0]

In [X]: true_positive(l1, l2)
Out[X]: 2

In [X]: false_positive(l1, l2)
Out[X]: 1

In [X]: false_negative(l1, l2)
Out[X]: 2

In [X]: true_negative(l1, l2)
Out[X]: 3
```

If we have to define accuracy using the terms described above, we can write:

$$Accuracy\ Score = (TP + TN) / (TP + TN + FP + FN)$$

We can now quickly implement accuracy score using TP, TN, FP and FN in python. Let's call it *accuracy_v2*.

```
def accuracy_v2(y_true, y_pred):
    """
    Function to calculate accuracy using tp/tn/fp/fn
    :param y_true: list of true values
    :param y_pred: list of predicted values
    :return: accuracy score
    """
    tp = true_positive(y_true, y_pred)
    fp = false_positive(y_true, y_pred)
    fn = false_negative(y_true, y_pred)
    tn = true_negative(y_true, y_pred)
    accuracy_score = (tp + tn) / (tp + tn + fp + fn)
    return accuracy_score
```

We can quickly check the correctness of this function by comparing it to our previous implementation and scikit-learn version.

```
In [X]: l1 = [0,1,1,1,0,0,0,1]
   ...: l2 = [0,1,0,1,0,1,0,0]

In [X]: accuracy(l1, l2)
Out[X]: 0.625

In [X]: accuracy_v2(l1, l2)
Out[X]: 0.625

In [X]: metrics.accuracy_score(l1, l2)
Out[X]: 0.625
```

Please note that in this code, *metrics.accuracy_score* comes from scikit-learn.

Great. All values match. This means we have not made any mistakes in the implementation.

Now, we can move to other important metrics.

First one is precision. **Precision** is defined as:

$$Precision = TP / (TP + FP)$$

Let's say we make a new model on the new skewed dataset and our model correctly identified 80 non-pneumothorax out of 90 and 8 pneumothorax out of 10. Thus, we identify 88 images out of 100 successfully. The accuracy is, therefore, 0.88 or 88%.

But, out of these 100 samples, 10 non-pneumothorax images are misclassified as having pneumothorax and 2 pneumothorax are misclassified as not having pneumothorax.

Thus, we have:

- TP : 8
- TN: 80
- FP: 10
- FN: 2

So, our precision is 8 / (8 + 10) = 0.444. This means our model is correct 44.4% times when it's trying to identify positive samples (pneumothorax).

Now, since we have implemented TP, TN, FP and FN, we can easily implement precision in python.

```python
def precision(y_true, y_pred):
    """
    Function to calculate precision
    :param y_true: list of true values
    :param y_pred: list of predicted values
    :return: precision score
    """
    tp = true_positive(y_true, y_pred)
    fp = false_positive(y_true, y_pred)
    precision = tp / (tp + fp)
    return precision
```

Let's try this implementation of precision.

```
In [X]: l1 = [0,1,1,1,0,0,0,1]
   ...: l2 = [0,1,0,1,0,1,0,0]
```

```
In [X]: precision(l1, l2)
Out[X]: 0.6666666666666666
```

This seems fine.

Next, we come to recall. **Recall** is defined as:

$$Recall = TP / (TP + FN)$$

In the above case recall is 8 / (8 + 2) = 0.80. This means our model identified 80% of positive samples correctly.

```
def recall(y_true, y_pred):
    """
    Function to calculate recall
    :param y_true: list of true values
    :param y_pred: list of predicted values
    :return: recall score
    """
    tp = true_positive(y_true, y_pred)
    fn = false_negative(y_true, y_pred)
    recall = tp / (tp + fn)
    return recall
```

In the case of our two small lists, we should have a recall of 0.5. Let's check.

```
In [X]: l1 = [0,1,1,1,0,0,0,1]
   ...: l2 = [0,1,0,1,0,1,0,0]

In [X]: recall(l1, l2)
Out[X]: 0.5
```

And that matches our calculated value!

For a "good" model, our precision and recall values should be high. We see that in the above example, the recall value is quite high. However, precision is very low! Our model produces quite a lot of false positives but less false negatives. Fewer false negatives are good in this type of problem because you don't want to say that patients do not have pneumothorax when they do. That is going to be more harmful. But we do have a lot of false positives, and that's not good either.

Most of the models predict a probability, and when we predict, we usually choose this threshold to be 0.5. This threshold is not always ideal, and depending on this threshold, your value of precision and recall can change drastically. If for every threshold we choose, we calculate the precision and recall values, we can create a plot between these sets of values. This plot or curve is known as the precision-recall curve.

Before looking into the precision-recall curve, let's assume two lists.

```
In [X]: y_true = [0, 0, 0, 1, 0, 0, 0, 0, 0, 0,
    ...:          1, 0, 0, 0, 0, 0, 0, 0, 1, 0]

In [X]: y_pred = [0.02638412, 0.11114267, 0.31620708,
    ...:          0.0490937,  0.0191491,  0.17554844,
    ...:          0.15952202, 0.03819563, 0.11639273,
    ...:          0.079377,   0.08584789, 0.39095342,
    ...:          0.27259048, 0.03447096, 0.04644807,
    ...:          0.03543574, 0.18521942, 0.05934905,
    ...:          0.61977213, 0.33056815]
```

So, y_true is our targets, and y_pred is the probability values for a sample being assigned a value of 1. So, now, we look at probabilities in prediction instead of the predicted value (which is most of the time calculated with a threshold at 0.5).

```
precisions = []
recalls = []
# how we assumed these thresholds is a long story
thresholds = [0.0490937 , 0.05934905, 0.079377,
              0.08584789, 0.11114267, 0.11639273,
              0.15952202, 0.17554844, 0.18521942,
              0.27259048, 0.31620708, 0.33056815,
              0.39095342, 0.61977213]

# for every threshold, calculate predictions in binary
# and append calculated precisions and recalls
# to their respective lists
for i in thresholds:
    temp_prediction = [1 if x >= i else 0 for x in y_pred]
```

```
p = precision(y_true, temp_prediction)
r = recall(y_true, temp_prediction)
precisions.append(p)
recalls.append(r)
```

Now, we can plot these values of precisions and recalls.

```
plt.figure(figsize=(7, 7))
plt.plot(recalls, precisions)
plt.xlabel('Recall', fontsize=15)
plt.ylabel('Precision', fontsize=15)
```

Figure 2 shows the precision-recall curve we get this way.

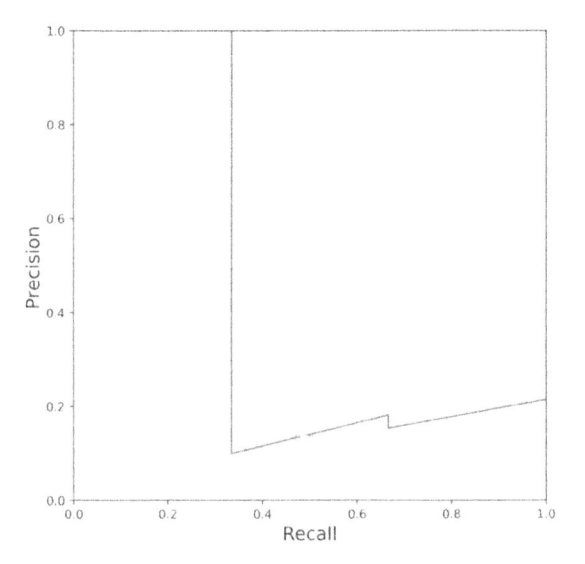

Figure 2: precision-recall curve

This **precision-recall curve** looks very different from what you might have seen on the internet. It's because we had only 20 samples, and only 3 of them were positive samples. But there's nothing to worry. It's the same old precision-recall curve.

You will notice that *it's challenging to choose a value of threshold that gives both good precision and recall values*. If the threshold is too high, you have a smaller number of true positives and a high number of false negatives. This decreases your recall; however, your precision score will be high. If you reduce the threshold too low, false positives will increase a lot, and precision will be less.

Both precision and recall range from 0 to 1 and a value closer to 1 is better.

F1 score is a metric that combines both precision and recall. It is defined as a simple weighted average (harmonic mean) of precision and recall. If we denote precision using P and recall using R, we can represent the F1 score as:

$$F1 = 2PR / (P + R)$$

A little bit of mathematics will lead you to the following equation of F1 based on TP, FP and FN

$$F1 = 2TP / (2TP + FP + FN)$$

A Python implementation is simple because we have already implemented these.

```python
def f1(y_true, y_pred):
    """
    Function to calculate f1 score
    :param y_true: list of true values
    :param y_pred: list of predicted values
    :return: f1 score
    """
    p = precision(y_true, y_pred)
    r = recall(y_true, y_pred)

    score = 2 * p * r / (p + r)

    return score
```

Let's see the results of this and compare it with scikit-learn.

```
In [X]: y_true = [0, 0, 0, 1, 0, 0, 0, 0, 0, 0,
   ...:           1, 0, 0, 0, 0, 0, 0, 0, 1, 0]
```

```
In [X]: y_pred = [0, 0, 1, 0, 0, 0, 1, 0, 0, 0,
   ...:           1, 0, 0, 0, 0, 0, 0, 0, 1, 0]

In [X]: f1(y_true, y_pred)
Out[X]: 0.5714285714285715
```

And from scikit learn for the same lists, we get:

```
In [X]: from sklearn import metrics

In [X]: metrics.f1_score(y_true, y_pred)
Out[X]: 0.5714285714285715
```

Instead of looking at precision and recall individually, you can also just look at **F1** score. Same as for precision, recall and accuracy, F1 score also ranges from 0 to 1, and a perfect prediction model has an F1 of 1. When dealing with datasets that have skewed targets, we should look at F1 (or precision and recall) instead of accuracy.

Then there are other crucial terms that we should know about.

The first one is **TPR or True Positive Rate**, which is the same as recall.

$$TPR = TP / (TP + FN)$$

Even though it is same as recall, we will make a python function for it for further use with this name.

```
def tpr(y_true, y_pred):
    """
    Function to calculate tpr
    :param y_true: list of true values
    :param y_pred: list of predicted values
    :return: tpr/recall
    """
    return recall(y_true, y_pred)
```

TPR or recall is also known as **sensitivity**.

And **FPR or False Positive Rate**, which is defined as:

$$FPR = FP / (TN + FP)$$

```
def fpr(y_true, y_pred):
    """
    Function to calculate fpr
    :param y_true: list of true values
    :param y_pred: list of predicted values
    :return: fpr
    """
    fp = false_positive(y_true, y_pred)
    tn = true_negative(y_true, y_pred)
    return fp / (tn + fp)
```

And **1 - FPR** is known as **specificity or True Negative Rate or TNR**.

These are a lot of terms, but the most important ones out of these are only TPR and FPR.

Let's assume that we have only 15 samples and their target values are binary:

Actual targets : [0, 0, 0, 0, 1, 0, 1, 0, 0, 1, 0, 1, 0, 0, 1, 0, 1]

We train a model like the random forest, and we can get the probability of when a sample is positive.

Predicted probabilities for 1: [0.1, 0.3, 0.2, 0.6, 0.8, 0.05, 0.9, 0.5, 0.3, 0.66, 0.3, 0.2, 0.85, 0.15, 0.99]

For a typical threshold of >= 0.5, we can evaluate all the above values of precision, recall/TPR, F1 and FPR. But we can do the same if we choose the value of the threshold to be 0.4 or 0.6. In fact, we can choose any value between 0 and 1 and calculate all the metrics described above.

Let's calculate only two values, though: TPR and FPR.

```
# empty lists to store tpr
# and fpr values
```

```
tpr_list = []
fpr_list = []

# actual targets
y_true = [0, 0, 0, 0, 1, 0, 1,
          0, 0, 1, 0, 1, 0, 0, 1]

# predicted probabilities of a sample being 1
y_pred = [0.1, 0.3, 0.2, 0.6, 0.8, 0.05,
          0.9, 0.5, 0.3, 0.66, 0.3, 0.2,
          0.85, 0.15, 0.99]

# handmade thresholds
thresholds = [0, 0.1, 0.2, 0.3, 0.4, 0.5,
              0.6, 0.7, 0.8, 0.85, 0.9, 0.99, 1.0]

# loop over all thresholds
for thresh in thresholds:
    # calculate predictions for a given threshold
    temp_pred = [1 if x >= thresh else 0 for x in y_pred]
    # calculate tpr
    temp_tpr = tpr(y_true, temp_pred)
    # calculate fpr
    temp_fpr = fpr(y_true, temp_pred)
    # append tpr and fpr to lists
    tpr_list.append(temp_tpr)
    fpr_list.append(temp_fpr)
```

We can thus get a tpr and fpr value for each threshold.

	threshold	tpr	fpr
0	0.00	1.0	1.0
1	0.10	1.0	0.9
2	0.20	1.0	0.7
3	0.30	0.8	0.6
4	0.40	0.8	0.3
5	0.50	0.8	0.3

Figure 3: Table for threshold, TPR and FPR values

If we plot the table as shown in figure 3, i.e. if we have TPR on the y-axis and FPR on the x-axis, we will get a curve as shown in figure 4.

```
plt.figure(figsize=(7, 7))
plt.fill_between(fpr_list, tpr_list, alpha=0.4)
plt.plot(fpr_list, tpr_list, lw=3)
plt.xlim(0, 1.0)
plt.ylim(0, 1.0)
plt.xlabel('FPR', fontsize=15)
plt.ylabel('TPR', fontsize=15)
plt.show()
```

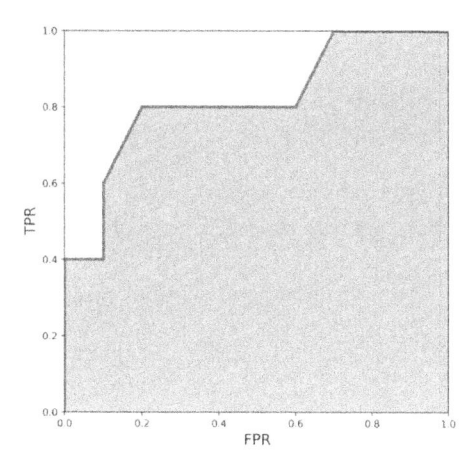

Figure 4: Receiver operating characteristic (ROC) curve

This curve is also known as the **Receiver Operating Characteristic (ROC)**. And if we calculate the area under this ROC curve, we are calculating another metric which is used very often when you have a dataset which has skewed binary targets.

This metric is known as the **Area Under ROC Curve** or **Area Under Curve** or just simply **AUC**. There are many ways to calculate the area under the ROC curve. For this particular purpose, we will stick to the fantastic implementation by scikit-learn.

```
In [X]: from sklearn import metrics
```

```
In [X]: y_true = [0, 0, 0, 0, 1, 0, 1,
   ...:           0, 0, 1, 0, 1, 0, 0, 1]

In [X]: y_pred = [0.1, 0.3, 0.2, 0.6, 0.8, 0.05,
   ...:           0.9, 0.5, 0.3, 0.66, 0.3, 0.2,
   ...:           0.85, 0.15, 0.99]

In [X]: metrics.roc_auc_score(y_true, y_pred)
Out[X]: 0.8300000000000001
```

AUC values range from 0 to 1.

- **AUC = 1** implies you have a perfect model. Most of the time, it means that you made some mistake with validation and should revisit data processing and validation pipeline of yours. If you didn't make any mistakes, then congratulations, you have the best model one can have for the dataset you built it on.

- **AUC = 0** implies that your model is very bad (or very good!). Try inverting the probabilities for the predictions, for example, if your probability for the positive class is p, try substituting it with $1-p$. This kind of AUC may also mean that there is some problem with your validation or data processing.

- **AUC = 0.5** implies that your predictions are random. So, for any binary classification problem, if I predict all targets as 0.5, I will get an AUC of 0.5.

AUC values between 0 and 0.5 imply that your model is worse than random. Most of the time, it's because you inverted the classes. If you try to invert your predictions, your AUC might become more than 0.5. AUC values closer to 1 are considered good.

But what does AUC say about our model?

Suppose you get an AUC of 0.85 when you build a model to detect pneumothorax from chest x-ray images. This means that if you select a random image from your dataset with pneumothorax (positive sample) and another random image without pneumothorax (negative sample), then the pneumothorax image will rank higher than a non-pneumothorax image with a probability of 0.85.

After calculating probabilities and AUC, you would want to make predictions on the test set. Depending on the problem and use-case, you might want to either have probabilities or actual classes. If you want to have probabilities, it's effortless. You already have them. If you want to have classes, you need to select a threshold. In the case of binary classification, you can do something like the following.

$$Prediction = Probability >= Threshold$$

Which means, that *prediction* is a new list which contains only binary variables. An item in *prediction* is 1 if the *probability* is greater than or equal to a given *threshold* else the value is 0.

And guess what, you can use the ROC curve to choose this threshold! The ROC curve will tell you how the threshold impacts false positive rate and true positive rate and thus, in turn, false positives and true positives. You should choose the threshold that is best suited for your problem and datasets.

For example, if you don't want to have too many false positives, you should have a high threshold value. This will, however, also give you a lot more false negatives. Observe the trade-off and select the best threshold. Let's see how these thresholds impact true positive and false positive values.

```
# empty lists to store true positive
# and false positive values
tp_list = []
fp_list = []

# actual targets
y_true = [0, 0, 0, 0, 1, 0, 1,
          0, 0, 1, 0, 1, 0, 0, 1]

# predicted probabilities of a sample being 1
y_pred = [0.1, 0.3, 0.2, 0.6, 0.8, 0.05,
          0.9, 0.5, 0.3, 0.66, 0.3, 0.2,
          0.85, 0.15, 0.99]

# some handmade thresholds
thresholds = [0, 0.1, 0.2, 0.3, 0.4, 0.5,
              0.6, 0.7, 0.8, 0.85, 0.9, 0.99, 1.0]

# loop over all thresholds
for thresh in thresholds:
```

```
# calculate predictions for a given threshold
temp_pred = [1 if x >= thresh else 0 for x in y_pred]
# calculate tp
temp_tp = true_positive(y_true, temp_pred)
# calculate fp
temp_fp = false_positive(y_true, temp_pred)
# append tp and fp to lists
tp_list.append(temp_tp)
fp_list.append(temp_fp)
```

Using this, we can create a table, as shown in Figure 5.

	threshold	tp	fp
0	0.00	5.0	10.0
1	0.10	5.0	9.0
2	0.20	5.0	7.0
3	0.30	4.0	6.0
4	0.40	4.0	3.0
5	0.50	4.0	3.0
6	0.60	4.0	2.0
7	0.70	3.0	1.0
8	0.80	3.0	1.0
9	0.85	2.0	1.0
10	0.90	2.0	0.0
11	0.99	1.0	0.0
12	1.00	0.0	0.0

Figure 5: TP and FP values for different thresholds

Most of the time, the top-left value on ROC curve should give you a quite good threshold, as shown in figure 6.

Comparing the table and the ROC curve, we see that a threshold of around 0.6 is quite good where we do not lose a lot of true positives and neither we have a lot of false positives.

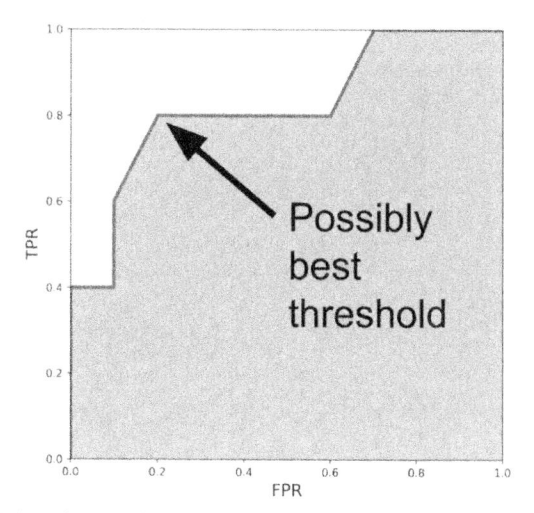

Figure 6: Select the best threshold from the leftmost top point in the ROC curve

AUC is a widely used metric for skewed binary classification tasks in the industry, and a metric everyone should know about. Once you understand the idea behind AUC, as explained in the paragraphs above, it is also easy to explain it to non-technical people who would probably be assessing your models in the industry.

Another important metric you should learn after learning AUC is **log loss**. In case of a binary classification problem, we define log loss as:

Log Loss = - 1.0 * (target * log(prediction) + (1 - target) * log(1 - prediction))

Where target is either 0 or 1 and prediction is a probability of a sample belonging to class 1.

For multiple samples in the dataset, the log-loss over all samples is a mere average of all individual log losses. One thing to remember is that log loss penalizes quite high for an incorrect or a far-off prediction, i.e. log loss punishes you for being very sure and very wrong.

```
import numpy as np

def log_loss(y_true, y_proba):
```

```
"""
Function to calculate log loss
:param y_true: list of true values
:param y_proba: list of probabilities for 1
:return: overall log loss
"""
# define an epsilon value
# this can also be an input
# this value is used to clip probabilities
epsilon = 1e-15
# initialize empty list to store
# individual losses
loss = []
# loop over all true and predicted probability values
for yt, yp in zip(y_true, y_proba):
    # adjust probability
    # 0 gets converted to 1e-15
    # 1 gets converted to 1-1e-15
    # Why? Think about it!
    yp = np.clip(yp, epsilon, 1 - epsilon)
    # calculate loss for one sample
    temp_loss = - 1.0 * (
        yt * np.log(yp)
        + (1 - yt) * np.log(1 - yp)
    )
    # add to loss list
    loss.append(temp_loss)
# return mean loss over all samples
return np.mean(loss)
```

Let's test our implementation:

```
In [X]: y_true = [0, 0, 0, 0, 1, 0, 1,
   ...:           0, 0, 1, 0, 1, 0, 0, 1]

In [X]: y_proba = [0.1, 0.3, 0.2, 0.6, 0.8, 0.05,
   ...:            0.9, 0.5, 0.3, 0.66, 0.3, 0.2,
   ...:            0.85, 0.15, 0.99]

In [X]: log_loss(y_true, y_proba)
Out[X]: 0.49882711861432294
```

We can compare this with scikit-learn:

```
In [X]: from sklearn import metrics

In [X]: metrics.log_loss(y_true, y_proba)
Out[X]: 0.49882711861432294
```

Thus, our implementation is correct. Implementation of log loss is easy. Interpretation may seem a bit difficult. You must remember that log loss penalizes a lot more than other metrics.

For example, if you are 51% sure about a sample belonging to class 1, log loss would be:

$$- 1.0 * (1 * \log(0.51) + (1 - 1) * \log(1 - 0.51)) = 0.67$$

And if you are 49% sure for a sample belonging to class 0, log loss would be:

$$- 1.0 * (0 * \log(0.49) + (1 - 0) * \log(1 - 0.49)) = 0.67$$

So, even though we can choose a cut off at 0.5 and get perfect predictions, we will still have a very high log loss. So, when dealing with log loss, you need to be very careful; any non-confident prediction will have a very high log loss.

Most of the metrics that we discussed until now can be converted to a multi-class version. The idea is quite simple. Let's take precision and recall. We can calculate precision and recall for each class in a **multi-class classification** problem.

There are three different ways to calculate this which might get confusing from time to time. Let's assume we are interested in precision first. We know that precision depends on true positives and false positives.

- **Macro averaged precision**: calculate precision for all classes individually and then average them

- **Micro averaged precision**: calculate class wise true positive and false positive and then use that to calculate overall precision

- **Weighted precision**: same as macro but in this case, it is weighted average depending on the number of items in each class

This seems complicated but is easy to understand by python implementations. Let's see how macro-averaged precision is implemented.

```python
import numpy as np


def macro_precision(y_true, y_pred):
    """
    Function to calculate macro averaged precision
    :param y_true: list of true values
    :param y_pred: list of predicted values
    :return: macro precision score
    """

    # find the number of classes by taking
    # length of unique values in true list
    num_classes = len(np.unique(y_true))

    # initialize precision to 0
    precision = 0

    # loop over all classes
    for class_ in range(num_classes):

        # all classes except current are considered negative
        temp_true = [1 if p == class_ else 0 for p in y_true]
        temp_pred = [1 if p == class_ else 0 for p in y_pred]

        # calculate true positive for current class
        tp = true_positive(temp_true, temp_pred)

        # calculate false positive for current class
        fp = false_positive(temp_true, temp_pred)

        # calculate precision for current class
        temp_precision = tp / (tp + fp)

        # keep adding precision for all classes
        precision += temp_precision

    # calculate and return average precision over all classes
    precision /= num_classes
    return precision
```

You will notice that it wasn't so difficult. Similarly, we have micro-averaged precision score.

```
import numpy as np


def micro_precision(y_true, y_pred):
    """
    Function to calculate micro averaged precision
    :param y_true: list of true values
    :param y_pred: list of predicted values
    :return: micro precision score
    """

    # find the number of classes by taking
    # length of unique values in true list
    num_classes = len(np.unique(y_true))

    # initialize tp and fp to 0
    tp = 0
    fp = 0

    # loop over all classes
    for class_ in range(num_classes):
        # all classes except current are considered negative
        temp_true = [1 if p == class_ else 0 for p in y_true]
        temp_pred = [1 if p == class_ else 0 for p in y_pred]

        # calculate true positive for current class
        # and update overall tp
        tp += true_positive(temp_true, temp_pred)

        # calculate false positive for current class
        # and update overall tp
        fp += false_positive(temp_true, temp_pred)

    # calculate and return overall precision
    precision = tp / (tp + fp)
    return precision
```

This isn't difficult, either. Then what is? Nothing. *Machine learning is easy*.

Now, let's look at the implementation of weighted precision.

```python
from collections import Counter
import numpy as np


def weighted_precision(y_true, y_pred):
    """
    Function to calculate weighted averaged precision
    :param y_true: list of true values
    :param y_pred: list of predicted values
    :return: weighted precision score
    """

    # find the number of classes by taking
    # length of unique values in true list
    num_classes = len(np.unique(y_true))

    # create class:sample count dictionary
    # it looks something like this:
    # {0: 20, 1:15, 2:21}
    class_counts = Counter(y_true)

    # initialize precision to 0
    precision = 0

    # loop over all classes
    for class_ in range(num_classes):
        # all classes except current are considered negative
        temp_true = [1 if p == class_ else 0 for p in y_true]
        temp_pred = [1 if p == class_ else 0 for p in y_pred]

        # calculate tp and fp for class
        tp = true_positive(temp_true, temp_pred)
        fp = false_positive(temp_true, temp_pred)

        # calculate precision of class
        temp_precision = tp / (tp + fp)

        # multiply precision with count of samples in class
        weighted_precision = class_counts[class_] * temp_precision

        # add to overall precision
        precision += weighted_precision
    # calculate overall precision by dividing by
    # total number of samples
    overall_precision = precision / len(y_true)
```

```
    return overall_precision
```

Let's compare our implementations with scikit-learn to know if we implemented it right.

```
In [X]: from sklearn import metrics

In [X]: y_true = [0, 1, 2, 0, 1, 2, 0, 2, 2]

In [X]: y_pred = [0, 2, 1, 0, 2, 1, 0, 0, 2]

In [X]: macro_precision(y_true, y_pred)
Out[X]: 0.3611111111111111

In [X]: metrics.precision_score(y_true, y_pred, average="macro")
Out[X]: 0.3611111111111111

In [X]: micro_precision(y_true, y_pred)
Out[X]: 0.4444444444444444

In [X]: metrics.precision_score(y_true, y_pred, average="micro")
Out[X]: 0.4444444444444444

In [X]: weighted_precision(y_true, y_pred)
Out[X]: 0.39814814814814814

In [X]: metrics.precision_score(y_true, y_pred, average="weighted")
Out[X]: 0.39814814814814814
```

It seems like we implemented everything correctly. Please note that the implementations shown here may not be the most efficient, but they are the easiest to understand.

Similarly, we can implement the **recall metric for multi-class**. Precision and recall depend on true positive, false positive and false negative while F1 depends on precision and recall.

Implementation for recall is left as an exercise for the reader and one version of F1 for multi-class, i.e., weighted average is implemented here.

```python
from collections import Counter
import numpy as np


def weighted_f1(y_true, y_pred):
    """
    Function to calculate weighted f1 score
    :param y_true: list of true values
    :param y_proba: list of predicted values
    :return: weighted f1 score
    """

    # find the number of classes by taking
    # length of unique values in true list
    num_classes = len(np.unique(y_true))

    # create class:sample count dictionary
    # it looks something like this:
    # {0: 20, 1:15, 2:21}
    class_counts = Counter(y_true)

    # initialize f1 to 0
    f1 = 0

    # loop over all classes
    for class_ in range(num_classes):
        # all classes except current are considered negative
        temp_true = [1 if p == class_ else 0 for p in y_true]
        temp_pred = [1 if p == class_ else 0 for p in y_pred]

        # calculate precision and recall for class
        p = precision(temp_true, temp_pred)
        r = recall(temp_true, temp_pred)

        # calculate f1 of class
        if p + r != 0:
            temp_f1 = 2 * p * r / (p + r)
        else:
            temp_f1 = 0

        # multiply f1 with count of samples in class
        weighted_f1 = class_counts[class_] * temp_f1

        # add to f1 precision
        f1 += weighted_f1
```

```
# calculate overall F1 by dividing by
# total number of samples
overall_f1 = f1 / len(y_true)
return overall_f1
```

Note that there are a few lines of code above which are new. *And that's why you should read the code carefully.*

```
In [X]: from sklearn import metrics

In [X]: y_true = [0, 1, 2, 0, 1, 2, 0, 2, 2]

In [X]: y_pred = [0, 2, 1, 0, 2, 1, 0, 0, 2]

In [X]: weighted_f1(y_true, y_pred)
Out[X]: 0.41269841269841273

In [X]: metrics.f1_score(y_true, y_pred, average="weighted")
Out[X]: 0.41269841269841273
```

Thus, we have precision, recall and F1 implemented for multi-class problems. You can similarly convert AUC and log loss to multi-class formats too. This format of conversion is known as **one-vs-all**. I'm not going to implement them here as the implementation is quite similar to what we have already discussed.

In binary or multi-class classification, it is also quite popular to take a look at **confusion matrix**. Don't be *confused*; it's quite easy. A confusion matrix is nothing but a table of TP, FP, TN and FN. Using the confusion matrix, you can quickly see how many samples were misclassified and how many were classified correctly.
One might argue that the confusion matrix should be covered quite early in this chapter, but I chose not to do it. If you understand TP, FP, TN, FN, precision, recall and AUC, it becomes quite easy to understand and interpret confusion matrix. Let's see what confusion matrix looks like for a binary classification problem in figure 7.

We see that the confusion matrix is made up of TP, FP, FN and TN. These are the only values we need to calculate precision, recall, F1 score and AUC. Sometimes, people also prefer calling FP as **Type-I error** and FN as **Type-II error**.

	Actual Targets	
	Class - 1	Class - 0
Class - 1 (Predictions)	TP	FP
Class - 0 (Predictions)	FN	TN

Figure 7: Confusion matrix for a binary classification task

We can also expand the binary confusion matrix to a multi-class confusion matrix. How would that look like? If we have N classes, it will be a matrix of size NxN. For every class, we calculate the total number of samples that went to the class in concern and other classes. This can be best understood by an example.

Suppose we have the following actual classes:

$$[0, 1, 2, 0, 1, 2, 0, 2, 2]$$

And our predictions are:

$$[0, 2, 1, 0, 2, 1, 0, 0, 2]$$

Then our confusion matrix will look as shown in figure 8.

What does figure 8 tell us?

Let's look at class 0. We see that there are 3 instances of class 0 in the actual target. However, in prediction, we have 3 instances that belong to class 0 and 1 instance that belongs to class 1. Ideally, for class 0 in the actual label, predicted labels 1 and 2 shouldn't have any instance. Let's see class 2. In actual labels, this count adds up to 4 while in predicted it adds up to 3. Only 1 instance has a perfect prediction for class 2 and 2 instances go to class 1.

A perfect confusion matrix should only be filled diagonally from left to right.

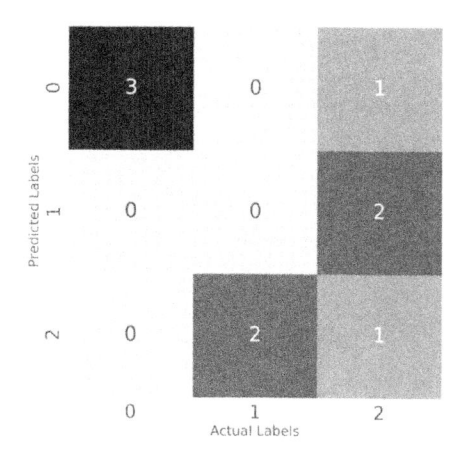

Figure 8: Confusion matrix for a multi-class problem

Confusion matrix gives an easy way to calculate different metrics that we have discussed before. Scikit-learn offers an easy and straightforward way to generate a confusion matrix. Please note that the confusion matrix that I have shown in figure 8 is a transpose of scikit-learn's confusion matrix and an original version can be plotted by the following code.

```
import matplotlib.pyplot as plt
import seaborn as sns
from sklearn import metrics

# some targets
y_true = [0, 1, 2, 0, 1, 2, 0, 2, 2]

#some predictions
y_pred = [0, 2, 1, 0, 2, 1, 0, 0, 2]

# get confusion matrix from sklearn
cm = metrics.confusion_matrix(y_true, y_pred)

# plot using matplotlib and seaborn
plt.figure(figsize=(10, 10))
cmap = sns.cubehelix_palette(50, hue=0.05, rot=0, light=0.9, dark=0,
as_cmap=True)
sns.set(font_scale=2.5)
sns.heatmap(cm, annot=True, cmap=cmap, cbar=False)
```

```
plt.ylabel('Actual Labels', fontsize=20)
plt.xlabel('Predicted Labels', fontsize=20)
```

So, until now, we have tackled metrics for binary and multi-class classification. Then comes another type of classification problem called **multi-label classification**. In multi-label classification, each sample can have one or more classes associated with it. One simple example of this type of problem would be a task in which you are asked to predict different objects in a given image.

Figure 9: Different objects in an image[4]

Figure 9 shows an example image from a well-known dataset. Note that this dataset's objective is something different but let's not go there. Let's assume that the aim is only to predict if an object is present in an image or not. For figure 9, we have a chair, flower-pot, window, but we don't have other objects such as computer, bed, tv, etc. So, one image can have multiple targets associated with it. This type of problem is the multi-label classification problem.

The metrics for this type of classification problem are a bit different. Some suitable and most common metrics are:

- Precision at k (P@k)
- Average precision at k (AP@k)

---
[4] https://www.flickr.com/photos/krakluski/2950388100 License: CC BY 2.0

- Mean average precision at k (MAP@k)
- Log loss

Let's start with **precision at k or P@k**. One must not confuse this precision with the precision discussed earlier. If you have a list of original classes for a given sample and list of predicted classes for the same, precision is defined as the number of hits in the predicted list considering only top-k predictions, divided by k.

If that's confusing, it will become apparent with python code.

```
def pk(y_true, y_pred, k):
    """
    This function calculates precision at k
    for a single sample
    :param y_true: list of values, actual classes
    :param y_pred: list of values, predicted classes
    :param k: the value for k
    :return: precision at a given value k
    """
    # if k is 0, return 0. we should never have this
    # as k is always >= 1
    if k == 0:
        return 0
    # we are interested only in top-k predictions
    y_pred = y_pred[:k]
    # convert predictions to set
    pred_set = set(y_pred)
    # convert actual values to set
    true_set = set(y_true)
    # find common values
    common_values = pred_set.intersection(true_set)
    # return length of common values over k
    return len(common_values) / len(y_pred[:k])
```

With code, everything becomes much easier to understand.

Now, we have **average precision at k or AP@k**. AP@k is calculated using P@k. For example, if we have to calculate AP@3, we calculate P@1, P@2 and P@3 and then divide the sum by 3.

Let's see its implementation.

```python
def apk(y_true, y_pred, k):
    """
    This function calculates average precision at k
    for a single sample
    :param y_true: list of values, actual classes
    :param y_pred: list of values, predicted classes
    :return: average precision at a given value k
    """
    # initialize p@k list of values
    pk_values = []
    # loop over all k. from 1 to k + 1
    for i in range(1, k + 1):
        # calculate p@i and append to list
        pk_values.append(pk(y_true, y_pred, i))

    # if we have no values in the list, return 0
    if len(pk_values) == 0:
        return 0
    # else, we return the sum of list over length of list
    return sum(pk_values) / len(pk_values)
```

These two functions can be used to calculate average precision at k (AP@k) for two given lists; let's see how.

```
In [X]: y_true = [
   ...:     [1, 2, 3],
   ...:     [0, 2],
   ...:     [1],
   ...:     [2, 3],
   ...:     [1, 0],
   ...:     []
   ...: ]

In [X]: y_pred = [
   ...:     [0, 1, 2],
   ...:     [1],
   ...:     [0, 2, 3],
   ...:     [2, 3, 4, 0],
   ...:     [0, 1, 2],
   ...:     [0]
   ...: ]

In [X]: for i in range(len(y_true)):
   ...:     for j in range(1, 4):
   ...:         print(
```

```
...:            f"""
...:            y_true={y_true[i]},
...:            y_pred={y_pred[i]},
...:            AP@{j}={apk(y_true[i], y_pred[i], k=j)}
...:            """
...:        )
...:

y_true=[1, 2, 3],
y_pred=[0, 1, 2],
AP@1=0.0


y_true=[1, 2, 3],
y_pred=[0, 1, 2],
AP@2=0.25


y_true=[1, 2, 3],
y_pred=[0, 1, 2],
AP@3=0.38888888888888884
.
.
```

Please note that I have omitted many values from the output, but you get the point. So, this is how we can calculate AP@k which is per sample. In machine learning, we are interested in all samples, and that's why we have **mean average precision at k or MAP@k**. MAP@k is just an average of AP@k and can be calculated easily by the following python code.

```
def mapk(y_true, y_pred, k):
    """
    This function calculates mean avg precision at k
    for a single sample
    :param y_true: list of values, actual classes
    :param y_pred: list of values, predicted classes
    :return: mean avg precision at a given value k
    """
    # initialize empty list for apk values
    apk_values = []
    # loop over all samples
    for i in range(len(y_true)):
        # store apk values for every sample
        apk_values.append(
```

```
        apk(y_true[i], y_pred[i], k=k)
    )
    # return mean of apk values list
    return sum(apk_values) / len(apk_values)
```

Now, we can calculate MAP@k for k=1, 2, 3 and 4 for the same list of lists.

```
In [X]: y_true = [
   ...:     [1, 2, 3],
   ...:     [0, 2],
   ...:     [1],
   ...:     [2, 3],
   ...:     [1, 0],
   ...:     []
   ...: ]

In [X]: y_pred = [
   ...:     [0, 1, 2],
   ...:     [1],
   ...:     [0, 2, 3],
   ...:     [2, 3, 4, 0],
   ...:     [0, 1, 2],
   ...:     [0]
   ...: ]

In [X]: mapk(y_true, y_pred, k=1)
Out[X]: 0.3333333333333333

In [X]: mapk(y_true, y_pred, k=2)
Out[X]: 0.375

In [X]: mapk(y_true, y_pred, k=3)
Out[X]: 0.3611111111111111

In [X]: mapk(y_true, y_pred, k=4)
Out[X]: 0.34722222222222215
```

P@k, AP@k and MAP@k all range from 0 to 1 with 1 being the best.

Please note that sometimes you might see different implementations of P@k and AP@k on the internet. For example, let's take a look at one of these implementations.

```python
# taken from:
# https://github.com/benhamner/Metrics/blob/
# master/Python/ml_metrics/average_precision.py
import numpy as np

def apk(actual, predicted, k=10):
    """
    Computes the average precision at k.
    This function computes the AP at k between two lists of
    items.
    Parameters
    ----------
    actual : list
             A list of elements to be predicted (order doesn't matter)
    predicted : list
             A list of predicted elements (order does matter)
    k : int, optional
             The maximum number of predicted elements
    Returns
    -------
    score : double
             The average precision at k over the input lists
    """
    if len(predicted)>k:
        predicted = predicted[:k]

    score = 0.0
    num_hits = 0.0

    for i,p in enumerate(predicted):
        if p in actual and p not in predicted[:i]:
            num_hits += 1.0
            score += num_hits / (i+1.0)

    if not actual:
        return 0.0

    return score / min(len(actual), k)
```

This implementation is another version of AP@k where order matters and we weigh the predictions. This implementation will have slightly different results from what I have presented.

Now, we come to **log loss for multi-label classification**. This is quite easy. You can convert the targets to binary format and then use a log loss for each column. In the end, you can take the average of log loss in each column. This is also known as mean column-wise log loss. Of course, there are other ways you can implement this, and you should explore it as you come across it.

We have now reached a stage where we can say that we now know all binary, multi-class and multi-label classification metrics, and now we can move to regression metrics.

The most common metric in regression is error. **Error** is simple and very easy to understand.

$$Error = True\ Value - Predicted\ Value$$

Absolute error is just absolute of the above.

$$Absolute\ Error = Abs\ (\ True\ Value - Predicted\ Value\ )$$

Then we have **mean absolute error (MAE).** It's just mean of all absolute errors.

```python
import numpy as np

def mean_absolute_error(y_true, y_pred):
    """
    This function calculates mae
    :param y_true: list of real numbers, true values
    :param y_pred: list of real numbers, predicted values
    :return: mean absolute error
    """
    # initialize error at 0
    error = 0
    # loop over all samples in the true and predicted list
    for yt, yp in zip(y_true, y_pred):
        # calculate absolute error
        # and add to error
        error += np.abs(yt - yp)
    # return mean error
    return error / len(y_true)
```

Similarly, we have squared error and **mean squared error (MSE)**.

$$Squared\ Error = (\ True\ Value - Predicted\ Value\ )^2$$

And mean squared error (MSE) can be implemented as follows.

```python
def mean_squared_error(y_true, y_pred):
    """
    This function calculates mse
    :param y_true: list of real numbers, true values
    :param y_pred: list of real numbers, predicted values
    :return: mean squared error
    """
    # initialize error at 0
    error = 0
    # loop over all samples in the true and predicted list
    for yt, yp in zip(y_true, y_pred):
        # calculate squared error
        # and add to error
        error += (yt - yp) ** 2
    # return mean error
    return error / len(y_true)
```

MSE and **RMSE (root mean squared error)** are the most popular metrics used in evaluating regression models.

$$RMSE = SQRT\ (\ MSE\ )$$

Another type of error in same class is **squared logarithmic error**. Some people call it **SLE,** and when we take mean of this error across all samples, it is known as **MSLE (mean squared logarithmic error)** and implemented as follows.

```python
import numpy as np


def mean_squared_log_error(y_true, y_pred):
    """
    This function calculates msle
    :param y_true: list of real numbers, true values
    :param y_pred: list of real numbers, predicted values
    :return: mean squared logarithmic error
    """
```

```
"""
# initialize error at 0
error = 0
# loop over all samples in true and predicted list
for yt, yp in zip(y_true, y_pred):
    # calculate squared log error
    # and add to error
    error += (np.log(1 + yt) - np.log(1 + yp)) ** 2
# return mean error
return error / len(y_true)
```

Root mean squared logarithmic error is just a square root of this. It is also known as **RMSLE**.

Then we have the percentage error:

*Percentage Error = ((True Value – Predicted Value) / True Value) * 100*

Same can be converted to mean percentage error for all samples.

```
def mean_percentage_error(y_true, y_pred):
    """
    This function calculates mpe
    :param y_true: list of real numbers, true values
    :param y_pred: list of real numbers, predicted values
    :return: mean percentage error
    """
    # initialize error at 0
    error = 0

    # loop over all samples in true and predicted list
    for yt, yp in zip(y_true, y_pred):
        # calculate percentage error
        # and add to error
        error += (yt - yp) / yt

    # return mean percentage error
    return error / len(y_true)
```

And an absolute version of the same (and more common version) is known as **mean absolute percentage error or MAPE**.

```
import numpy as np


def mean_abs_percentage_error(y_true, y_pred):
    """
    This function calculates MAPE
    :param y_true: list of real numbers, true values
    :param y_pred: list of real numbers, predicted values
    :return: mean absolute percentage error
    """
    # initialize error at 0
    error = 0
    # loop over all samples in true and predicted list
    for yt, yp in zip(y_true, y_pred):
        # calculate percentage error
        # and add to error
        error += np.abs(yt - yp) / yt
    # return mean percentage error
    return error / len(y_true)
```

The best thing about regression is that there are only a few most popular metrics that can be applied to almost every regression problem. And it is much easier to understand when we compare it to classification metrics.

Let's talk about another regression metric known as **R² (R-squared)**, also known as the **coefficient of determination**.

In simple words, R-squared says how good your model fits the data. R-squared closer to 1.0 says that the model fits the data quite well, whereas closer 0 means that model isn't that good. R-squared can also be negative when the model just makes absurd predictions.

The formula for R-squared is shown in figure 10, but as always a python implementation makes things more clear.

$$R^2 = 1 - \frac{\sum_{i=1}^{N}(y_{t_i} - y_{p_i})^2}{\sum_{i=1}^{N}(y_{t_i} - y_{t_{mean}})}$$

Figure 10: Formula for R-squared

```python
import numpy as np


def r2(y_true, y_pred):
    """
    This function calculates r-squared score
    :param y_true: list of real numbers, true values
    :param y_pred: list of real numbers, predicted values
    :return: r2 score
    """

    # calculate the mean value of true values
    mean_true_value = np.mean(y_true)

    # initialize numerator with 0
    numerator = 0
    # initialize denominator with 0
    denominator = 0

    # loop over all true and predicted values
    for yt, yp in zip(y_true, y_pred):
        # update numerator
        numerator += (yt - yp) ** 2
        # update denominator
        denominator += (yt - mean_true_value) ** 2
    # calculate the ratio
    ratio = numerator / denominator
    # return 1 - ratio
    return 1 - ratio
```

There are many more evaluation metrics, and this list is never-ending. I can write a book which is only about different evaluation metrics. Maybe I will. For now, these evaluations metrics will fit almost every problem you want to attempt. Please note that I have implemented these metrics in the most straightforward manner, and that means they are not efficient enough. You can make most of them in a very efficient way by properly using numpy. For example, take a look at the implementation of mean absolute error without any loops.

```python
import numpy as np

def mae_np(y_true, y_pred):
    return np.mean(np.abs(y_true - y_pred))
```

I could have implemented all the metrics this way but to learn it's better to look at low-level implementation. Once you learn the low-level implementation in pure python, and without using a lot of numpy, you can easily convert it to numpy and make it much faster.

Then, there are some advanced metrics.

One of them which is quite widely used is **quadratic weighted kappa,** also known as QWK. It is also known as **Cohen's kappa**. QWK measures the "agreement" between two "ratings". The ratings can be any real numbers in 0 to N. And predictions are also in the same range. An agreement can be defined as how close these ratings are to each other. So, it's suitable for a classification problem with N different categories/classes. If the agreement is high, the score is closer towards 1.0. In the case of low agreement, the score is close to 0. Cohen's kappa has a good implementation in scikit-learn, and detailed discussion of this metric is beyond the scope of this book.

```
In [X]: from sklearn import metrics

In [X]: y_true = [1, 2, 3, 1, 2, 3, 1, 2, 3]

In [X]: y_pred = [2, 1, 3, 1, 2, 3, 3, 1, 2]

In [X]: metrics.cohen_kappa_score(y_true, y_pred, weights="quadratic")
Out[X]: 0.33333333333333337

In [X]: metrics.accuracy_score(y_true, y_pred)
Out[X]: 0.4444444444444444
```

You can see that even though accuracy is high, QWK is less. A QWK greater than 0.85 is considered to be very good!

An important metric is **Matthew's Correlation Coefficient (MCC)**. MCC ranges from -1 to 1. 1 is perfect prediction, -1 is imperfect prediction, and 0 is random prediction. The formula for MCC is quite simple.

$$MCC = \frac{TP * TN - FP * FN}{[(TP + FP) * (FN + TN) * (FP + TN) * (TP + FN)]^{\wedge}(0.5)}$$

We see that MCC takes into consideration TP, FP, TN and FN and thus can be used for problems where classes are skewed. You can quickly implement it in python by using what we have already implemented.

```python
def mcc(y_true, y_pred):
    """
    This function calculates Matthew's Correlation Coefficient
    for binary classification.
    :param y_true: list of true values
    :param y_pred: list of predicted values
    :return: mcc score
    """
    tp = true_positive(y_true, y_pred)
    tn = true_negative(y_true, y_pred)
    fp = false_positive(y_true, y_pred)
    fn = false_negative(y_true, y_pred)

    numerator = (tp * tn) - (fp * fn)

    denominator = (
        (tp + fp) *
        (fn + tn) *
        (fp + tn) *
        (tp + fn)
    )

    denominator = denominator ** 0.5

    return numerator/denominator
```

These are the metrics that can help you get started and will apply to almost every machine learning problem.

One thing to keep in mind is that to evaluate un-supervised methods, for example, some kind of clustering, it's better to create or manually label the test set and keep it separate from everything that is going on in your modelling part. When you are done with clustering, you can evaluate the performance on the test set simply by using any of the supervised learning metrics.

Once we understand what metric to use for a given problem, we can start looking more deeply into our models for improvements.

Arranging machine learning projects

Finally, we are at a stage where we can start building our very first machine learning models.

Or are we?

Before we start, we must take care of a few things. Please remember that we will work in an IDE/text editor rather than jupyter notebooks. You can also work in jupyter notebooks, and it's totally up to you. However, I will be using jupyter only for things like data exploration and for plotting charts and graphs. We will build the classification framework in such a way that most problems will become plug n' play. You will be able to train a model without making too many changes to the code, and when you improve your models, you will be able to track them using git.

Let's look at the structure of the files first of all. For any project that you are doing, create a new folder. For this example, I am calling the project "**project**".

The inside of the project folder should look something like the following.

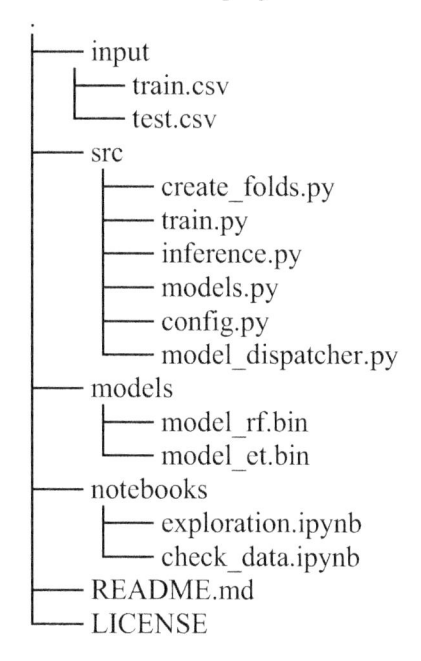

```
├── input
│   ├── train.csv
│   └── test.csv
├── src
│   ├── create_folds.py
│   ├── train.py
│   ├── inference.py
│   ├── models.py
│   ├── config.py
│   └── model_dispatcher.py
├── models
│   ├── model_rf.bin
│   └── model_et.bin
├── notebooks
│   ├── exploration.ipynb
│   └── check_data.ipynb
├── README.md
└── LICENSE
```

Let's see what these folders and file are about.

input/: This folder consists of all the input files and data for your machine learning project. If you are working on NLP projects, you can keep your embeddings here. If you are working on image projects, all images go to a subfolder inside this folder.

src/: We will keep all the python scripts associated with the project here. If I talk about a python script, i.e. any *.py file, it is stored in the src folder.

models/: This folder keeps all the trained models.

notebooks/: All jupyter notebooks (i.e. any *.ipynb file) are stored in the notebooks folder.

README.md: This is a markdown file where you can describe your project and write instructions on how to train the model or to serve this in a production environment.

LICENSE: This is a simple text file that consists of a license for the project, such as MIT, Apache, etc. Going into details of the licenses is beyond the scope of this book.

Let's assume you are building a model to classify MNIST dataset (a dataset that has been used in almost every machine learning book). If you remember, we touched MNIST dataset in cross-validation chapter too. So, I am not going to explain how this dataset looks like. There are many different formats of MNIST dataset available online, but we will be using the CSV format of the dataset.

In this format of the dataset, each row of the CSV consists of the label of the image and 784 pixel values ranging from 0 to 255. The dataset consists of 60000 images in this format.

We can use pandas to read this data format easily.

Please note that even though Figure 1 shows all pixel values as zeros, it is not the case.

	label	1x1	1x2	1x3	1x4	1x5	1x6	1x7	1x8	1x9	...	28x19	28x20	28x21	28x22	28x23	28x24	28x25	28x26	28x27
0	5	0	0	0	0	0	0	0	0	0	...	0	0	0	0	0	0	0	0	0
1	0	0	0	0	0	0	0	0	0	0	...	0	0	0	0	0	0	0	0	0
2	4	0	0	0	0	0	0	0	0	0	...	0	0	0	0	0	0	0	0	0
3	1	0	0	0	0	0	0	0	0	0	...	0	0	0	0	0	0	0	0	0
4	9	0	0	0	0	0	0	0	0	0	...	0	0	0	0	0	0	0	0	0

Figure 1: MNIST dataset in CSV format

Let's take a look at the counts of the label column in this dataset.

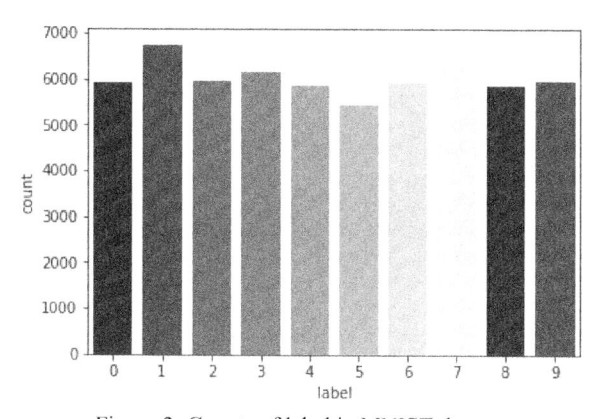

Figure 2: Counts of label in MNIST dataset

We don't need much more exploration for this dataset. We already know what we have, and there is no need to make plots on different pixel values. From figure 2, it is quite clear that the distribution of labels is quite good and even. We can thus use accuracy/F1 as metrics. This is the first step when approaching a machine learning problem: decide the metric!

Now, we can code a little bit. We need to create the *src/* folder and some python scripts.

Please note that the training CSV file is located in the *input/* folder and is called *mnist_train.csv*.

How should these files look like for such a project?

The first script that one should create is ***create_folds.py***.

This will create a new file in the *input/* folder called *mnist_train_folds.csv,* and it's the same as *mnist_train.csv*. The only differences are that this CSV is shuffled and has a new column called *kfold*.

Once we have decided what kind of evaluation metric we want to use and have created the folds, we are good to go with creating a basic model. This is done in ***train.py***.

```
# src/train.py
import joblib
import pandas as pd
from sklearn import metrics
from sklearn import tree


def run(fold):
    # read the training data with folds
    df = pd.read_csv("../input/mnist_train_folds.csv")

    # training data is where kfold is not equal to provided fold
    # also, note that we reset the index
    df_train = df[df.kfold != fold].reset_index(drop=True)

    # validation data is where kfold is equal to provided fold
    df_valid = df[df.kfold == fold].reset_index(drop=True)

    # drop the label column from dataframe and convert it to
    # a numpy array by using .values.
    # target is label column in the dataframe
    x_train = df_train.drop("label", axis=1).values
    y_train = df_train.label.values

    # similarly, for validation, we have
    x_valid = df_valid.drop("label", axis=1).values
    y_valid = df_valid.label.values

    # initialize simple decision tree classifier from sklearn
    clf = tree.DecisionTreeClassifier()

    # fit the model on training data
    clf.fit(x_train, y_train)

    # create predictions for validation samples
    preds = clf.predict(x_valid)
```

```
    # calculate & print accuracy
    accuracy = metrics.accuracy_score(y_valid, preds)
    print(f"Fold={fold}, Accuracy={accuracy}")

    # save the model
    joblib.dump(clf, f"../models/dt_{fold}.bin")

if __name__ == "__main__":
    run(fold=0)
    run(fold=1)
    run(fold=2)
    run(fold=3)
    run(fold=4)
```

You can run this script by calling *python train.py* in the console.

```
> python train.py
Fold=0, Accuracy=0.8680833333333333
Fold=1, Accuracy=0.8685
Fold=2, Accuracy=0.8674166666666666
Fold=3, Accuracy=0.8703333333333333
Fold=4, Accuracy=0.8699166666666667
```

When you look at the training script, you will see that there are still a few more things that are hardcoded, for example, the fold numbers, the training file and the output folder.

We can thus create a config file with all this information: **config.py**.

```
# config.py

TRAINING_FILE = "../input/mnist_train_folds.csv"

MODEL_OUTPUT = "../models/"
```

And we make some changes to our training script too. The training file utilizes the config file now. Thus making it easier to change data or the model output.

```python
# train.py
import os

import config

import joblib
import pandas as pd
from sklearn import metrics
from sklearn import tree


def run(fold):
    # read the training data with folds
    df = pd.read_csv(config.TRAINING_FILE)

    # training data is where kfold is not equal to provided fold
    # also, note that we reset the index
    df_train = df[df.kfold != fold].reset_index(drop=True)

    # validation data is where kfold is equal to provided fold
    df_valid = df[df.kfold == fold].reset_index(drop=True)

    # drop the label column from dataframe and convert it to
    # a numpy array by using .values.
    # target is label column in the dataframe
    x_train = df_train.drop("label", axis=1).values
    y_train = df_train.label.values

    # similarly, for validation, we have
    x_valid = df_valid.drop("label", axis=1).values
    y_valid = df_valid.label.values

    # initialize simple decision tree classifier from sklearn
    clf = tree.DecisionTreeClassifier()

    # fir the model on training data
    clf.fit(x_train, y_train)

    # create predictions for validation samples
    preds = clf.predict(x_valid)

    # calculate & print accuracy
    accuracy = metrics.accuracy_score(y_valid, preds)
    print(f"Fold={fold}, Accuracy={accuracy}")

    # save the model
```

```
        joblib.dump(
            clf,
            os.path.join(config.MODEL_OUTPUT, f"dt_{fold}.bin")
        )

if __name__ == "__main__":
    run(fold=0)
    run(fold=1)
    run(fold=2)
    run(fold=3)
    run(fold=4)
```

Please note that I am not showing the difference between this training script and the one before. Please take a careful look at both of them and find the differences yourself. There aren't many of them.

There is still one more thing related to the training script that can be improved. As you can see, we call the *run* function multiple times for every fold. Sometimes it's not advisable to run multiple folds in the same script as the memory consumption may keep increasing, and your program may crash. To take care of this problem, we can pass arguments to the training script. I like doing it using *argparse*.

```
# train.py
import argparse
.
.
.

if __name__ == "__main__":
    # initialize ArgumentParser class of argparse
    parser = argparse.ArgumentParser()

    # add the different arguments you need and their type
    # currently, we only need fold
    parser.add_argument(
        "--fold",
        type=int
    )
    # read the arguments from the command line
    args = parser.parse_args()

    # run the fold specified by command line arguments
```

```
run(fold=args.fold)
```

Now, we can run the python script again, but only for a given fold.

```
> python train.py --fold 0
Fold=0, Accuracy=0.8656666666666667
```

If you see carefully, our fold 0 score was a bit different before. This is because of the randomness in the model. We will come to handling randomness in later chapters.

Now, if you want, you can create a **shell script** with different commands for different folds and run them all together, as shown below.

```
#!/bin/sh

python train.py --fold 0
python train.py --fold 1
python train.py --fold 2
python train.py --fold 3
python train.py --fold 4
```

And you can run this by the following command.

```
> sh run.sh
Fold=0, Accuracy=0.8675
Fold=1, Accuracy=0.8693333333333333
Fold=2, Accuracy=0.8683333333333333
Fold=3, Accuracy=0.8704166666666666
Fold=4, Accuracy=0.8685
```

We have made quite some progress now, but if we look at our training script, we still are limited by a few things, for example, the model. The model is hardcoded in the training script, and the only way to change it is to modify the script. So, we will create a new python script called ***model_dispatcher.py***. *model_dispatcher.py,* as the name suggests, will dispatch our models to our training script.

```
# model_dispatcher.py
from sklearn import tree


models = {
    "decision_tree_gini": tree.DecisionTreeClassifier(
        criterion="gini"
    ),
    "decision_tree_entropy": tree.DecisionTreeClassifier(
        criterion="entropy"
    ),
}
```

model_dispatcher.py imports tree from scikit-learn and defines a dictionary with keys that are names of the models and values are the models themselves. Here, we define two different decision trees, one with gini criterion and one with entropy. To use *model_dispatcher.py*, we need to make a few changes to our training script.

```
# train.py
import argparse
import os

import joblib
import pandas as pd
from sklearn import metrics

import config
import model_dispatcher


def run(fold, model):
    # read the training data with folds
    df = pd.read_csv(config.TRAINING_FILE)

    # training data is where kfold is not equal to provided fold
    # also, note that we reset the index
    df_train = df[df.kfold != fold].reset_index(drop=True)

    # validation data is where kfold is equal to provided fold
    df_valid = df[df.kfold == fold].reset_index(drop=True)

    # drop the label column from dataframe and convert it to
    # a numpy array by using .values.
```

```python
    # target is label column in the dataframe
    x_train = df_train.drop("label", axis=1).values
    y_train = df_train.label.values

    # similarly, for validation, we have
    x_valid = df_valid.drop("label", axis=1).values
    y_valid = df_valid.label.values

    # fetch the model from model_dispatcher
    clf = model_dispatcher.models[model]

    # fir the model on training data
    clf.fit(x_train, y_train)

    # create predictions for validation samples
    preds = clf.predict(x_valid)

    # calculate & print accuracy
    accuracy = metrics.accuracy_score(y_valid, preds)
    print(f"Fold={fold}, Accuracy={accuracy}")

    # save the model
    joblib.dump(
        clf,
        os.path.join(config.MODEL_OUTPUT, f"dt_{fold}.bin")
    )


if __name__ == "__main__":
    parser = argparse.ArgumentParser()

    parser.add_argument(
        "--fold",
        type=int
    )
    parser.add_argument(
        "--model",
        type=str
    )

    args = parser.parse_args()

    run(
        fold=args.fold,
        model=args.model
    )
```

There are a few major changes to train.py:
- import *model_dispatcher*
- add *--model* argument to *ArgumentParser*
- add *model* argument to *run()* function
- use the dispatcher to fetch the model given the name

Now, we can run the script using the following command:

```
> python train.py --fold 0 --model decision_tree_gini
Fold=0, Accuracy=0.8665833333333334
```

Or the following command

```
> python train.py --fold 0 --model decision_tree_entropy
Fold=0, Accuracy=0.8705833333333334
```

Now, if you add a new model, all you have to do is make changes to *model_dispatcher.py*. Let's try adding random forest and see what happens to our accuracy.

```
# model_dispatcher.py
from sklearn import ensemble
from sklearn import tree


models = {
    "decision_tree_gini": tree.DecisionTreeClassifier(
        criterion="gini"
    ),
    "decision_tree_entropy": tree.DecisionTreeClassifier(
        criterion="entropy"
    ),
    "rf": ensemble.RandomForestClassifier(),
}
```

Let's run this code.

```
> python train.py --fold 0 --model rf
Fold=0, Accuracy=0.9670833333333333
```

Wow, a simple change gave such a massive improvement in the score! Let's run all 5 folds using our *run.sh* script now!

```
#!/bin/sh

python train.py --fold 0 --model rf
python train.py --fold 1 --model rf
python train.py --fold 2 --model rf
python train.py --fold 3 --model rf
python train.py --fold 4 --model rf
```

And the scores look like the following.

```
> sh run.sh
Fold=0, Accuracy=0.9674166666666667
Fold=1, Accuracy=0.9698333333333333
Fold=2, Accuracy=0.96575
Fold=3, Accuracy=0.9684166666666667
Fold=4, Accuracy=0.9666666666666667
```

MNIST is a problem that is discussed in almost every book and every blog. But I tried to convert this problem to more fun and show you how to write a basic framework for almost any machine learning project you are doing, or you plan to do in the near future. There are many different ways to improve on this MNIST model and also this framework, and we will see that in future chapters.

I used some scripts like *model_dispatcher.py* and *config.py* and imported them in my training script. Please note that *I did not import * and neither should you. If I had imported *, you would have never known where the models dictionary came from*. Writing good, understandable code is an essential quality one can have, and many data scientists ignore it. If you work on a project that others can understand and use without consulting you, you save their time and your own time and can invest that time to improve your project or work on a new one.

Approaching categorical variables

Many people struggle a lot with the handling of categorical variables, and thus this deserves a full chapter. In this chapter, I will talk about different types of categorical data and how to approach a problem with categorical variables.

What are categorical variables?

Categorical variables/features are any feature type can be classified into two major types:
- Nominal
- Ordinal

Nominal variables are variables that have two or more categories which do not have any kind of order associated with them. For example, if gender is classified into two groups, i.e. male and female, it can be considered as a nominal variable.

Ordinal variables, on the other hand, have "levels" or categories with a particular order associated with them. For example, an ordinal categorical variable can be a feature with three different levels: low, medium and high. Order is important.

As far as definitions are concerned, we can also categorize categorical variables as **binary**, i.e., a categorical variable with only two categories. Some even talk about a type called "**cyclic**" for categorical variables. Cyclic variables are present in "cycles" for example, days in a week: Sunday, Monday, Tuesday, Wednesday, Thursday, Friday and Saturday. After Saturday, we have Sunday again. This is a cycle. Another example would be hours in a day if we consider them to be categories.

There are many different definitions of categorical variables, and many people talk about handling categorical variables differently depending on the type of categorical variable. However, I do not see any need for it. All problems with categorical variables can be approached in the same way.

Before we start, we need a dataset to work with (as always). One of the best free datasets to understand categorical variables is *cat-in-the-dat* from Categorical Features Encoding Challenge from Kaggle. There were two challenges, and we will be using the data from the second challenge as it had more variables and was more difficult than its previous version.

Let's take a look at the data.

bin_0	bin_1	nom_0	nom_1	ord_0	ord_1	day	month	target
NaN	0.0	Green	Polygon	3.0	Novice	6.0	8.0	0
0.0	0.0	Red	Square	1.0	Expert	7.0	1.0	0
0.0	0.0	Blue	Trapezoid	1.0	Expert	5.0	8.0	0
0.0	0.0	Green	Circle	1.0	Contributor	3.0	6.0	0
0.0	0.0	Blue	Circle	1.0	Expert	2.0	4.0	0
...	...	...	...	...	...	...	...	...
0.0	0.0	Red	Triangle	2.0	Expert	3.0	11.0	1
0.0	1.0	Blue	Circle	3.0	Novice	4.0	5.0	0
0.0	0.0	Red	Polygon	3.0	Grandmaster	1.0	8.0	0
1.0	1.0	Blue	Trapezoid	2.0	Novice	7.0	5.0	0
0.0	1.0	Red	Circle	1.0	Novice	2.0	11.0	0

Figure 1: Viewing a subset of the data. Cat-in-the-dat-ii challenge[5]

The dataset consists of all kinds of categorical variables:
- Nominal
- Ordinal
- Cyclical
- Binary

In Figure 1, we see only a subset of all the variables that are present and the target variable.

It is a binary classification problem.

The target is not very important for us to learn categorical variables, but in the end, we will be building an end-to-end model so let's take a look at the target distribution in figure 2. We see that the target is **skewed** and thus the best metric for this binary classification problem would be Area Under the ROC Curve (AUC). We can use precision and recall too, but AUC combines these two metrics. Thus, we will be using AUC to evaluate the model that we build on this dataset.

---

[5] https://www.kaggle.com/c/cat-in-the-dat-ii

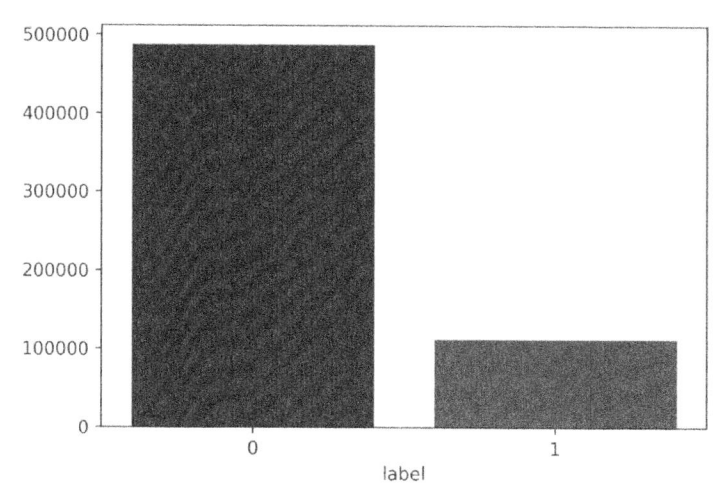

Figure 2: Count of targets. the x-axis shows the label, and the y-axis shows the count of the label

Overall, there are:
- Five binary variables
- Ten nominal variables
- Six ordinal variables
- Two cyclic variables
- And a target variable

Let's look at *ord_2* feature in the dataset. It consists of six different categories:
- Freezing
- Warm
- Cold
- Boiling Hot
- Hot
- Lava Hot

We have to know that computers do not understand text data and thus, we need to convert these categories to numbers. A simple way of doing this would be to create a dictionary that maps these values to numbers starting from 0 to N-1, where N is the total number of categories in a given feature.

```
mapping = {
    "Freezing": 0,
    "Warm": 1,
    "Cold": 2,
    "Boiling Hot": 3,
    "Hot": 4,
    "Lava Hot": 5
}
```

Now, we can read the dataset and convert these categories to numbers easily.

```
import pandas as pd

df = pd.read_csv("../input/cat_train.csv")

df.loc[:, "ord_2"] = df.ord_2.map(mapping)
```

Value counts before mapping:

```
df.ord_2.value_counts()

Freezing       142726
Warm           124239
Cold            97822
Boiling Hot     84790
Hot             67508
Lava Hot        64840
Name: ord_2, dtype: int64
```

Value counts after mapping:

```
0.0    142726
1.0    124239
2.0     97822
3.0     84790
4.0     67508
5.0     64840
Name: ord_2, dtype: int64
```

This type of encoding of categorical variables is known as **Label Encoding**, i.e., we are encoding every category as a numerical label.

We can do the same by using *LabelEncoder* from scikit-learn.

```
import pandas as pd
from sklearn import preprocessing

# read the data
df = pd.read_csv("../input/cat_train.csv")

# fill NaN values in ord_2 column
df.loc[:, "ord_2"] = df.ord_2.fillna("NONE")

# initialize LabelEncoder
lbl_enc = preprocessing.LabelEncoder()

# fit label encoder and transform values on ord_2 column
# P.S: do not use this directly. fit first, then transform
df.loc[:, "ord_2"] = lbl_enc.fit_transform(df.ord_2.values)
```

You will see that I use *fillna* from pandas. The reason is *LabelEncoder* from scikit-learn does not handle NaN values, and *ord_2* column has NaN values in it.

We can use this directly in many tree-based models:

- Decision trees
- Random forest
- Extra Trees
- Or any kind of boosted trees model
    - XGBoost
    - GBM
    - LightGBM

This type of encoding cannot be used in linear models, support vector machines or neural networks as they expect data to be normalized (or standardized).

For these types of models, we can binarize the data.

```
Freezing       --> 0 --> 0 0 0
Warm           --> 1 --> 0 0 1
Cold           --> 2 --> 0 1 0
Boiling Hot    --> 3 --> 0 1 1
Hot            --> 4 --> 1 0 0
Lava Hot       --> 5 --> 1 0 1
```

This is just converting the categories to numbers and then converting them to their binary representation. We are thus splitting one feature into three (in this case) features (or columns). If we have more categories, we might end up splitting into a lot more columns.

It becomes easy to store lots of **binarized variables** like this if we store them in a sparse format. **A sparse format** is nothing but a representation or way of storing data in memory in which you do not store all the values but only the values that matter. In the case of binary variables described above, all that matters is where we have ones (1s).

It's difficult to imagine a format like this but should become clear with an example.

Let's assume that we are provided with only one feature in the dataframe above: *ord_2*.

Index	Feature
0	Warm
1	Hot
2	Lava hot

Currently, we are looking at only three samples in the dataset. Let's convert this to binary representation where we have three items for each sample.

These three items are the three features.

Index	Feature_0	Feature_1	Feature_2
0	0	0	1
1	1	0	0
2	1	0	1

So, our features are stored in a matrix which has 3 rows and 3 columns - 3x3. Each element of this matrix occupies 8 bytes. So, our total memory requirement for this array is 8x3x3 = 72 bytes.

We can also check this using a simple python snippet.

```
import numpy as np

# create our example feature matrix
example = np.array(
    [
        [0, 0, 1],
        [1, 0, 0],
        [1, 0, 1]
    ]
)

# print size in bytes
print(example.nbytes)
```

This code will print 72 as we calculated before. But do we need to store all the elements of this matrix? No. As mentioned before we are only interested in 1s. 0s are not that important because anything multiplied with 0 will be zero and 0 added/subtracted to/from anything doesn't make any difference. One way to represent this matrix only with ones would be some kind of dictionary method in which keys are indices of rows and columns and value is 1:

```
(0, 2)    1
(1, 0)    1
(2, 0)    1
(2, 2)    1
```

A notation like this will occupy much less memory because it has to store only four values (in this case). The total memory used will be 8x4 = 32 bytes. Any numpy array can be converted to a sparse matrix by simple python code.

```python
import numpy as np
from scipy import sparse

# create our example feature matrix
example = np.array(
    [
        [0, 0, 1],
        [1, 0, 0],
        [1, 0, 1]
    ]
)

# convert numpy array to sparse CSR matrix
sparse_example = sparse.csr_matrix(example)

# print size of this sparse matrix
print(sparse_example.data.nbytes)
```

This will print 32, which is so less than our dense array! The total size of the **sparse csr matrix** is the sum of three values.

```python
print(
    sparse_example.data.nbytes +
    sparse_example.indptr.nbytes +
    sparse_example.indices.nbytes
)
```

This will print 64, which is still less than our dense array. Unfortunately, I will not go into the details of these elements. You can read more about them in **scipy** docs. The difference in size becomes vast when we have much larger arrays, let's say with thousands of samples and tens of thousands of features. For example, a text dataset where we are using count-based features.

```python
import numpy as np
from scipy import sparse
```

```
# number of rows
n_rows = 10000

# number of columns
n_cols = 100000

# create random binary matrix with only 5% values as 1s
example = np.random.binomial(1, p=0.05, size=(n_rows, n_cols))

# print size in bytes
print(f"Size of dense array: {example.nbytes}")

# convert numpy array to sparse CSR matrix
sparse_example = sparse.csr_matrix(example)

# print size of this sparse matrix
print(f"Size of sparse array: {sparse_example.data.nbytes}")

full_size = (
    sparse_example.data.nbytes +
    sparse_example.indptr.nbytes +
    sparse_example.indices.nbytes
)

# print full size of this sparse matrix
print(f"Full size of sparse array: {full_size}")
```

This prints:

```
Size of dense array: 8000000000
Size of sparse array: 399932496
Full size of sparse array: 599938748
```

So, dense array takes ~8000MB or approximately 8GB of memory. The sparse array, on the other hand, takes only 399MB of memory.

And, that's why we prefer sparse arrays over dense whenever we have a lot of zeros in our features.

Please note that there are many different ways of representing a sparse matrix. Here I have shown only one such (and probably the most popular) way. Going deep into these is beyond the scope of this book and is left as an exercise to the reader.

Even though the sparse representation of binarized features takes much less memory than its dense representation, there is another transformation for categorical variables that takes even less memory. This is known as **One Hot Encoding**.

One hot encoding is a binary encoding too in the sense that there are only two values, 0s and 1s. However, it must be noted that it's not a binary representation. Its representation can be understood by looking at the following example.

Suppose we represent each category of the *ord_2* variable by a vector. This vector is of the same size as the number of categories in the *ord_2* variable. In this specific case, each vector is of size six and has all zeros except at one position. Let's look at this particular table of vectors.

Freezing	0	0	0	0	0	1
Warm	0	0	0	0	1	0
Cold	0	0	0	1	0	0
Boiling Hot	0	0	1	0	0	0
Hot	0	1	0	0	0	0
Lava Hot	1	0	0	0	0	0

We see that the size of vectors is 1x6, i.e. there are six elements in the vector. Where does this number come from? If you look carefully, you will see that there are six categories, as mentioned before. When one-hot encoding, the vector size has to be same as the number of categories we are looking at. Each vector has a 1 and rest all other values are 0s. Now, let's use these features instead of the binarized feature as before and see how much memory can we save.

If you remember the old data, it looked as follows:

Index	Feature
0	Warm
1	Hot
2	Lava hot

And we had three features for each sample. But one-hot vectors, in this case, are of size 6. Thus, we have six features instead of 3.

Index	F_0	F_1	F_2	F_3	F_4	F_5
0	0	0	0	0	1	0
1	0	1	0	0	0	0
2	1	0	0	0	0	0

So, we have six features, and in this 3x6 array, there are only 3 ones. Finding size using numpy is very similar to the binarization size calculation script. All you need to change is the array. Let's take a look at this code.

```python
import numpy as np
from scipy import sparse
# create binary matrix
example = np.array(
    [
        [0, 0, 0, 0, 1, 0],
        [0, 1, 0, 0, 0, 0],
        [1, 0, 0, 0, 0, 0]
    ]
)

# print size in bytes
print(f"Size of dense array: {example.nbytes}")

# convert numpy array to sparse CSR matrix
sparse_example = sparse.csr_matrix(example)

# print size of this sparse matrix
print(f"Size of sparse array: {sparse_example.data.nbytes}")

full_size = (
    sparse_example.data.nbytes +
    sparse_example.indptr.nbytes +
    sparse_example.indices.nbytes
)

# print full size of this sparse matrix
print(f"Full size of sparse array: {full_size}")
```

This will print the sizes as:

```
Size of dense array: 144
Size of sparse array: 24
Full size of sparse array: 52
```

We see that the dense array size is much larger than the one with binarization. However, the size of the sparse array is much less. Let's try this with a much larger array. In this example, we will use *OneHotEncoder* from scikit-learn to transform our feature array with 1001 categories into dense and sparse matrices.

```
import numpy as np
from sklearn import preprocessing

# create random 1-d array with 1001 different categories (int)
example = np.random.randint(1000, size=1000000)

# initialize OneHotEncoder from scikit-learn
# keep sparse = False to get dense array
ohe = preprocessing.OneHotEncoder(sparse=False)

# fit and transform data with dense one hot encoder
ohe_example = ohe.fit_transform(example.reshape(-1, 1))

# print size in bytes for dense array
print(f"Size of dense array: {ohe_example.nbytes}")

# initialize OneHotEncoder from scikit-learn
# keep sparse = True to get sparse array
ohe = preprocessing.OneHotEncoder(sparse=True)

# fit and transform data with sparse one-hot encoder
ohe_example = ohe.fit_transform(example.reshape(-1, 1))

# print size of this sparse matrix
print(f"Size of sparse array: {ohe_example.data.nbytes}")

full_size = (
    ohe_example.data.nbytes +
    ohe_example.indptr.nbytes + ohe_example.indices.nbytes
)

# print full size of this sparse matrix
print(f"Full size of sparse array: {full_size}")
```

And this code prints:

```
Size of dense array: 8000000000
Size of sparse array: 8000000
Full size of sparse array: 16000004
```

Dense array size here is approximately 8GB and sparse array is 8MB. If you had a choice, which one would you choose? Seems like a quite simple choice to me, isn't it?

These three methods are the most important ways to handle categorical variables. There are, however, many other different methods you can use to handle categorical variables. An example of one such method is about converting categorical variables to numerical variables.

Suppose we go back to the categorical features dataframe (original cat-in-the-dat-ii) that we had. How many *ids* do we have in the dataframe where the value of *ord_2* is *Boiling Hot*?

We can easily calculate this value by calculating the shape of the dataframe where *ord_2* column has the value *Boiling Hot*.

```
In [X]: df[df.ord_2 == "Boiling Hot"].shape
Out[X]: (84790, 25)
```

We see that there are 84790 rows with this value. We can also calculate this value for all the categories using *groupby* in pandas.

```
In [X]: df.groupby(["ord_2"])["id"].count()
Out[X]:
ord_2
Boiling Hot     84790
Cold            97822
Freezing       142726
Hot             67508
Lava Hot        64840
Warm           124239
Name: id, dtype: int64
```

If we just replace *ord_2* column with its count values, we have converted it to a feature which is kind of numerical now. We can create a new column or replace this column by using the *transform* function of pandas along with *groupby*.

```
In [X]: df.groupby(["ord_2"])["id"].transform("count")
Out[X]:
0            67508.0
1           124239.0
2           142726.0
3            64840.0
4            97822.0
             ...
599995      142726.0
599996       84790.0
599997      142726.0
599998      124239.0
599999       84790.0
Name: id, Length: 600000, dtype: float64
```

You can add counts of all the features or can also replace them or maybe group by multiple columns and their counts. For example, the following code counts by grouping on *ord_1* and *ord_2* columns.

```
In [X]: df.groupby(
   ...:         [
   ...:             "ord_1",
   ...:             "ord_2"
   ...:         ]
   ...: )["id"].count().reset_index(name="count")
Out[X]:
          ord_1         ord_2  count
0   Contributor   Boiling Hot  15634
1   Contributor          Cold  17734
2   Contributor      Freezing  26082
3   Contributor           Hot  12428
4   Contributor      Lava Hot  11919
5   Contributor          Warm  22774
6        Expert   Boiling Hot  19477
7        Expert          Cold  22956
8        Expert      Freezing  33249
9        Expert           Hot  15792
10       Expert      Lava Hot  15078
11       Expert          Warm  28900
```

```
12     Grandmaster   Boiling Hot    13623
13     Grandmaster          Cold    15464
14     Grandmaster      Freezing    22818
15     Grandmaster           Hot    10805
16     Grandmaster      Lava Hot    10363
17     Grandmaster          Warm    19899
18          Master   Boiling Hot    10800
.
.
.
.
```

Please note that I have eliminated some rows from the output to fit them in one page. This is another kind of count that you can add as a feature. You must have noted by now that I am using the *id* column for counts. You can, however, also count other columns by grouping by on combinations of the columns.

One more trick is to *create new features from these categorical variables*. You can create new categorical features from existing features, and this can be done in an effortless manner.

```
In [X]: df["new_feature"] = (
   ...:      df.ord_1.astype(str)
   ...:      + "_"
   ...:      + df.ord_2.astype(str)
   ...: )

In [X]: df.new_feature

Out[X]:
0                   Contributor_Hot
1                  Grandmaster_Warm
2                      nan_Freezing
3                   Novice_Lava Hot
4                  Grandmaster_Cold
                    ...
599995                Novice_Freezing
599996            Novice_Boiling Hot
599997          Contributor_Freezing
599998                   Master_Warm
599999       Contributor_Boiling Hot
Name: new_feature, Length: 600000, dtype: object
```

Here, we have combined *ord_1* and *ord_2* by an underscore, and before that, we convert these columns to string types. Note that NaN will also convert to string. But it's okay. We can also treat NaN as a new category. Thus, we have a new feature which is a combination of these two features. You can also combine more than three columns or four or even more.

```
In [X]: df["new_feature"] = (
   ...:     df.ord_1.astype(str)
   ...:     + "_"
   ...:     + df.ord_2.astype(str)
   ...:     + "_"
   ...:     + df.ord_3.astype(str)
   ...: )

In [X]: df.new_feature
Out[X]:
0            Contributor_Hot_c
1            Grandmaster_Warm_e
2                nan_Freezing_n
3              Novice_Lava_Hot_a
4            Grandmaster_Cold_h
                 ...
599995          Novice_Freezing_a
599996         Novice_Boiling Hot_n
599997       Contributor_Freezing_n
599998              Master_Warm_m
599999     Contributor_Boiling Hot_b
Name: new_feature, Length: 600000, dtype: object
```

So which categories should we combine? Well, there isn't an easy answer to that. It depends on your data and the types of features. Some domain knowledge might be useful for creating features like this. But if you don't have concerns about memory and CPU usage, you can go for a greedy approach where you can create many such combinations and then use a model to decide which features are useful and keep them. We will read about it later in this book.

Whenever you get categorical variables, follow these simple steps:
- fill the NaN values (this is very important!)
- convert them to integers by applying label encoding using *LabelEncoder* of scikit-learn or by using a mapping dictionary. If you didn't fill up NaN values with something, you might have to take care of them in this step

- create one-hot encoding. Yes, you can skip binarization!
- go for modelling! I mean the machine learning one. Not on the ramp.

Handling NaN data in categorical features is quite essential else you can get the infamous error from scikit-learn's LabelEncoder:

```
ValueError: y contains previously unseen labels: [nan, nan, nan, nan, nan, nan, nan, nan]
```

This simply means that when you are transforming the test data, you have NaN values in it. It's because you forgot to handle them during training. One simple way to **handle NaN values** would be to drop them. Well, it's simple but not ideal. NaN values may have a lot of information in them, and you will lose it if you just drop these values. There might also be many situations where most of your data has NaN values, and thus, you cannot drop rows/samples with NaN values. Another way of handling NaN values is to treat them as a completely new category. This is the most preferred way of handling NaN values. And can be achieved in a very simple manner if you are using *pandas*.

Check this out on *ord_2* column of the data we have been looking at till now.

```
In [X]: df.ord_2.value_counts()
Out[X]:
Freezing       142726
Warm           124239
Cold            97822
Boiling Hot     84790
Hot             67508
Lava Hot        64840
Name: ord_2, dtype: int64
```

And after filling the NaN values, it becomes:

```
In [X]: df.ord_2.fillna("NONE").value_counts()
Out[X]:
Freezing       142726
Warm           124239
Cold            97822
Boiling Hot     84790
Hot             67508
```

```
Lava Hot         64840
NONE             18075
Name: ord_2, dtype: int64
```

Wow! There were 18075 NaN values in this column that we didn't even consider using previously. With the addition of this new category, the total number of categories have now increased from 6 to 7. This is okay because now when we build our models, we will also consider NaN. The more relevant information we have, the better the model is.

Let's assume that *ord_2* did not have any NaN values. We see that all categories in this column have a significant count. There are no "rare" categories; i.e. the categories which appear only a small percentage of the total number of samples. Now, let's assume that you have deployed this model which uses this column in production and when the model or the project is live, you get a category in *ord_2* column that is not present in train. You model pipeline, in this case, will throw an error and there is nothing that you can do about it. If this happens, then probably something is wrong with your pipeline in production. If this is expected, then you must modify your model pipeline and include a new category to these six categories.

This new category is known as the "rare" category. **A rare category** is a category which is not seen very often and can include many different categories. You can also try to "predict" the unknown category by using a nearest neighbour model. Remember, if you predict this category, it will become one of the categories from the training data.

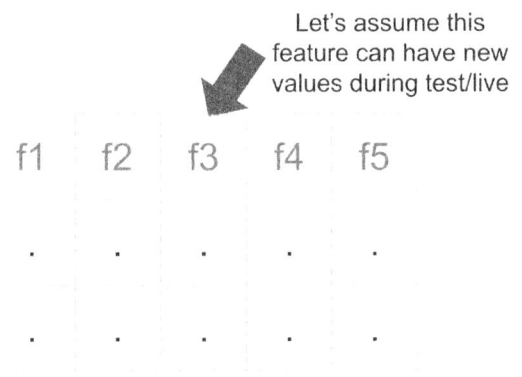

Figure 3: An illustration of a data set with different features and no targets where one feature might assume a new value when it's seen in the test set or live data

When we have a dataset like as shown in figure 3, we can build a simple model that's trained on all features except "f3". Thus, you will be creating a model that predicts "f3" when it's not known or not available in training. I can't say if this kind of model is going to give you an excellent performance but might be able to handle those missing values in test set or live data and one can't say without trying just like everything else when it comes to machine learning.

If you have a fixed test set, you can add your test data to training to know about the categories in a given feature. This is very similar to semi-supervised learning in which you use data which is not available for training to improve your model. This will also take care of rare values that appear very less number of times in training data but are in abundance in test data. Your model will be more robust.

Many people think that this idea overfits. It may or may not overfit. There is a simple fix for that. *If you design your cross-validation in such a way that it replicates the prediction process when you run your model on test data, then it's never going to overfit.* It means that the first step should be the separation of folds, and in each fold, you should apply the same pre-processing that you want to apply to test data. Suppose you want to concatenate training and test data, then in each fold you must concatenate training and validation data and also make sure that your validation dataset replicates the test set. In this specific case, you must design your validation sets in such a way that it has categories which are "unseen" in the training set.

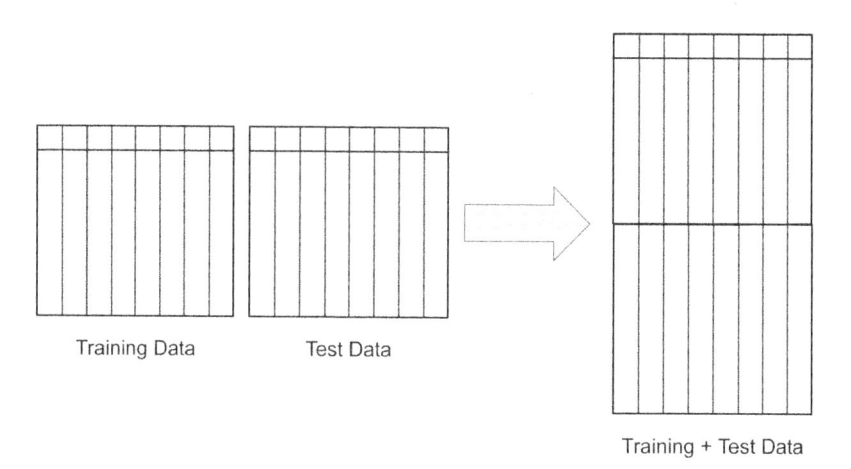

Figure 4: A simple concatenation of training and test sets to learn about the categories present in the test set but not in the training set or rare categories in the training set.

How this works is can be understood easily by looking at figure 4 and the following code.

```python
import pandas as pd
from sklearn import preprocessing

# read training data
train = pd.read_csv("../input/cat_train.csv")

#read test data
test = pd.read_csv("../input/cat_test.csv")

# create a fake target column for test data
# since this column doesn't exist
test.loc[:, "target"] = -1

# concatenate both training and test data
data = pd.concat([train, test]).reset_index(drop=True)

# make a list of features we are interested in
# id and target is something we should not encode
features = [x for x in train.columns if x not in ["id", "target"]]

# loop over the features list
for feat in features:
    # create a new instance of LabelEncoder for each feature
    lbl_enc = preprocessing.LabelEncoder()

    # note the trick here
    # since its categorical data, we fillna with a string
    # and we convert all the data to string type
    # so, no matter its int or float, its converted to string
    # int/float but categorical!!!
    temp_col = data[feat].fillna("NONE").astype(str).values

    # we can use fit_transform here as we do not
    # have any extra test data that we need to
    # transform on separately
    data.loc[:, feat] = lbl_enc.fit_transform(temp_col)

# split the training and test data again
train = data[data.target != -1].reset_index(drop=True)
test = data[data.target == -1].reset_index(drop=True)
```

This trick works when you have a problem where you already have the test dataset. It must be noted that this trick will not work in a live setting. For example, let's say you are in a company that builds a real-time bidding solution (RTB). RTB systems bid on every user they see online to buy ad space. The features that can be used for such a model may include pages viewed in a website. Let's assume that features are the last five categories/pages visited by the user. In this case, if the website introduces new categories, we will no longer be able to predict accurately. Our model, in this case, will fail. A situation like this can be avoided by using an **"unknown" category**.

In our *cat-in-the-dat* dataset, we already have unknowns in *ord_2* column.

```
In [X]: df.ord_2.fillna("NONE").value_counts()
Out[X]:
Freezing        142726
Warm            124239
Cold             97822
Boiling Hot      84790
Hot              67508
Lava Hot         64840
NONE             18075
Name: ord_2, dtype: int64
```

We can treat "NONE" as unknown. So, if during live testing, we get new categories that we have not seen before, we will mark them as "NONE".

This is very similar to natural language processing problems. We always build a model based on a fixed vocabulary. Increasing the size of the vocabulary increases the size of the model. Transformer models like BERT are trained on ~30000 words (for English). So, when we have a new word coming in, we mark it as UNK (unknown).

So, you can either assume that your test data will have the same categories as training or you can introduce a rare or unknown category to training to take care of new categories in test data.

Let's see the value counts in ord_4 column after filling NaN values:

```
In [X]: df.ord_4.fillna("NONE").value_counts()
```

```
Out[X]:
N          39978
P          37890
Y          36657
A          36633
R          33045
U          32897
 .
 .
 .
K          21676
I          19805
NONE       17930
D          17284
F          16721
W           8268
Z           5790
S           4595
G           3404
V           3107
J           1950
L           1657
Name: ord_4, dtype: int64
```

We see that some values appear only a couple thousand times, and some appear almost 40000 times. NaNs are also seen a lot. Please note that I have removed some values from the output.

We can now define our criteria for calling a value "rare". Let's say the requirement for a value being rare in this column is a count of less than 2000. So, it seems, J and L can be marked as rare values. With pandas, it is quite easy to replace categories based on count threshold. Let's take a look at how it's done.

```
In [X]: df.ord_4 = df.ord_4.fillna("NONE")

In [X]: df.loc[
   ...:       df["ord_4"].value_counts()[df["ord_4"]].values < 2000,
   ...:       "ord_4"
   ...: ] = "RARE"

In [X]: df.ord_4.value_counts()
Out[X]:
N          39978
```

```
P        37890
Y        36657
A        36633
R        33045
U        32897
M        32504
.
.
.
B        25212
E        21871
K        21676
I        19805
NONE     17930
D        17284
F        16721
W         8268
Z         5790
S         4595
RARE      3607
G         3404
V         3107
Name: ord_4, dtype: int64
```

We say that wherever the value count for a certain category is less than 2000, replace it with rare. So, now, when it comes to test data, all the new, unseen categories will be mapped to "RARE", and all missing values will be mapped to "NONE".

This approach will also ensure that the model works in a live setting, even if you have new categories.

Now we have everything we need to approach any kind of problem with categorical variables in it. Let's try building our first model and try to improve its performance in a step-wise manner.

Before going to any kind of model building, it's essential to take care of cross-validation. We have already seen the label/target distribution, and we know that it is a binary classification problem with skewed targets. Thus, we will be using *StratifiedKFold* to split the data here.

```
# create_folds.py
# import pandas and model_selection module of scikit-learn
import pandas as pd
from sklearn import model_selection

if __name__ == "__main__":
    # Read training data
    df = pd.read_csv("../input/cat_train.csv")

    # we create a new column called kfold and fill it with -1
    df["kfold"] = -1

    # the next step is to randomize the rows of the data
    df = df.sample(frac=1).reset_index(drop=True)

    # fetch labels
    y = df.target.values

    # initiate the kfold class from model_selection module
    kf = model_selection.StratifiedKFold(n_splits=5)

    # fill the new kfold column
    for f, (t_, v_) in enumerate(kf.split(X=df, y=y)):
        df.loc[v_, 'kfold'] = f

    # save the new csv with kfold column
    df.to_csv("../input/cat_train_folds.csv", index=False)
```

We can now check our new folds csv to see the number of samples per fold:

```
In [X]: import pandas as pd

In [X]: df = pd.read_csv("../input/cat_train_folds.csv")

In [X]: df.kfold.value_counts()
Out[X]:
4    120000
3    120000
2    120000
1    120000
0    120000
Name: kfold, dtype: int64
```

All folds have 120000 samples. This is expected as training data has 600000 samples, and we made five folds. So far, so good.

Now, we can also check the target distribution per fold.

```
In [X]: df[df.kfold==0].target.value_counts()
Out[X]:
0    97536
1    22464
Name: target, dtype: int64

In [X]: df[df.kfold==1].target.value_counts()
Out[X]:
0    97536
1    22464
Name: target, dtype: int64

In [X]: df[df.kfold==2].target.value_counts()
Out[X]:
0    97535
1    22465
Name: target, dtype: int64


In [X]: df[df.kfold==3].target.value_counts()
Out[X]:
0    97535
1    22465
Name: target, dtype: int64

In [X]: df[df.kfold==4].target.value_counts()
Out[X]:
0    97535
1    22465
Name: target, dtype: int64
```

We see that in each fold, the distribution of targets is the same. This is what we need. It can also be similar and doesn't have to be the same all the time. Now, when we build our models, we will have the same distribution of targets across every fold.

One of the simplest models we can build is by one-hot encoding all the data and using logistic regression.

```
# ohe_logres.py
import pandas as pd

from sklearn import linear_model
from sklearn import metrics
from sklearn import preprocessing

def run(fold):
    # load the full training data with folds
    df = pd.read_csv("../input/cat_train_folds.csv")

    # all columns are features except id, target and kfold columns
    features = [
        f for f in df.columns if f not in ("id", "target", "kfold")
    ]

    # fill all NaN values with NONE
    # note that I am converting all columns to "strings"
    # it doesn't matter because all are categories
    for col in features:
        df.loc[:, col] = df[col].astype(str).fillna("NONE")

    # get training data using folds
    df_train = df[df.kfold != fold].reset_index(drop=True)

    # get validation data using folds
    df_valid = df[df.kfold == fold].reset_index(drop=True)

    # initialize OneHotEncoder from scikit-learn
    ohe = preprocessing.OneHotEncoder()

    # fit ohe on training + validation features
    full_data = pd.concat(
        [df_train[features], df_valid[features]],
        axis=0
    )
    ohe.fit(full_data[features])

    # transform training data
    x_train = ohe.transform(df_train[features])

    # transform validation data
    x_valid = ohe.transform(df_valid[features])

    # initialize Logistic Regression model
    model = linear_model.LogisticRegression()
```

```python
    # fit model on training data (ohe)
    model.fit(x_train, df_train.target.values)

    # predict on validation data
    # we need the probability values as we are calculating AUC
    # we will use the probability of 1s
    valid_preds = model.predict_proba(x_valid)[:, 1]

    # get roc auc score
    auc = metrics.roc_auc_score(df_valid.target.values, valid_preds)

    # print auc
    print(auc)


if __name__ == "__main__":
    # run function for fold = 0
    # we can just replace this number and
    # run this for any fold
    run(0)
```

So, what's happening?

We have created a function that splits data into training and validation, given a fold number, handles NaN values, applies one-hot encoding on all the data and trains a simple **Logistic Regression** model.

When we run this chunk of code, it produces an output like this:

```
❯ python ohe_logres.py
/home/abhishek/miniconda3/envs/ml/lib/python3.7/site-
packages/sklearn/linear_model/_logistic.py:939: ConvergenceWarning: lbfgs
failed to converge (status=1):
STOP: TOTAL NO. of ITERATIONS REACHED LIMIT.
Increase the number of iterations (max_iter) or scale the data as shown
in:
    https://scikit-learn.org/stable/modules/preprocessing.html.
Please also refer to the documentation for alternative solver options:
    https://scikit-learn.org/stable/modules/linear_model.html#logistic-
regression
  extra_warning_msg=_LOGISTIC_SOLVER_CONVERGENCE_MSG)
0.7847865042255127
```

There are a few warnings. It seems logistic regression did not converge for the max number of iterations. We didn't play with the parameters, so that is fine. We see that AUC is ~ 0.785.

Let's run it for all folds now with a simple change in code.

```
# ohe_logres.py
    .
    .
    .
    # initialize Logistic Regression model
    model = linear_model.LogisticRegression()

    # fit model on training data (ohe)
    model.fit(x_train, df_train.target.values)

    # predict on validation data
    # we need the probability values as we are calculating AUC
    # we will use the probability of 1s
    valid_preds = model.predict_proba(x_valid)[:, 1]

    # get roc auc score
    auc = metrics.roc_auc_score(df_valid.target.values, valid_preds)

    # print auc
    print(f"Fold = {fold}, AUC = {auc}")

if __name__ == "__main__":
    for fold_ in range(5):
        run(fold_)
```

Please note that we are not making a lot of changes and that's why I have shown only some lines of the code; some of which have changes.

This gives:

```
> python -W ignore ohe_logres.py
Fold = 0, AUC = 0.7847865042255127
Fold = 1, AUC = 0.7853553605899214
Fold = 2, AUC = 0.7879321942914885
```

```
Fold = 3, AUC = 0.7870315929550808
Fold = 4, AUC = 0.7864668243125608
```

Note that I use "-*W ignore*" to ignore all the warnings.

We see that AUC scores are quite stable across all folds. The average AUC is 0.78631449527. Quite good for our first model!

Many people will start this kind of problem with a tree-based model, such as random forest. For applying random forest in this dataset, instead of one-hot encoding, we can use label encoding and convert every feature in every column to an integer as discussed previously.

The code is not very different from one hot encoding code. Let's take a look.

```python
# lbl_rf.py
import pandas as pd

from sklearn import ensemble
from sklearn import metrics
from sklearn import preprocessing


def run(fold):
    # load the full training data with folds
    df = pd.read_csv("../input/cat_train_folds.csv")

    # all columns are features except id, target and kfold columns
    features = [
        f for f in df.columns if f not in ("id", "target", "kfold")
    ]

    # fill all NaN values with NONE
    # note that I am converting all columns to "strings"
    # it doesnt matter because all are categories
    for col in features:
        df.loc[:, col] = df[col].astype(str).fillna("NONE")

    # now its time to label encode the features
    for col in features:

        # initialize LabelEncoder for each feature column
```

```
        lbl = preprocessing.LabelEncoder()

        # fit label encoder on all data
        lbl.fit(df[col])

        # transform all the data
        df.loc[:, col] = lbl.transform(df[col])

    # get training data using folds
    df_train = df[df.kfold != fold].reset_index(drop=True)

    # get validation data using folds
    df_valid = df[df.kfold == fold].reset_index(drop=True)

    # get training data
    x_train = df_train[features].values

    # get validation data
    x_valid = df_valid[features].values

    # initialize random forest model
    model = ensemble.RandomForestClassifier(n_jobs=-1)

    # fit model on training data (ohe)
    model.fit(x_train, df_train.target.values)

    # predict on validation data
    # we need the probability values as we are calculating AUC
    # we will use the probability of 1s
    valid_preds = model.predict_proba(x_valid)[:, 1]

    # get roc auc score
    auc = metrics.roc_auc_score(df_valid.target.values, valid_preds)

    # print auc
    print(f"Fold = {fold}, AUC = {auc}")

if __name__ == "__main__":
    for fold_ in range(5):
        run(fold_)
```

We use **random forest** from scikit-learn and have removed one-hot encoding. Instead of one-hot encoding, we use label encoding. Scores are as follows:

```
> python lbl_rf.py
Fold = 0, AUC = 0.7167390828113697
Fold = 1, AUC = 0.7165459672958506
Fold = 2, AUC = 0.7159709909587376
Fold = 3, AUC = 0.7161589664189556
Fold = 4, AUC = 0.7156020216155978
```

Wow! Huge difference! The random forest model, without any tuning of hyperparameters, performs a lot worse than simple logistic regression.

And this is a reason why we should always start with simple models first. A fan of random forest would begin with it here and will ignore logistic regression model thinking it's a very simple model that cannot bring any value better than random forest. That kind of person will make a huge mistake. In our implementation of random forest, the folds take a much longer time to complete compared to logistic regression. So, we are not only losing on AUC but also taking much longer to complete the training. Please note that inference is also time-consuming with random forest and it also takes much larger space.

If we want, we can also try to run random forest on sparse one-hot encoded data, but that is going to take a lot of time. We can also try reducing the sparse one-hot encoded matrices using singular value decomposition. This is a very common method of extracting topics in natural language processing.

```
# ohe_svd_rf.py
import pandas as pd

from scipy import sparse
from sklearn import decomposition
from sklearn import ensemble
from sklearn import metrics
from sklearn import preprocessing


def run(fold):
    # load the full training data with folds
    df = pd.read_csv("../input/cat_train_folds.csv")

    # all columns are features except id, target and kfold columns
    features = [
        f for f in df.columns if f not in ("id", "target", "kfold")
```

```python
]

# fill all NaN values with NONE
# note that I am converting all columns to "strings"
# it doesnt matter because all are categories
for col in features:
    df.loc[:, col] = df[col].astype(str).fillna("NONE")

# get training data using folds
df_train = df[df.kfold != fold].reset_index(drop=True)

# get validation data using folds
df_valid = df[df.kfold == fold].reset_index(drop=True)

# initialize OneHotEncoder from scikit-learn
ohe = preprocessing.OneHotEncoder()

# fit ohe on training + validation features
full_data = pd.concat(
    [df_train[features], df_valid[features]],
    axis=0
)
ohe.fit(full_data[features])

# transform training data
x_train = ohe.transform(df_train[features])

# transform validation data
x_valid = ohe.transform(df_valid[features])

# initialize Truncated SVD
# we are reducing the data to 120 components
svd = decomposition.TruncatedSVD(n_components=120)

# fit svd on full sparse training data
full_sparse = sparse.vstack((x_train, x_valid))
svd.fit(full_sparse)

# transform sparse training data
x_train = svd.transform(x_train)

# transform sparse validation data
x_valid = svd.transform(x_valid)

# initialize random forest model
model = ensemble.RandomForestClassifier(n_jobs=-1)
```

```python
    # fit model on training data (ohe)
    model.fit(x_train, df_train.target.values)

    # predict on validation data
    # we need the probability values as we are calculating AUC
    # we will use the probability of 1s
    valid_preds = model.predict_proba(x_valid)[:, 1]

    # get roc auc score
    auc = metrics.roc_auc_score(df_valid.target.values, valid_preds)

    # print auc
    print(f"Fold = {fold}, AUC = {auc}")


if __name__ == "__main__":
    for fold_ in range(5):
        run(fold_)
```

We one-hot encode the full data and then fit *TruncatedSVD* from scikit-learn on sparse matrix with training + validation data. In this way, we reduce the high dimensional sparse matrix to 120 features and then fit random forest classifier.

Below is the output of this model:

```
❯ python ohe_svd_rf.py
Fold = 0, AUC = 0.7064863038754249
Fold = 1, AUC = 0.706050102937374
Fold = 2, AUC = 0.7086069243167242
Fold = 3, AUC = 0.7066819080085971
Fold = 4, AUC = 0.7058154015055585
```

We see that it is even worse. It seems like the best method for this problem is one-hot encoding with logistic regression. Random forest appears to be taking way too much time. Maybe we can give **XGBoost** a try. In case you don't know about XGBoost, it is one of the most popular gradient boosting algorithms. Since it's a tree-based algorithm, we will use label encoded data.

```python
# lbl_xgb.py
import pandas as pd
```

```python
import xgboost as xgb

from sklearn import metrics
from sklearn import preprocessing


def run(fold):
    # load the full training data with folds
    df = pd.read_csv("../input/cat_train_folds.csv")

    # all columns are features except id, target and kfold columns
    features = [
        f for f in df.columns if f not in ("id", "target", "kfold")
    ]

    # fill all NaN values with NONE
    # note that I am converting all columns to "strings"
    # it doesnt matter because all are categories
    for col in features:
        df.loc[:, col] = df[col].astype(str).fillna("NONE")

    # now it's time to label encode the features
    for col in features:

        # initialize LabelEncoder for each feature column
        lbl = preprocessing.LabelEncoder()

        # fit label encoder on all data
        lbl.fit(df[col])

        # transform all the data
        df.loc[:, col] = lbl.transform(df[col])

    # get training data using folds
    df_train = df[df.kfold != fold].reset_index(drop=True)

    # get validation data using folds
    df_valid = df[df.kfold == fold].reset_index(drop=True)

    # get training data
    x_train = df_train[features].values

    # get validation data
    x_valid = df_valid[features].values

    # initialize xgboost model
    model = xgb.XGBClassifier(
```

```
        n_jobs=-1,
        max_depth=7,
        n_estimators=200
    )

    # fit model on training data (ohe)
    model.fit(x_train, df_train.target.values)

    # predict on validation data
    # we need the probability values as we are calculating AUC
    # we will use the probability of 1s
    valid_preds = model.predict_proba(x_valid)[:, 1]

    # get roc auc score
    auc = metrics.roc_auc_score(df_valid.target.values, valid_preds)

    # print auc
    print(f"Fold = {fold}, AUC = {auc}")

if __name__ == "__main__":
    for fold_ in range(5):
        run(fold_)
```

It must be noted that in this code, I modified xgboost parameters a bit. Default *max_depth* for xgboost is 3, and I changed it to 7, and I also changed the number of estimators (*n_estimators*) from 100 to 200.

The 5 fold scores from this model are as follows:

```
❯ python lbl_xgb.py
Fold = 0, AUC = 0.7656768851999011
Fold = 1, AUC = 0.7633006564148015
Fold = 2, AUC = 0.7654277821434345
Fold = 3, AUC = 0.7663609758878182
Fold = 4, AUC = 0.764914671468069
```

We see that we have much better scores than plain random forest without any tuning and we can probably improve this further with more tuning of hyperparameters.

You can also try some feature engineering, dropping certain columns which don't add any value to the model, etc. But it seems like there is not much we can do here to demonstrate improvements in the model. Let's change the dataset to another dataset with a lot of categorical variables. One more famous dataset is **US adult census data**. The dataset contains some features, and your job is to predict the salary bracket. Let's take a look at this dataset. Figure 5 shows some of the columns from this dataset.

	age	education	marital.status	race	sex	capital.loss	income
0	90	HS-grad	Widowed	White	Female	4356	<=50K
1	82	HS-grad	Widowed	White	Female	4356	<=50K
2	66	Some-college	Widowed	Black	Female	4356	<=50K
3	54	7th-8th	Divorced	White	Female	3900	<=50K
4	41	Some-college	Separated	White	Female	3900	<=50K
...	...	...	...	...	...	...	...
32556	22	Some-college	Never-married	White	Male	0	<=50K
32557	27	Assoc-acdm	Married-civ-spouse	White	Female	0	<=50K
32558	40	HS-grad	Married-civ-spouse	White	Male	0	>50K
32559	58	HS-grad	Widowed	White	Female	0	<=50K
32560	22	HS-grad	Never-married	White	Male	0	<=50K

Figure 5: Snapshot with few columns from the adult dataset[6]

This dataset has the following columns:
- age
- workclass
- fnlwgt
- education
- education.num
- marital.status
- occupation
- relationship
- race
- sex
- capital.gain
- capital.loss
- hours.per.week

---

[6] https://archive.ics.uci.edu/ml/datasets/adult

- native.country
- income

Most of these columns are self-explanatory. Those which are not, we can forget about it. Let's try to build a model first.

We see that the income column is a string. Let's do a value counts on that column.

```
In [X]: import pandas as pd

In [X]: df = pd.read_csv("../input/adult.csv")

In [X]: df.income.value_counts()
Out[X]:
<=50K     24720
>50K       7841
```

We see that there are 7841 instances with income greater than 50K USD. This is ~24% of the total number of samples. Thus, we will keep the evaluation same as the cat-in-the-dat dataset, i.e. AUC. Before we start modelling, for simplicity, we will be dropping a few columns, which are numerical, namely:

- fnlwgt
- age
- capital.gain
- capital.loss
- hours.per.week

Let's try to quickly throw in one hot encoder with logistic regression and see what happens. The first step is always making cross-validation. I'm not going to show that part of the code here. It is left as an exercise for the reader.

```
# ohe_logres.py
import pandas as pd

from sklearn import linear_model
from sklearn import metrics
from sklearn import preprocessing
```

```python
def run(fold):
    # load the full training data with folds
    df = pd.read_csv("../input/adult_folds.csv")

    # list of numerical columns
    num_cols = [
        "fnlwgt",
        "age",
        "capital.gain",
        "capital.loss",
        "hours.per.week"
    ]

    # drop numerical columns
    df = df.drop(num_cols, axis=1)

    # map targets to 0s and 1s
    target_mapping = {
        "<=50K": 0,
        ">50K": 1
    }
    df.loc[:, "income"] = df.income.map(target_mapping)

    # all columns are features except income and kfold columns
    features = [
        f for f in df.columns if f not in ("kfold", "income")
    ]

    # fill all NaN values with NONE
    # note that I am converting all columns to "strings"
    # it doesnt matter because all are categories
    for col in features:
        df.loc[:, col] = df[col].astype(str).fillna("NONE")

    # get training data using folds
    df_train = df[df.kfold != fold].reset_index(drop=True)

    # get validation data using folds
    df_valid = df[df.kfold == fold].reset_index(drop=True)

    # initialize OneHotEncoder from scikit-learn
    ohe = preprocessing.OneHotEncoder()

    # fit ohe on training + validation features
    full_data = pd.concat(
        [df_train[features], df_valid[features]],
        axis=0
```

```
    )
    ohe.fit(full_data[features])

    # transform training data
    x_train = ohe.transform(df_train[features])

    # transform validation data
    x_valid = ohe.transform(df_valid[features])

    # initialize Logistic Regression model
    model = linear_model.LogisticRegression()

    # fit model on training data (ohe)
    model.fit(x_train, df_train.income.values)

    # predict on validation data
    # we need the probability values as we are calculating AUC
    # we will use the probability of 1s
    valid_preds = model.predict_proba(x_valid)[:, 1]

    # get roc auc score
    auc = metrics.roc_auc_score(df_valid.income.values, valid_preds)

    # print auc
    print(f"Fold = {fold}, AUC = {auc}")

if __name__ == "__main__":
    for fold_ in range(5):
        run(fold_)
```

And when we run this code, we get:

```
> python -W ignore ohe_logres.py
Fold = 0, AUC = 0.8794809708119079
Fold = 1, AUC = 0.8875785068274882
Fold = 2, AUC = 0.8852609687685753
Fold = 3, AUC = 0.8681236223251438
Fold = 4, AUC = 0.8728581541840037
```

This is a very good AUC for a model which is that simple!

Let's try the label encoded xgboost without tuning any of hyperparameters now.

```
# lbl_xgb.py
import pandas as pd
import xgboost as xgb

from sklearn import metrics
from sklearn import preprocessing


def run(fold):
    # load the full training data with folds
    df = pd.read_csv("../input/adult_folds.csv")

    # list of numerical columns
    num_cols = [
        "fnlwgt",
        "age",
        "capital.gain",
        "capital.loss",
        "hours.per.week"
    ]

    # drop numerical columns
    df = df.drop(num_cols, axis=1)

    # map targets to 0s and 1s
    target_mapping = {
        "<=50K": 0,
        ">50K": 1
    }
    df.loc[:, "income"] = df.income.map(target_mapping)

    # all columns are features except kfold & income columns
    features = [
        f for f in df.columns if f not in ("kfold", "income")
    ]

    # fill all NaN values with NONE
    # note that I am converting all columns to "strings"
    # it doesnt matter because all are categories
    for col in features:
        df.loc[:, col] = df[col].astype(str).fillna("NONE")

    # now its time to label encode the features
    for col in features:

        # initialize LabelEncoder for each feature column
```

```python
        lbl = preprocessing.LabelEncoder()

        # fit label encoder on all data
        lbl.fit(df[col])

        # transform all the data
        df.loc[:, col] = lbl.transform(df[col])

    # get training data using folds
    df_train = df[df.kfold != fold].reset_index(drop=True)

    # get validation data using folds
    df_valid = df[df.kfold == fold].reset_index(drop=True)

    # get training data
    x_train = df_train[features].values

    # get validation data
    x_valid = df_valid[features].values

    # initialize xgboost model
    model = xgb.XGBClassifier(
        n_jobs=-1
    )

    # fit model on training data (ohe)
    model.fit(x_train, df_train.income.values)

    # predict on validation data
    # we need the probability values as we are calculating AUC
    # we will use the probability of 1s
    valid_preds = model.predict_proba(x_valid)[:, 1]

    # get roc auc score
    auc = metrics.roc_auc_score(df_valid.income.values, valid_preds)

    # print auc
    print(f"Fold = {fold}, AUC = {auc}")

if __name__ == "__main__":
    for fold_ in range(5):
        run(fold_)
```

Let's run this!

```
> python lbl_xgb.py
Fold = 0, AUC = 0.8800810634234078
Fold = 1, AUC = 0.886811884948154
Fold = 2, AUC = 0.8854421433318472
Fold = 3, AUC = 0.8676319549361007
Fold = 4, AUC = 0.8714450054900602
```

This seems quite good already. Let's see the scores when we increase *max_depth* to 7 and *n_estimators* to 200.

```
> python lbl_xgb.py
Fold = 0, AUC = 0.8764108944332032
Fold = 1, AUC = 0.8840708537662638
Fold = 2, AUC = 0.8816601162613102
Fold = 3, AUC = 0.8662335762581732
Fold = 4, AUC = 0.8698983461709926
```

It looks like it doesn't improve.

This shows that parameters from one dataset are not transferrable to another dataset. We must try tuning the parameters again, but we will do it in more details in next chapters.

Now, let's try to include **numerical features in the xgboost model** without parameter tuning.

```python
# lbl_xgb_num.py
import pandas as pd
import xgboost as xgb

from sklearn import metrics
from sklearn import preprocessing


def run(fold):
    # load the full training data with folds
    df = pd.read_csv("../input/adult_folds.csv")

    # list of numerical columns
```

```python
num_cols = [
    "fnlwgt",
    "age",
    "capital.gain",
    "capital.loss",
    "hours.per.week"
]

# map targets to 0s and 1s
target_mapping = {
    "<=50K": 0,
    ">50K": 1
}
df.loc[:, "income"] = df.income.map(target_mapping)

# all columns are features except kfold & income columns
features = [
    f for f in df.columns if f not in ("kfold", "income")
]

# fill all NaN values with NONE
# note that I am converting all columns to "strings"
# it doesnt matter because all are categories
for col in features:
    # do not encode the numerical columns
    if col not in num_cols:
        df.loc[:, col] = df[col].astype(str).fillna("NONE")

# now its time to label encode the features
for col in features:
    if col not in num_cols:
        # initialize LabelEncoder for each feature column
        lbl = preprocessing.LabelEncoder()

        # fit label encoder on all data
        lbl.fit(df[col])

        # transform all the data
        df.loc[:, col] = lbl.transform(df[col])

# get training data using folds
df_train = df[df.kfold != fold].reset_index(drop=True)

# get validation data using folds
df_valid = df[df.kfold == fold].reset_index(drop=True)

# get training data
```

```
    x_train = df_train[features].values

    # get validation data
    x_valid = df_valid[features].values

    # initialize xgboost model
    model = xgb.XGBClassifier(
        n_jobs=-1
    )

    # fit model on training data (ohe)
    model.fit(x_train, df_train.income.values)

    # predict on validation data
    # we need the probability values as we are calculating AUC
    # we will use the probability of 1s
    valid_preds = model.predict_proba(x_valid)[:, 1]

    # get roc auc score
    auc = metrics.roc_auc_score(df_valid.income.values, valid_preds)

    # print auc
    print(f"Fold = {fold}, AUC = {auc}")

if __name__ == "__main__":
    for fold_ in range(5):
        run(fold_)
```

So, we keep the numerical columns; we just do not label encode it. So, our final feature matrix consists of numerical columns (as it is) and encoded categorical columns. Any tree-based algorithm can handle this mix easily.

Please note that we do not need to normalize data when we use tree-based models. This is, however, a vital thing to do and cannot be missed when we are using linear models such as logistic regression.

Let's run this script now!

```
❯ python lbl_xgb_num.py
Fold = 0, AUC = 0.9209790185449889
Fold = 1, AUC = 0.9247157449144706
```

```
Fold = 2, AUC = 0.9269329887598243
Fold = 3, AUC = 0.9119349082169275
Fold = 4, AUC = 0.9166408030141667
```

Whoa!

That's an excellent score!

Now, we can try to add some features. We will take all the categorical columns and create all combinations of degree two. Take a look at *feature_engineering* function in the snippet below to know how this is done.

```python
# lbl_xgb_num_feat.py
import itertools
import pandas as pd
import xgboost as xgb

from sklearn import metrics
from sklearn import preprocessing


def feature_engineering(df, cat_cols):
    """
    This function is used for feature engineering
    :param df: the pandas dataframe with train/test data
    :param cat_cols: list of categorical columns
    :return: dataframe with new features
    """
    # this will create all 2-combinations of values
    # in this list
    # for example:
    # list(itertools.combinations([1,2,3], 2)) will return
    # [(1, 2), (1, 3), (2, 3)]
    combi = list(itertools.combinations(cat_cols, 2))
    for c1, c2 in combi:
        df.loc[
            :,
            c1 + "_" + c2
        ] = df[c1].astype(str) + "_" + df[c2].astype(str)
    return df


def run(fold):
    # load the full training data with folds
```

```python
df = pd.read_csv("../input/adult_folds.csv")

# list of numerical columns
num_cols = [
    "fnlwgt",
    "age",
    "capital.gain",
    "capital.loss",
    "hours.per.week"
]

# map targets to 0s and 1s
target_mapping = {
    "<=50K": 0,
    ">50K": 1
}
df.loc[:, "income"] = df.income.map(target_mapping)

# list of categorical columns for feature engineering
cat_cols = [
    c for c in df.columns if c not in num_cols
    and c not in ("kfold", "income")
]

# add new features
df = feature_engineering(df, cat_cols)

# all columns are features except kfold & income columns
features = [
    f for f in df.columns if f not in ("kfold", "income")
]

# fill all NaN values with NONE
# note that I am converting all columns to "strings"
# it doesnt matter because all are categories
for col in features:
    # do not encode the numerical columns
    if col not in num_cols:
        df.loc[:, col] = df[col].astype(str).fillna("NONE")

# now its time to label encode the features
for col in features:
    if col not in num_cols:
        # initialize LabelEncoder for each feature column
        lbl = preprocessing.LabelEncoder()

        # fit label encoder on all data
```

```python
            lbl.fit(df[col])

            # transform all the data
            df.loc[:, col] = lbl.transform(df[col])

        # get training data using folds
        df_train = df[df.kfold != fold].reset_index(drop=True)

        # get validation data using folds
        df_valid = df[df.kfold == fold].reset_index(drop=True)

        # get training data
        x_train = df_train[features].values

        # get validation data
        x_valid = df_valid[features].values

        # initialize xgboost model
        model = xgb.XGBClassifier(
            n_jobs=-1
        )

        # fit model on training data (ohe)
        model.fit(x_train, df_train.income.values)

        # predict on validation data
        # we need the probability values as we are calculating AUC
        # we will use the probability of 1s
        valid_preds = model.predict_proba(x_valid)[:, 1]

        # get roc auc score
        auc = metrics.roc_auc_score(df_valid.income.values, valid_preds)

        # print auc
        print(f"Fold = {fold}, AUC = {auc}")


if __name__ == "__main__":
    for fold_ in range(5):
        run(fold_)
```

This is a very naïve way of creating features from categorical columns. One should take a look at the data and see which combinations make the most sense. If you use this method, you might end up creating a lot of features, and in that case, you will need to use some kind of feature selection to select the best features. We will read more about feature selection later. Let's see the scores now.

```
> python lbl_xgb_num_feat.py
Fold = 0, AUC = 0.9211483465031423
Fold = 1, AUC = 0.9251499446866125
Fold = 2, AUC = 0.9262344766486692
Fold = 3, AUC = 0.9114264068794995
Fold = 4, AUC = 0.9177914453099201
```

It seems that even without changing any hyperparameters and just by adding a bunch of features, we can improve our fold scores a bit. Let's see if increasing *max_depth* to 7 helps.

```
> python lbl_xgb_num_feat.py
Fold = 0, AUC = 0.9286668430204137
Fold = 1, AUC = 0.9329340656165378
Fold = 2, AUC = 0.9319817543218744
Fold = 3, AUC = 0.919046187194538
Fold = 4, AUC = 0.9245692057162671
```

And yet again, we have been able to improve our model.

Note that we have not yet used rare values, binary features, a combination of one-hot and label encoded features and several other methods.

One more way of feature engineering from categorical features is to use **target encoding**. However, you have to be very careful here as this might overfit your model. Target encoding is a technique in which you map each category in a given feature to its mean target value, but this must always be done in a cross-validated manner. It means that the first thing you do is create the folds, and then use those folds to create target encoding features for different columns of the data in the same way you fit and predict the model on folds. So, if you have created 5 folds, you have to create target encoding 5 times such that in the end, you have encoding for variables in each fold which are not derived from the same fold. And then when you fit your model, you must use the same folds again. Target encoding for unseen test data can be derived from the full training data or can be an average of all the 5 folds.

Let's see how we can use target encoding on the same adult dataset so that we can compare.

```python
# target_encoding.py
import copy
import pandas as pd

from sklearn import metrics
from sklearn import preprocessing
import xgboost as xgb


def mean_target_encoding(data):

    # make a copy of dataframe
    df = copy.deepcopy(data)

    # list of numerical columns
    num_cols = [
        "fnlwgt",
        "age",
        "capital.gain",
        "capital.loss",
        "hours.per.week"
    ]

    # map targets to 0s and 1s
    target_mapping = {
        "<=50K": 0,
        ">50K": 1
    }

    df.loc[:, "income"] = df.income.map(target_mapping)

    # all columns are features except income and kfold columns
    features = [
        f for f in df.columns if f not in ("kfold", "income")
        and f not in num_cols
    ]

    # fill all NaN values with NONE
    # note that I am converting all columns to "strings"
    # it doesnt matter because all are categories
    for col in features:
        # do not encode the numerical columns
        if col not in num_cols:
```

```python
            df.loc[:, col] = df[col].astype(str).fillna("NONE")

    # now its time to label encode the features
    for col in features:
        if col not in num_cols:
            # initialize LabelEncoder for each feature column
            lbl = preprocessing.LabelEncoder()

            # fit label encoder on all data
            lbl.fit(df[col])

            # transform all the data
            df.loc[:, col] = lbl.transform(df[col])

    # a list to store 5 validation dataframes
    encoded_dfs = []

    # go over all folds
    for fold in range(5):
        # fetch training and validation data
        df_train = df[df.kfold != fold].reset_index(drop=True)
        df_valid = df[df.kfold == fold].reset_index(drop=True)
        # for all feature columns, i.e. categorical columns
        for column in features:
            # create dict of category:mean target
            mapping_dict = dict(
                df_train.groupby(column)["income"].mean()
            )
            # column_enc is the new column we have with mean encoding
            df_valid.loc[
                :, column + "_enc"
            ] = df_valid[column].map(mapping_dict)
        # append to our list of encoded validation dataframes
        encoded_dfs.append(df_valid)
    # create full data frame again and return
    encoded_df = pd.concat(encoded_dfs, axis=0)
    return encoded_df


def run(df, fold):
    # note that folds are same as before
    # get training data using folds
    df_train = df[df.kfold != fold].reset_index(drop=True)

    # get validation data using folds
    df_valid = df[df.kfold == fold].reset_index(drop=True)
```

```python
    # all columns are features except income and kfold columns
    features = [
        f for f in df.columns if f not in ("kfold", "income")
    ]
    # scale training data
    x_train = df_train[features].values

    # scale validation data
    x_valid = df_valid[features].values

    # initialize xgboost model
    model = xgb.XGBClassifier(
        n_jobs=-1,
        max_depth=7
    )

    # fit model on training data (ohe)
    model.fit(x_train, df_train.income.values)

    # predict on validation data
    # we need the probability values as we are calculating AUC
    # we will use the probability of 1s
    valid_preds = model.predict_proba(x_valid)[:, 1]

    # get roc auc score
    auc = metrics.roc_auc_score(df_valid.income.values, valid_preds)

    # print auc
    print(f"Fold = {fold}, AUC = {auc}")


if __name__ == "__main__":
    # read data
    df = pd.read_csv("../input/adult_folds.csv")

    # create mean target encoded categories and
    # munge data
    df = mean_target_encoding(df)

    # run training and validation for 5 folds
    for fold_ in range(5):
        run(df, fold_)
```

It must be noted that in the above snippet, I had not dropped categorical columns when I did the target encoding. I kept all the features and added target encoded features on top of it. Also, I used mean. You can use mean, median, standard deviation or any other function of targets.

Let's see the results.

```
Fold = 0, AUC = 0.9332240662017529
Fold = 1, AUC = 0.9363551625140347
Fold = 2, AUC = 0.9375013544556173
Fold = 3, AUC = 0.92237621307625
Fold = 4, AUC = 0.9292131180445478
```

Nice! It seems like we have improved again. However, you must be very careful when using target encoding as it is too prone to overfitting. When we use target encoding, it's better to use some kind of smoothing or adding noise in the encoded values. Scikit-learn has contrib repository which has target encoding with smoothing, or you can create your own smoothing. Smoothing introduces some kind of regularization that helps with not overfitting the model. It's not very difficult.

Handling categorical features is a complicated task. There is a lot of information floating around in several resources. This chapter should help you get started with any problem with categorical variables. For most of the problems, however, you won't need anything more than one-hot encoding and label encoding. For improving the models further, you might need a lot more!

We cannot end this chapter without using a neural network on this data. So, let's take a look at a technique known as entity embedding. In **entity embeddings**, the categories are represented as vectors. We represent categories by vectors in both binarization and one hot encoding approaches. But what if we have tens of thousands of categories. This will create huge matrices and will take a long time for us to train complicated models. We can thus represent them by vectors with float values instead.

The idea is super simple. You have an embedding layer for each categorical feature. So, every category in a column can now be mapped to an embedding (like mapping words to embeddings in natural language processing). You then reshape these embeddings to their dimension to make them flat and then concatenate all the flattened inputs embeddings. Then add a bunch of dense layers, an output layer and you are done.

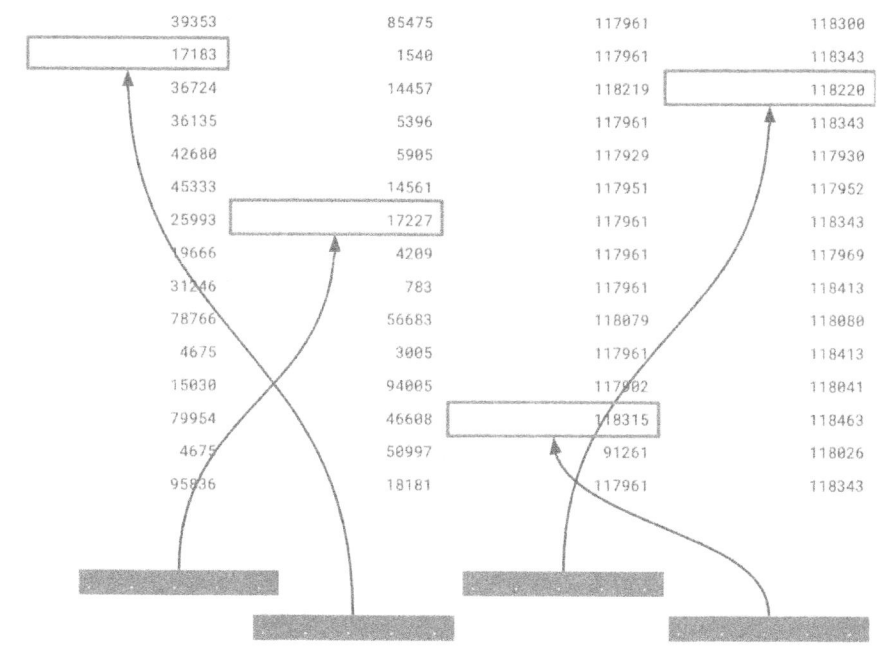

Figure 6: Categories are converted to vectors of float or embeddings

For some reason, I find it super easy to do using TF/Keras. So, let's see how it's implemented using TF/Keras. Also, this is the only example using TF/Keras in this book and its super easy to convert it to PyTorch (using cat-in-the-dat-ii dataset).

```
# entity_emebddings.py
import os
import gc
import joblib
import pandas as pd
import numpy as np
from sklearn import metrics, preprocessing
from tensorflow.keras import layers
from tensorflow.keras import optimizers
from tensorflow.keras.models import Model, load_model
from tensorflow.keras import callbacks
from tensorflow.keras import backend as K
from tensorflow.keras import utils
```

```python
def create_model(data, catcols):
    """
    This function returns a compiled tf.keras model
    for entity embeddings
    :param data: this is a pandas dataframe
    :param catcols: list of categorical column names
    :return: compiled tf.keras model
    """
    # init list of inputs for embeddings
    inputs = []

    # init list of outputs for embeddings
    outputs = []

    # loop over all categorical columns
    for c in catcols:
        # find the number of unique values in the column
        num_unique_values = int(data[c].nunique())
        # simple dimension of embedding calculator
        # min size is half of the number of unique values
        # max size is 50. max size depends on the number of unique
        # categories too. 50 is quite sufficient most of the times
        # but if you have millions of unique values, you might need
        # a larger dimension
        embed_dim = int(min(np.ceil((num_unique_values)/2), 50))

        # simple keras input layer with size 1
        inp = layers.Input(shape=(1,))

        # add embedding layer to raw input
        # embedding size is always 1 more than unique values in input
        out = layers.Embedding(
            num_unique_values + 1, embed_dim, name=c
        )(inp)

        # 1-d spatial dropout is the standard for emebedding layers
        # you can use it in NLP tasks too
        out = layers.SpatialDropout1D(0.3)(out)

        # reshape the input to the dimension of embedding
        # this becomes our output layer for current feature
        out = layers.Reshape(target_shape=(embed_dim, ))(out)

        # add input to input list
        inputs.append(inp)

        # add output to output list
```

```python
        outputs.append(out)

    # concatenate all output layers
    x = layers.Concatenate()(outputs)

    # add a batchnorm layer.
    # from here, everything is up to you
    # you can try different architectures
    # this is the architecture I like to use
    # if you have numerical features, you should add
    # them here or in concatenate layer
    x = layers.BatchNormalization()(x)

    # a bunch of dense layers with dropout.
    # start with 1 or two layers only
    x = layers.Dense(300, activation="relu")(x)
    x = layers.Dropout(0.3)(x)
    x = layers.BatchNormalization()(x)

    x = layers.Dense(300, activation="relu")(x)
    x = layers.Dropout(0.3)(x)
    x = layers.BatchNormalization()(x)

    # using softmax and treating it as a two class problem
    # you can also use sigmoid, then you need to use only one
    # output class
    y = layers.Dense(2, activation="softmax")(x)

    # create final model
    model = Model(inputs=inputs, outputs=y)

    # compile the model
    # we use adam and binary cross entropy.
    # feel free to use something else and see how model behaves
    model.compile(loss='binary_crossentropy', optimizer='adam')
    return model


def run(fold):
    # load the full training data with folds
    df = pd.read_csv("../input/cat_train_folds.csv")

    # all columns are features except id, target and kfold columns
    features = [
        f for f in df.columns if f not in ("id", "target", "kfold")
    ]
```

```python
# fill all NaN values with NONE
# note that I am converting all columns to "strings"
# it doesnt matter because all are categories
for col in features:
    df.loc[:, col] = df[col].astype(str).fillna("NONE")

# encode all features with label encoder individually
# in a live setting you need to save all label encoders
for feat in features:
    lbl_enc = preprocessing.LabelEncoder()
    df.loc[:, feat] = lbl_enc.fit_transform(df[feat].values)

# get training data using folds
df_train = df[df.kfold != fold].reset_index(drop=True)

# get validation data using folds
df_valid = df[df.kfold == fold].reset_index(drop=True)

# create tf.keras model
model = create_model(df, features)

# our features are lists of lists
xtrain = [
    df_train[features].values[:, k] for k in range(len(features))
]
xvalid = [
    df_valid[features].values[:, k] for k in range(len(features))
]
# fetch target columns
ytrain = df_train.target.values
yvalid = df_valid.target.values

# convert target columns to categories
# this is just binarization
ytrain_cat = utils.to_categorical(ytrain)
yvalid_cat = utils.to_categorical(yvalid)

# fit the model
model.fit(xtrain,
          ytrain_cat,
          validation_data=(xvalid, yvalid_cat),
          verbose=1,
          batch_size=1024,
          epochs=3
          )

# generate validation predictions
```

```
        valid_preds = model.predict(xvalid)[:, 1]

        # print roc auc score
        print(metrics.roc_auc_score(yvalid, valid_preds))

        # clear session to free up some GPU memory
        K.clear_session()

if __name__ == "__main__":
    run(0)
    run(1)
    run(2)
    run(3)
    run(4)
```

You will notice that this approach gives the best results and is also super-fast if you have a GPU! This can also be improved further, and you don't need to worry about feature engineering as neural network handles it on its own. This is definitely worth a try when dealing with a large dataset of categorical features. When embedding size is the same as the number of unique categories, we have one-hot-encoding.

This chapter is basically all about feature engineering. Let's see how you can do some more feature engineering when it comes to numerical features and combination of different types of features in the next chapter.

Feature engineering

Feature engineering is one of the most crucial parts of building a good machine learning model. If we have useful features, the model will perform better. There are many situations where you can avoid large, complicated models and use simple models with crucially engineered features. We must keep in mind that feature engineering is something that is done in the best possible manner only when you have some knowledge about the domain of the problem and depends a lot on the data in concern. However, there are some general techniques that you can try to create features from almost all kinds of numerical and categorical variables. *Feature engineering is not just about creating new features from data but also includes different types of normalization and transformations.*

In the chapter about categorical features, we have seen a way to combine different categorical variables, how we can convert categorical variables to counts, target encoding and using embeddings. These are almost all kinds of ways to engineer features from categorical variables. Thus, in this chapter, our focus will be limited to numerical variables and a combination of numerical and categorical variables.

Let's start with the most simple but most widely used feature engineering techniques. Let's say that you are dealing with **date and time data**. So, we have a pandas dataframe with a datetime type column. Using this column, we can create features like:

- Year
- Week of year
- Month
- Day of week
- Weekend
- Hour
- And many more.

And this can be done using pandas very easily.

```
df.loc[:, 'year'] = df['datetime_column'].dt.year
df.loc[:, 'weekofyear'] = df['datetime_column'].dt.weekofyear
df.loc[:, 'month'] = df['datetime_column'].dt.month
df.loc[:, 'dayofweek'] = df['datetime_column'].dt.dayofweek
```

```
df.loc[:, 'weekend'] = (df.datetime_column.dt.weekday >=5).astype(int)
df.loc[:, 'hour'] = df['datetime_column'].dt.hour
```

So, we are creating a bunch of new columns using the datetime column. Let's see some of the sample features that can be created.

```
import pandas as pd

# create a series of datetime with a frequency of 10 hours
s = pd.date_range('2020-01-06', '2020-01-10', freq='10H').to_series()

# create some features based on datetime
features = {
    "dayofweek": s.dt.dayofweek.values,
    "dayofyear": s.dt.dayofyear.values,
    "hour": s.dt.hour.values,
    "is_leap_year": s.dt.is_leap_year.values,
    "quarter": s.dt.quarter.values,
    "weekofyear": s.dt.weekofyear.values
}
```

This will generate a dictionary of features from a given series. You can apply this to any datetime column in a pandas dataframe. These are some of the many date time features that pandas offer. Date time features are critical when you are dealing with time-series data, for example, predicting sales of a store but would like to use a model like xgboost on **aggregated features**.

Suppose we have a dataframe that looks like the following:

date	customer_id	cat1	cat2	cat3	num1
2016-09-01	146361	2	2	0	-0.518679
2017-04-01	180838	4	1	0	0.415853
2017-08-01	157857	3	3	1	-2.061687
2017-12-01	159772	5	1	1	-0.276558
2017-09-01	80014	3	2	1	-1.456827

Figure 1: A sample dataframe with categorical and date features

In figure 1, we see that we have a date column, and we can easily extract features like the year, month, quarter, etc. from that. Then we have a *customer_id* column which has multiple entries, so a customer is seen many times (not visible in the screenshot). And each date and customer id has three categorical and one numerical feature attached to it. There are a bunch of features we can create from it:

- What's the month a customer is most active in
- What is the count of cat1, cat2, cat3 for a customer
- What is the count of cat1, cat2, cat3 for a customer for a given week of the year
- What is the mean of num1 for a given customer
- And so on.

Using aggregates in pandas, it is quite easy to create features like these. Let's see how.

```python
def generate_features(df):
    # create a bunch of features using the date column
    df.loc[:, 'year'] = df['date'].dt.year
    df.loc[:, 'weekofyear'] = df['date'].dt.weekofyear
    df.loc[:, 'month'] = df['date'].dt.month
    df.loc[:, 'dayofweek'] = df['date'].dt.dayofweek
    df.loc[:, 'weekend'] = (df['date'].dt.weekday >=5).astype(int)

    # create an aggregate dictionary
    aggs = {}
    # for aggregation by month, we calculate the
    # number of unique month values and also the mean
    aggs['month'] = ['nunique', 'mean']
    aggs['weekofyear'] = ['nunique', 'mean']
    # we aggregate by num1 and calculate sum, max, min
    # and mean values of this column
    aggs['num1'] = ['sum','max','min','mean']
    # for customer_id, we calculate the total count
    aggs['customer_id'] = ['size']
    # again for customer_id, we calculate the total unique
    aggs['customer_id'] = ['nunique']

    # we group by customer_id and calculate the aggregates
    agg_df = df.groupby('customer_id').agg(aggs)
    agg_df = agg_df.reset_index()
    return agg_df
```

Please note that in the above function, we have skipped the categorical variables, but you can use them in the same way as other aggregates.

customer_id	month		weekofyear		customer_id	num1			
	nunique	mean	nunique	mean	size	sum	max	min	mean
0	1	2	1	5	1	0.134077	0.134077	0.134077	0.134077
1	1	7	1	26	1	0.884295	0.884295	0.884295	0.884295
2	1	9	1	35	1	-0.264433	-0.264433	-0.264433	-0.264433
3	1	5	1	18	1	0.812872	0.812872	0.812872	0.812872
4	1	4	1	13	1	1.288514	1.288514	1.288514	1.288514
...	...	...	...	...	...	...	...	...	...
201912	1	4	1	13	1	0.362965	0.362965	0.362965	0.362965
201913	1	11	1	44	1	-0.085357	-0.085357	-0.085357	-0.085357
201914	1	8	1	31	1	1.530061	1.530061	1.530061	1.530061
201915	1	1	1	1	1	-0.600063	-0.600063	-0.600063	-0.600063
201916	1	8	1	31	1	-1.073077	-1.073077	-1.073077	-1.073077

Figure 2: Aggregate and other features

Now, we can join this dataframe in figure 2 with the original dataframe with *customer_id* column to start training a model. Here, we are not trying to predict anything; we are just creating generic features. However, it would have been easier to create features if we were trying to predict something here.

Sometimes, for example, when dealing with time-series problems, you might have features which are not individual values but a list of values. For example, transactions by a customer in a given period of time. In these cases, we create different types of features such as: with numerical features, when you are grouping on a categorical column, you will get features like a list of values which are time distributed. In these cases, you can create a bunch of statistical features such as:

- Mean
- Max
- Min
- Unique
- Skew
- Kurtosis
- Kstat
- Percentile
- Quantile

- Peak to peak
- And many more

These can be created using simple numpy functions, as shown in the following python snippet.

```python
import numpy as np

feature_dict = {}

# calculate mean
feature_dict['mean'] = np.mean(x)

# calculate max
feature_dict['max'] = np.max(x)

# calculate min
feature_dict['min'] = np.min(x)

# calculate standard deviation
feature_dict['std'] = np.std(x)

# calculate variance
feature_dict['var'] = np.var(x)

# peak-to-peak
feature_dict['ptp'] = np.ptp(x)

# percentile features
feature_dict['percentile_10'] = np.percentile(x, 10)
feature_dict['percentile_60'] = np.percentile(x, 60)
feature_dict['percentile_90'] = np.percentile(x, 90)

# quantile features
feature_dict['quantile_5'] = np.quantile(x, 0.05)
feature_dict['quantile_95'] = np.quantile(x, 0.95)
feature_dict['quantile_99'] = np.quantile(x, 0.99)
```

The **time series data** (list of values) can be converted to a lot of features.

A python library called *tsfresh* is instrumental in this case.

```
from tsfresh.feature_extraction import feature_calculators as fc

# tsfresh based features
feature_dict['abs_energy'] = fc.abs_energy(x)
feature_dict['count_above_mean'] = fc.count_above_mean(x)
feature_dict['count_below_mean'] = fc.count_below_mean(x)
feature_dict['mean_abs_change'] = fc.mean_abs_change(x)
feature_dict['mean_change'] = fc.mean_change(x)
```

This is not all; tsfresh offers hundreds of features and tens of variations of different features that you can use for time series (list of values) based features. In the examples above, x is a list of values. But that's not all. There are many other features that you can create for numerical data with or without categorical data. A simple way to generate many features is just to create a bunch of **polynomial features**. For example, a second-degree polynomial feature from two features "a" and "b" would include: "a", "b", "ab", "a^2" and "b^2".

```
import numpy as np

# generate a random dataframe with
# 2 columns and 100 rows
df = pd.DataFrame(
    np.random.rand(100, 2),
    columns=[f"f_{i}" for i in range(1, 3)]
)
```

Which gives a dataframe, as shown in figure 3.

	f_1	f_2
	0.118305	0.648567
	0.503417	0.117854
	0.067735	0.158106
	0.907574	0.436235
	0.134100	0.824813

Figure 3: A random dataframe with two numerical features

And we can create two-degree polynomial features using *PolynomialFeatures* from scikit-learn.

```
from sklearn import preprocessing

# initialize polynomial features class object
# for two-degree polynomial features
pf = preprocessing.PolynomialFeatures(
    degree=2,
    interaction_only=False,
    include_bias=False
)

# fit to the features
pf.fit(df)

# create polynomial features
poly_feats = pf.transform(df)

# create a dataframe with all the features
num_feats = poly_feats.shape[1]
df_transformed = pd.DataFrame(
    poly_feats,
    columns=[f"f_{i}" for i in range(1, num_feats + 1)]
)
```

And that would give a dataframe, as shown in figure 4.

f_1	f_2	f_3	f_4	f_5
0.118305	0.648567	0.013996	0.076729	0.420639
0.503417	0.117854	0.253429	0.059330	0.013890
0.067735	0.158106	0.004588	0.010709	0.024997
0.907574	0.436235	0.823691	0.395916	0.190301
0.134100	0.824813	0.017983	0.110608	0.680317

Figure 4: A sample dataframe with polynomial features

So, now we have created some polynomial features. If you create third-degree polynomial features, you will end up with nine features in total. The more the number of features, the more the number of polynomial features and you must also remember that if you have a lot of samples in the dataset, it is going to take a while creating these kinds of features.

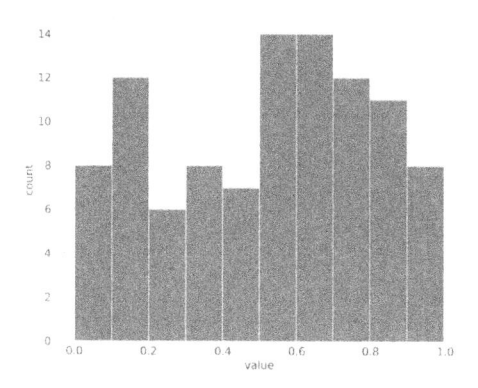

Figure 5: Histogram of a numerical feature column

Another interesting feature converts the numbers to categories. It's known as **binning**. Let's look at figure 5, which shows a sample histogram of a random numerical feature. We use ten bins for this figure, and we see that we can divide the data into ten parts. This is accomplished using the pandas' *cut* function.

```
# create bins of the numerical columns
# 10 bins
df["f_bin_10"] = pd.cut(df["f_1"], bins=10, labels=False)
# 100 bins
df["f_bin_100"] = pd.cut(df["f_1"], bins=100, labels=False)
```

Which generates two new features in the dataframe, as shown in figure 6.

f_1	f_2	f_bin_10	f_bin_100
0.143246	0.286327	1	12
0.421268	0.967212	4	41
0.224104	0.075204	2	21
0.859183	0.651964	8	86
0.082291	0.669589	0	6

Figure 6: Binning numerical features

When you bin, you can use both the bin and the original feature. We will learn a bit more about selecting features later in this chapter. *Binning also enables you to treat numerical features as categorical.*

Yet another interesting type of feature that you can create from numerical features is log transformation. Take a look at feature f_3 in figure 7.

f_1	f_2	f_bin_10	f_bin_100	f_3
0.143246	0.286327	1	12	8048
0.421268	0.967212	4	41	7433
0.224104	0.075204	2	21	2289
0.859183	0.651964	8	86	1153
0.082291	0.669589	0	6	2201

Figure 7: Example of a feature that has a high variance

f_3 is a special feature with a very high variance. Compared to other features that have a low variance (let's assume that). Thus, we would want to reduce the variance of this column, and that can be done by taking a log transformation.

The values in column f_3 range from 0 to 10000 and a histogram is shown in figure 8.

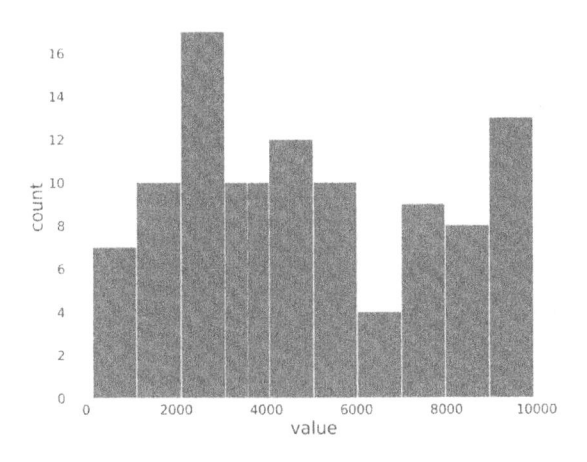

Figure 8: Histogram of feature f_3.

And we can apply log(1 + x) to this column to reduce its variance. Figure 9 shows what happens to the histogram when the log transformation is applied.

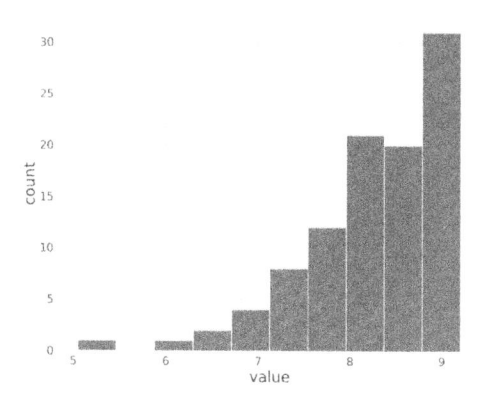

Figure 9: Histogram of f_3 after applying log transformation.

Let's take a look at the variance without and with the log transformation.

```
In [X]: df.f_3.var()
Out[X]: 8077265.875858586

In [X]: df.f_3.apply(lambda x: np.log(1 + x)).var()
Out[X]: 0.6058771732119975
```

Sometimes, instead of log, you can also take exponential. A very interesting case is when you use a log-based evaluation metric, for example, RMSLE. In that case, you can train on log-transformed targets and convert back to original using exponential on the prediction. That would help optimize the model for the metric.

Most of the time, these kinds of numerical features are created based on intuition. There is no formula. If you are working in an industry, you will create your industry-specific features.

When dealing with both categorical and numerical variables, you might encounter missing values. We saw some ways to handle missing values in categorical features in the previous chapter, but there are many more ways to handle missing/NaN values. This is also considered feature engineering.

For categorical features, let's keep it super simple. *If you ever encounter missing values in categorical features, treat is as a new category*! As simple as this is, it (almost) always works!

One way to fill missing values in numerical data would be to choose a value that does not appear in the specific feature and fill using that. For example, let's say 0 is not seen in the feature. So, we fill all the missing values using 0. This is one of the ways but might not be the most effective. One of the methods that works better than filling 0s for numerical data is to fill with mean instead. You can also try to fill with the median of all the values for that feature, or you can use the most common value to fill the missing values. There are just so many ways to do this.

A fancy way of filling in the missing values would be to use a **k-nearest neighbour** method. You can select a sample with missing values and find the nearest neighbours utilising some kind of distance metric, for example, Euclidean distance. Then you can take the mean of all nearest neighbours and fill up the missing value. You can use the KNN imputer implementation for filling missing values like this.

```
[  4., nan, 10., nan, 10., 11.]
[ 14.,  2., 14.,  6., 10., 14.]
[  7.,  6., 12.,  8.,  6.,  2.]
[nan, 14., nan,  1.,  2.,  5.]
[  1.,  7.,  6., 13., 14.,  9.]
[ 10.,  2., 14., nan, nan,  1.]
[  3., 14.,  3.,  7., 13.,  9.]
[ 11., nan,  1., nan,  4.,  7.]
[  4.,  8.,  2.,  2.,  6., nan]
[  2., nan, 13.,  9.,  2., 12.]
```
Figure 10: A 2d array with missing values

Let's see how a matrix with missing values, as shown in figure 10 is handled by *KNNImputer*.

```
import numpy as np
from sklearn import impute

# create a random numpy array with 10 samples
# and 6 features and values ranging from 1 to 15
X = np.random.randint(1, 15, (10, 6))
```

```
# convert the array to float
X = X.astype(float)

# randomly assign 10 elements to NaN (missing)
X.ravel()[np.random.choice(X.size, 10, replace=False)] = np.nan

# use 2 nearest neighbours to fill na values
knn_imputer = impute.KNNImputer(n_neighbors=2)
knn_imputer.fit_transform(X)
```

Which fills the above matrix, as shown in figure 11.

```
[ 4. , 10.5, 10. , 10. , 10. , 11. ]
[14. ,  2. , 14. ,  6. , 10. , 14. ]
[ 7. ,  6. , 12. ,  8. ,  6. ,  2. ]
[ 7.5, 14. ,  1.5,  1. ,  2. ,  5. ]
[ 1. ,  7. ,  6. , 13. , 14. ,  9. ]
[10. ,  2. , 14. ,  7. ,  8. ,  1. ]
[ 3. , 14. ,  3. ,  7. , 13. ,  9. ]
[11. , 11. ,  1. ,  1.5,  4. ,  7. ]
[ 4. ,  8. ,  2. ,  2. ,  6. ,  6. ]
[ 2. , 10. , 13. ,  9. ,  2. , 12. ]
```
Figure 11: Values imputed by KNN Imputer

Another way of imputing missing values in a column would be to train a regression model that tries to predict missing values in a column based on other columns. So, you start with one column that has a missing value and treat this column as the target column for regression model without the missing values. Using all the other columns, you now train a model on samples for which there is no missing value in the concerned column and then try to predict target (the same column) for the samples that were removed earlier. This way, you have a more robust model based imputation.

Always remember that imputing values for tree-based models is unnecessary as they can handle it themselves.

What I have shown until now are some of the ways of creating features in general. Now, let's say you are working on a problem of predicting store sales of different items (per week or month). You have items, and you have store ids. So, you can create features like items per store. Now, this is one of the features that is not discussed above. These kinds of features cannot be generalized and come purely from domain, data and business knowledge. Look at the data and see what fits and create features accordingly. And always remember to scale or normalize your features if you are using linear models like logistic regression or a model like SVM. Tree-based models will always work fine without any normalization of features.

Feature selection

When you are done creating hundreds of thousands of features, it's time for selecting a few of them. Well, we should never create hundreds of thousands of useless features. Having too many features pose a problem well known as the curse of dimensionality. If you have a lot of features, you must also have a lot of training samples to capture all the features. What's considered a "lot" is not defined correctly and is up to you to figure out by validating your models properly and checking how much time it takes to train your models.

The simplest form of selecting features would be to **remove features with very low variance**. If the features have a very low variance (i.e. very close to 0), they are close to being constant and thus, do not add any value to any model at all. It would just be nice to get rid of them and hence lower the complexity. Please note that the variance also depends on scaling of the data. Scikit-learn has an implementation for *VarianceThreshold* that does precisely this.

```
from sklearn.feature_selection import VarianceThreshold
data = ...
var_thresh = VarianceThreshold(threshold=0.1)
transformed_data = var_thresh.fit_transform(data)
# transformed data will have all columns with variance less
# than 0.1 removed
```

We can also remove features which have a high correlation. For calculating the correlation between different numerical features, you can use the **Pearson correlation**.

```
import pandas as pd
from sklearn.datasets import fetch_california_housing

# fetch a regression dataset
data = fetch_california_housing()
X = data["data"]
col_names = data["feature_names"]
y = data["target"]

# convert to pandas dataframe
```

```python
df = pd.DataFrame(X, columns=col_names)
# introduce a highly correlated column
df.loc[:, "MedInc_Sqrt"] = df.MedInc.apply(np.sqrt)

# get correlation matrix (pearson)
df.corr()
```

Which gives a correlation matrix, as shown in figure 1.

	MedInc	HouseAge	AveRooms	AveBedrms	Population	AveOccup	Latitude	Longitude	MedInc_Sqrt
MedInc	1.000000	-0.119034	0.326895	-0.062040	0.004834	0.018766	-0.079809	-0.015176	0.984329
HouseAge	-0.119034	1.000000	-0.153277	-0.077747	-0.296244	0.013191	0.011173	-0.108197	-0.132797
AveRooms	0.326895	-0.153277	1.000000	0.847621	-0.072213	-0.004852	0.106389	-0.027540	0.326688
AveBedrms	-0.062040	-0.077747	0.847621	1.000000	-0.066197	-0.006181	0.069721	0.013344	-0.066910
Population	0.004834	-0.296244	-0.072213	-0.066197	1.000000	0.069863	-0.108785	0.099773	0.018415
AveOccup	0.018766	0.013191	-0.004852	-0.006181	0.069863	1.000000	0.002366	0.002476	0.015266
Latitude	-0.079809	0.011173	0.106389	0.069721	-0.108785	0.002366	1.000000	-0.924664	-0.084303
Longitude	-0.015176	-0.108197	-0.027540	0.013344	0.099773	0.002476	-0.924664	1.000000	-0.015569
MedInc_Sqrt	0.984329	-0.132797	0.326688	-0.066910	0.018415	0.015266	-0.084303	-0.015569	1.000000

Figure 1: A sample Pearson correlation matrix

We see that the feature *MedInc_Sqrt* has a very high correlation with *MedInc*. We can thus remove one of them.

And now we can move to some univariate ways of feature selection. **Univariate feature selection** is nothing but a scoring of each feature against a given target. **Mutual information, ANOVA F-test** and **chi^2** are some of the most popular methods for univariate feature selection. There are two ways of using these in scikit-learn.
- *SelectKBest*: It keeps the top-k scoring features
- *SelectPercentile*: It keeps the top features which are in a percentage specified by the user

It must be noted that you can use chi^2 only for data which is non-negative in nature. This is a particularly useful feature selection technique in natural language processing when we have a bag of words or tf-idf based features. It's best to create a wrapper for univariate feature selection that you can use for almost any new problem.

```python
from sklearn.feature_selection import chi2
from sklearn.feature_selection import f_classif
from sklearn.feature_selection import f_regression
from sklearn.feature_selection import mutual_info_classif
from sklearn.feature_selection import mutual_info_regression
from sklearn.feature_selection import SelectKBest
from sklearn.feature_selection import SelectPercentile


class UnivariateFeatureSelction:
    def __init__(self, n_features, problem_type, scoring):
        """
        Custom univariate feature selection wrapper on
        different univariate feature selection models from
        scikit-learn.
        :param n_features: SelectPercentile if float else SelectKBest
        :param problem_type: classification or regression
        :param scoring: scoring function, string
        """
        # for a given problem type, there are only
        # a few valid scoring methods
        # you can extend this with your own custom
        # methods if you wish
        if problem_type == "classification":
            valid_scoring = {
                "f_classif": f_classif,
                "chi2": chi2,
                "mutual_info_classif": mutual_info_classif
            }
        else:
            valid_scoring = {
                "f_regression": f_regression,
                "mutual_info_regression": mutual_info_regression
            }

        # raise exception if we do not have a valid scoring method
        if scoring not in valid_scoring:
            raise Exception("Invalid scoring function")

        # if n_features is int, we use selectkbest
        # if n_features is float, we use selectpercentile
        # please note that it is int in both cases in sklearn
        if isinstance(n_features, int):
            self.selection = SelectKBest(
                valid_scoring[scoring],
                k=n_features
```

```
        )
    elif isinstance(n_features, float):
        self.selection = SelectPercentile(
            valid_scoring[scoring],
            percentile=int(n_features * 100)
        )
    else:
        raise Exception("Invalid type of feature")

# same fit function
def fit(self, X, y):
    return self.selection.fit(X, y)

# same transform function
def transform(self, X):
    return self.selection.transform(X)

# same fit_transform function
def fit_transform(self, X, y):
    return self.selection.fit_transform(X, y)
```

Using this class is pretty simple.

```
ufs = UnivariateFeatureSelction(
    n_features=0.1,
    problem_type="regression",
    scoring="f_regression"
)
ufs.fit(X, y)
X_transformed = ufs.transform(X)
```

That should take care of most of your univariate feature selection needs. Please note that it's usually better to create less and important features than to create hundreds of features in the first place. Univariate feature selection may not always perform well. Most of the time, people prefer doing feature selection using a machine learning model. Let's see how that is done.

The simplest form of feature selection that uses a model for selection is known as **greedy feature selection**. In greedy feature selection, the first step is to choose a model. The second step is to select a loss/scoring function. And the third and final step is to iteratively evaluate each feature and add it to the list of "good" features if it improves loss/score. It can't get simpler than this. But you must keep in mind that this is known as greedy feature selection for a reason. This feature selection process will fit a given model each time it evaluates a feature. The computational cost associated with this kind of method is very high. It will also take a lot of time for this kind of feature selection to finish. And if you do not use this feature selection properly, then you might even end up overfitting the model.

Let's see how it works by looking at how its implemented.

```python
# greedy.py
import pandas as pd

from sklearn import linear_model
from sklearn import metrics
from sklearn.datasets import make_classification


class GreedyFeatureSelection:
    """
    A simple and custom class for greedy feature selection.
    You will need to modify it quite a bit to make it suitable
    for your dataset.
    """
    def evaluate_score(self, X, y):
        """
        This function evaluates model on data and returns
        Area Under ROC Curve (AUC)
        NOTE: We fit the data and calculate AUC on same data.
        WE ARE OVERFITTING HERE.
        But this is also a way to achieve greedy selection.
        k-fold will take k times longer.

        If you want to implement it in really correct way,
        calculate OOF AUC and return mean AUC over k folds.
        This requires only a few lines of change and has been
        shown a few times in this book.

        :param X: training data
        :param y: targets
        :return: overfitted area under the roc curve
        """
        # fit the logistic regression model,
        # and calculate AUC on same data
        # again: BEWARE
        # you can choose any model that suits your data
```

```python
        model = linear_model.LogisticRegression()
        model.fit(X, y)
        predictions = model.predict_proba(X)[:, 1]
        auc = metrics.roc_auc_score(y, predictions)
        return auc

    def _feature_selection(self, X, y):
        """
        This function does the actual greedy selection
        :param X: data, numpy array
        :param y: targets, numpy array
        :return: (best scores, best features)
        """
        # initialize good features list
        # and best scores to keep track of both
        good_features = []
        best_scores = []

        # calculate the number of features
        num_features = X.shape[1]

        # infinite loop
        while True:
            # initialize best feature and score of this loop
            this_feature = None
            best_score = 0

            # loop over all features
            for feature in range(num_features):
                # if feature is already in good_features,
                # skip this for loop
                if feature in good_features:
                    continue
                # selected features are all good features till now
                # and current feature
                selected_features = good_features + [feature]
                # remove all other features from data
                xtrain = X[:, selected_features]
                # calculate the score, in our case, AUC
                score = self.evaluate_score(xtrain, y)
                # if score is greater than the best score
                # of this loop, change best score and best feature
                if score > best_score:
                    this_feature = feature
                    best_score = score

            # if we have selected a feature, add it
```

```python
            # to the good feature list and update best scores list
            if this_feature != None:
                good_features.append(this_feature)
                best_scores.append(best_score)

            # if we didnt improve during the previous round,
            # exit the while loop
            if len(best_scores) > 2:
                if best_scores[-1] < best_scores[-2]:
                    break
        # return best scores and good features
        # why do we remove the last data point?
        return best_scores[:-1], good_features[:-1]

    def __call__(self, X, y):
        """
        Call function will call the class on a set of arguments
        """
        # select features, return scores and selected indices
        scores, features = self._feature_selection(X, y)
        # transform data with selected features
        return X[:, features], scores

if __name__ == "__main__":
    # generate binary classification data
    X, y = make_classification(n_samples=1000, n_features=100)

    # transform data by greedy feature selection
    X_transformed, scores = GreedyFeatureSelection()(X, y)
```

The greedy feature selection implemented the way returns scores and a list of feature indices. Figure 2 shows how this score improves with the addition of a new feature in every iteration. We see that we are not able to improve our score after a certain point, and that's where we stop.

Another greedy approach is known as **recursive feature elimination (RFE)**. In the previous method, we started with one feature and kept adding new features, but in RFE, we start with all features and keep removing one feature in every iteration that provides the least value to a given model. But how to do we know which feature offers the least value? Well, if we use models like linear support vector machine (SVM) or logistic regression, we get a coefficient for each feature which decides the importance of the features. In case of any tree-based models, we get feature importance in place of coefficients. In each iteration, we can eliminate the least important feature and keep eliminating it until we reach the number of features needed. So, yes, we have the ability to decide how many features we want to keep.

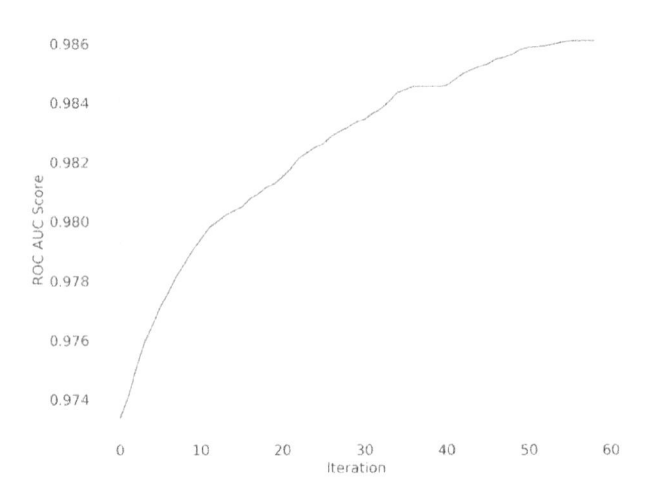

Figure 2: How AUC score varies in greedy feature selection with the addition of new features

When we are doing recursive feature elimination, in each iteration, we remove the feature which has the feature importance or the feature which has a coefficient close to 0. Please remember that when you use a model like logistic regression for binary classification, the coefficients for features are more positive if they are important for the positive class and more negative if they are important for the negative class. It's very easy to modify our greedy feature selection class to create a new class for recursive feature elimination, but scikit-learn also provides RFE out of the box. A simple usage is shown in the following example.

```
import pandas as pd

from sklearn.feature_selection import RFE
from sklearn.linear_model import LinearRegression
from sklearn.datasets import fetch_california_housing

# fetch a regression dataset
data = fetch_california_housing()
X = data["data"]
col_names = data["feature_names"]
y = data["target"]
```

```
# initialize the model
model = LinearRegression()
# initialize RFE
rfe = RFE(
    estimator=model,
    n_features_to_select=3
)

# fit RFE
rfe.fit(X, y)

# get the transformed data with
# selected columns
X_transformed = rfe.transform(X)
```

We saw two different greedy ways to select features from a model. But you can also fit the model to the data and select features from the model by the **feature coefficients or the importance of features**. If you use coefficients, you can select a threshold, and if the coefficient is above that threshold, you can keep the feature else eliminate it.

Let's see how we can get feature importance from a model like random forest.

```
import pandas as pd
from sklearn.datasets import load_diabetes
from sklearn.ensemble import RandomForestRegressor

# fetch a regression dataset
# in diabetes data we predict diabetes progression
# after one year based on some features
data = load_diabetes()
X = data["data"]
col_names = data["feature_names"]
y = data["target"]

# initialize the model
model = RandomForestRegressor()

# fit the model
model.fit(X, y)
```

Feature importance from random forest (or any model) can be plotted as follows.

```
importances = model.feature_importances_
idxs = np.argsort(importances)
plt.title('Feature Importances')
plt.barh(range(len(idxs)), importances[idxs], align='center')
plt.yticks(range(len(idxs)), [col_names[i] for i in idxs])
plt.xlabel('Random Forest Feature Importance')
plt.show()
```

The resulting plot is shown in figure 3.

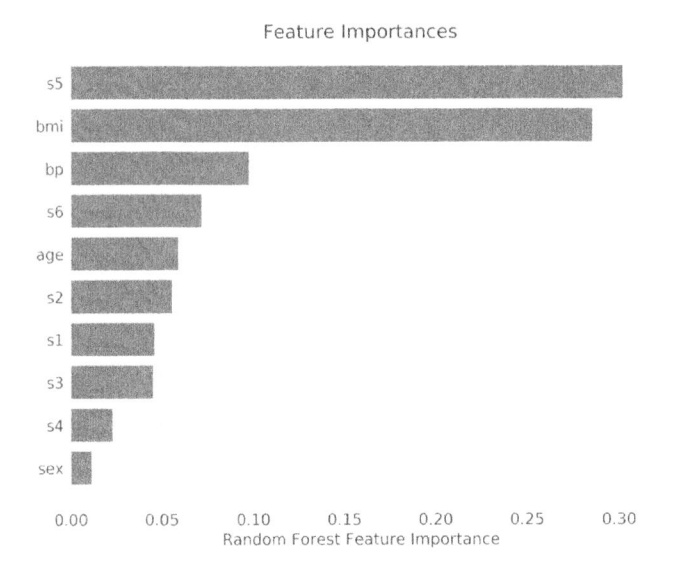

Figure 3: Plot of feature importance

Well, selecting the best features from the model is nothing new. You can choose features from one model and use another model to train. For example, you can use Logistic Regression coefficients to select the features and then use Random Forest to train the model on chosen features. Scikit-learn also offers *SelectFromModel* class that helps you choose features directly from a given model. You can also specify the threshold for coefficients or feature importance if you want and the maximum number of features you want to select.

Take a look at the following snippet where we select the features using default parameters in *SelectFromModel*.

```
import pandas as pd
from sklearn.datasets import load_diabetes
from sklearn.ensemble import RandomForestRegressor
from sklearn.feature_selection import SelectFromModel

# fetch a regression dataset
# in diabetes data we predict diabetes progression
# after one year based on some features
data = load_diabetes()
X = data["data"]
col_names = data["feature_names"]
y = data["target"]

# initialize the model
model = RandomForestRegressor()

# select from the model
sfm = SelectFromModel(estimator=model)
X_transformed = sfm.fit_transform(X, y)

# see which features were selected
support = sfm.get_support()

# get feature names
print([
    x for x, y in zip(col_names, support) if y == True
])
```

Which prints: ['bmi', 's5']. When we look at figure 3, we see that these are the top-2 features. Thus, we could have also selected directly from feature importance provided by random forest. One more thing that we are missing here is feature selection using models that have **L1 (Lasso) penalization**. When we have L1 penalization for regularization, most coefficients will be 0 (or close to 0), and we select the features with non-zero coefficients. You can do it by just replacing random forest in the snippet of selection from a model with a model that supports L1 penalty, e.g. lasso regression. All tree-based models provide feature importance so all the model-based snippets shown in this chapter can be used for XGBoost, LightGBM or CatBoost. The feature importance function names might be different and may produce results in a different format, but the usage will remain the same. In the end, you must be careful when doing feature selection. Select features on training data and validate the model on validation data for proper selection of features without overfitting the model.

Hyperparameter optimization

With great models, comes the great problem of optimizing hyper-parameters to get the best scoring model. So, what is this hyper-parameter optimization? Suppose there is a simple pipeline for your machine learning project. There is a dataset, you directly apply a model, and then you have results. The parameters that the model has here are known as hyper-parameters, i.e. the parameters that control the training/fitting process of the model. If we train a linear regression with SGD, parameters of a model are the slope and the bias and hyperparameter is learning rate. You will notice that I use these terms interchangeably in this chapter and throughout this book. Let's say there are three parameters a, b, c in the model, and all these parameters can be integers between 1 and 10. A "correct" combination of these parameters will provide you with the best result. So, it's kind of like a suitcase with a 3-dial combination lock. However, in 3 dial combination lock has only one correct answer. The model has many right answers. So, how would you find the best parameters? A method would be to evaluate all the combinations and see which one improves the metric. Let's see how this is done.

```
# define the best accuracy to be 0
# if you choose loss as a metric,
# you can make best loss to be inf (np.inf)
best_accuracy = 0
best_parameters = {"a": 0, "b": 0, "c": 0}

# loop over all values for a, b & c
for a in range(1, 11):
    for b in range(1, 11):
        for c in range(1, 11):
            # inititalize model with current parameters
            model = MODEL(a, b, c)
            # fit the model
            model.fit(training_data)
            # make predictions
            preds = model.predict(validation_data)
            # calculate accuracy
            accuracy = metrics.accuracy_score(targets, preds)
            # save params if current accuracy
            # is greater than best accuracy
            if accuracy > best_accuracy:
                best_accuracy = accuracy
                best_parameters["a"] = a
```

```
            best_parameters["b"] = b
            best_parameters["c"] = c
```

In the above code, we go through all the parameters from 1 to 10. So, we have a total of 1000 (10 x 10 x 10) fits for the model. Well, that might be expensive because the model can take a long time to train. In this situation, it should, however, be okay, but in a real-world scenario, there are not only three parameters and not only ten values for each parameter. Most models parameters are real-valued, and the combinations of different parameters can be infinite.

Let's look at the random forest model from scikit-learn.

```
RandomForestClassifier(
    n_estimators=100,
    criterion='gini',
    max_depth=None,
    min_samples_split=2,
    min_samples_leaf=1,
    min_weight_fraction_leaf=0.0,
    max_features='auto',
    max_leaf_nodes=None,
    min_impurity_decrease=0.0,
    min_impurity_split=None,
    bootstrap=True,
    oob_score=False,
    n_jobs=None,
    random_state=None,
    verbose=0,
    warm_start=False,
    class_weight=None,
    ccp_alpha=0.0,
    max_samples=None,
)
```

There are nineteen parameters, and all the combinations of all these parameters for all the values they can assume are going to be infinite. Normally, we don't have the resource and time to do this. Thus, we specify a *grid* of parameters. A search over this grid to find the best combination of parameters is known as **grid search**. We can say that *n_estimators* can be 100, 200, 250, 300, 400, 500; *max_depth* can be 1, 2, 5, 7, 11, 15 and *criterion* can be gini or entropy. These may not look like a lot of parameters, but it would take a lot of time for computation if the dataset is too large. We can make this grid search work by creating three for loops like before and calculating the score on the validation set. It must also be noted that if you have k-fold cross-validation, you need even more loops which implies even more time to find the perfect parameters. Grid search is therefore not very popular. Let's look at how it's done with an example of **predicting mobile phone price range** given the specifications.

battery_power	blue	clock_speed	dual_sim	fc	four_g	int_memory	m_dep	price_range
842	0	2.2	0	1	0	7	0.6	1
1021	1	0.5	1	0	1	53	0.7	2
563	1	0.5	1	2	1	41	0.9	2
615	1	2.5	0	0	0	10	0.8	2
1821	1	1.2	0	13	1	44	0.6	1
...	...	...	...	...	...	...	...	...
794	1	0.5	1	0	1	2	0.8	0
1965	1	2.6	1	0	0	39	0.2	2

Figure 1: A snapshot of the mobile price dataset[7]

We have 20 features like dual sim, battery power, etc. and a range of price which has 4 categories from 0 to 3. There are only 2000 samples in the training set. We can easily use stratified kfold and accuracy as a metric to evaluate. We will use a random forest model with the aforementioned parameter ranges and see how we can do a grid search in the following example.

```
# rf_grid_search.py
import numpy as np
import pandas as pd

from sklearn import ensemble
from sklearn import metrics
from sklearn import model_selection

if __name__ == "__main__":
    # read the training data
    df = pd.read_csv("../input/mobile_train.csv")

    # features are all columns without price_range
    # note that there is no id column in this dataset
```

---

[7] https://www.kaggle.com/iabhishekofficial/mobile-price-classification

```python
# here we have training features
X = df.drop("price_range", axis=1).values
# and the targets
y = df.price_range.values

# define the model here
# i am using random forest with n_jobs=-1
# n_jobs=-1 => use all cores
classifier = ensemble.RandomForestClassifier(n_jobs=-1)

# define a grid of parameters
# this can be a dictionary or a list of
# dictionaries
param_grid = {
    "n_estimators": [100, 200, 250, 300, 400, 500],
    "max_depth": [1, 2, 5, 7, 11, 15],
    "criterion": ["gini", "entropy"]
}

# initialize grid search
# estimator is the model that we have defined
# param_grid is the grid of parameters
# we use accuracy as our metric. you can define your own
# higher value of verbose implies a lot of details are printed
# cv=5 means that we are using 5 fold cv (not stratified)
model = model_selection.GridSearchCV(
    estimator=classifier,
    param_grid=param_grid,
    scoring="accuracy",
    verbose=10,
    n_jobs=1,
    cv=5
)

# fit the model and extract best score
model.fit(X, y)
print(f"Best score: {model.best_score_}")

print("Best parameters set:")
best_parameters = model.best_estimator_.get_params()
for param_name in sorted(param_grid.keys()):
    print(f"\t{param_name}: {best_parameters[param_name]}")
```

This prints a lot of stuff, let's look at the last few lines.

```
[CV] criterion=entropy, max_depth=15, n_estimators=500, score=0.895,
total=   1.0s
[CV] criterion=entropy, max_depth=15, n_estimators=500 ...............
[CV] criterion=entropy, max_depth=15, n_estimators=500, score=0.890,
total=   1.1s
[CV] criterion=entropy, max_depth=15, n_estimators=500 ...............
[CV] criterion=entropy, max_depth=15, n_estimators=500, score=0.910,
total=   1.1s
[CV] criterion=entropy, max_depth=15, n_estimators=500 ...............
[CV] criterion=entropy, max_depth=15, n_estimators=500, score=0.880,
total=   1.1s
[CV] criterion=entropy, max_depth=15, n_estimators=500 ...............
[CV] criterion=entropy, max_depth=15, n_estimators=500, score=0.870,
total=   1.1s
[Parallel(n_jobs=1)]: Done 360 out of 360 | elapsed:   3.7min finished
Best score: 0.889
Best parameters set:
        criterion: 'entropy'
        max_depth: 15
        n_estimators: 500
```

In the end, we see that our best five fold accuracy score was 0.889, and we have the best parameters from our grid search. Next best thing that we can use is random search. In **random search**, we randomly select a combination of parameters and calculate the cross-validation score. The time consumed here is less than grid search because we do not evaluate over all different combinations of parameters. We choose how many times we want to evaluate our models, and that's what decides how much time the search takes. The code is not very different from above. Except for *GridSearchCV*, we use *RandomizedSearchCV*.

```
# rf_random_search.py
.
.
.
if __name__ == "__main__":
    .
    .
    .
    # define the model here
    # i am using random forest with n_jobs=-1
    # n_jobs=-1 => use all cores
```

```python
classifier = ensemble.RandomForestClassifier(n_jobs=-1)

# define a grid of parameters
# this can be a dictionary or a list of
# dictionaries
param_grid = {
    "n_estimators": np.arange(100, 1500, 100),
    "max_depth": np.arange(1, 31),
    "criterion": ["gini", "entropy"]
}
# initialize random search
# estimator is the model that we have defined
# param_distributions is the grid/distribution of parameters
# we use accuracy as our metric. you can define your own
# higher value of verbose implies a lot of details are printed
# cv=5 means that we are using 5 fold cv (not stratified)
# n_iter is the number of iterations we want
# if param_distributions has all the values as list,
# random search will be done by sampling without replacement
# if any of the parameters come from a distribution,
# random search uses sampling with replacement
model = model_selection.RandomizedSearchCV(
    estimator=classifier,
    param_distributions=param_grid,
    n_iter=20,
    scoring="accuracy",
    verbose=10,
    n_jobs=1,
    cv=5
)

# fit the model and extract best score
model.fit(X, y)
print(f"Best score: {model.best_score_}")

print("Best parameters set:")
best_parameters = model.best_estimator_.get_params()
for param_name in sorted(param_grid.keys()):
    print(f"\t{param_name}: {best_parameters[param_name]}")
```

We have changed the grid of parameters for random search, and it seems like we even improved the results a little bit.

```
Best score: 0.8905
Best parameters set:
```

```
            criterion: entropy
            max_depth: 25
            n_estimators: 300
```

Random search is faster than grid search if the number of iterations is less. Using these two, you can find the optimal (?) parameters for all kinds of models as long as they have a fit and predict function, which is the standard of scikit-learn. Sometimes, you might want to use a pipeline. For example, let's say that we are dealing with a multiclass classification problem. In this problem, the training data consists of two text columns, and you are required to build a model to predict the class. Let's assume that the pipeline you choose is to first apply tf-idf in a semi-supervised manner and then use SVD with SVM classifier. Now, the problem is we have to select the components of SVD and also need to tune the parameters of SVM. How to do this is shown in the following snippet.

```python
# pipeline_search.py
import numpy as np
import pandas as pd

from sklearn import metrics
from sklearn import model_selection
from sklearn import pipeline

from sklearn.decomposition import TruncatedSVD
from sklearn.feature_extraction.text import TfidfVectorizer
from sklearn.preprocessing import StandardScaler
from sklearn.svm import SVC


def quadratic_weighted_kappa(y_true, y_pred):
    """
    Create a wrapper for cohen's kappa
    with quadratic weights
    """
    return metrics.cohen_kappa_score(
        y_true,
        y_pred,
        weights="quadratic"
    )


if __name__ == '__main__':
    # Load the training file
```

```python
train = pd.read_csv('../input/train.csv')

# we dont need ID columns
idx = test.id.values.astype(int)
train = train.drop('id', axis=1)
test = test.drop('id', axis=1)

# create labels. drop useless columns
y = train.relevance.values

# do some lambda magic on text columns
traindata = list(
    train.apply(lambda x:'%s %s' % (x['text1'], x['text2']),axis=1)
)
testdata = list(
    test.apply(lambda x:'%s %s' % (x['text1'], x['text2']),axis=1)
)

# tfidf vectorizer
tfv = TfidfVectorizer(
    min_df=3,
    max_features=None,
    strip_accents='unicode',
    analyzer='word',
    token_pattern=r'\w{1,}',
    ngram_range=(1, 3),
    use_idf=1,
    smooth_idf=1,
    sublinear_tf=1,
    stop_words='english'
)

# Fit TFIDF
tfv.fit(traindata)
X =  tfv.transform(traindata)
X_test = tfv.transform(testdata)

# Initialize SVD
svd = TruncatedSVD()

# Initialize the standard scaler
scl = StandardScaler()

# We will use SVM here..
svm_model = SVC()

# Create the pipeline
```

```python
clf = pipeline.Pipeline(
    [
        ('svd', svd),
        ('scl', scl),
        ('svm', svm_model)
    ]
)

# Create a parameter grid to search for
# best parameters for everything in the pipeline
param_grid = {
    'svd__n_components' : [200, 300],
    'svm__C': [10, 12]
}

# Kappa Scorer
kappa_scorer = metrics.make_scorer(
    quadratic_weighted_kappa,
    greater_is_better=True
)

# Initialize Grid Search Model
model = model_selection.GridSearchCV(
    estimator=clf,
    param_grid=param_grid,
    scoring=kappa_scorer,
    verbose=10,
    n_jobs=-1,
    refit=True,
    cv=5
)

# Fit Grid Search Model
model.fit(X, y)
print("Best score: %0.3f" % model.best_score_)
print("Best parameters set:")
best_parameters = model.best_estimator_.get_params()
for param_name in sorted(param_grid.keys()):
    print("\t%s: %r" % (param_name, best_parameters[param_name]))

# Get best model
best_model = model.best_estimator_

# Fit model with best parameters optimized for QWK
best_model.fit(X, y)
preds = best_model.predict(...)
```

The pipeline shown here has SVD (Singular Value Decomposition), standard scaling and an SVM (Support Vector Machines) model. Please note that you won't be able to run the above code as it is as training data is not available.

When we go into advanced hyperparameter optimization techniques, we can take a look at **minimization of functions** using different kinds of minimization algorithms. This can be achieved by using many minimization functions such as downhill simplex algorithm, Nelder-Mead optimization, using a Bayesian technique with Gaussian process for finding optimal parameters or by using a genetic algorithm. I will talk more about the application of downhill simplex and Nelder-Mead in ensembling and stacking chapter. First, let's see how the gaussian process can be used for hyper-parameter optimization. These kinds of algorithms need a function they can optimize. Most of the time, it's about the minimization of this function, like we **minimize loss**.

So, let's say, you want to find the best parameters for best accuracy and obviously, the more the accuracy is better. Now we cannot minimize the accuracy, but we can minimize it when we multiply it by -1. This way, we are minimizing the negative of accuracy, but in fact, we are maximizing accuracy. Using **Bayesian optimization with gaussian process** can be accomplished by using *gp_minimize* function from scikit-optimize (skopt) library. Let's take a look at how we can tune the parameters of our random forest model using this function.

```
# rf_gp_minimize.py
import numpy as np
import pandas as pd

from functools import partial

from sklearn import ensemble
from sklearn import metrics
from sklearn import model_selection

from skopt import gp_minimize
from skopt import space


def optimize(params, param_names, x, y):
    """
    The main optimization function.
    This function takes all the arguments from the search space
    and training features and targets. It then initializes
```

```python
    the models by setting the chosen parameters and runs
    cross-validation and returns a negative accuracy score
    :param params: list of params from gp_minimize
    :param param_names: list of param names. order is important!
    :param x: training data
    :param y: labels/targets
    :return: negative accuracy after 5 folds
    """
    # convert params to dictionary
    params = dict(zip(param_names, params))

    # initialize model with current parameters
    model = ensemble.RandomForestClassifier(**params)

    # initialize stratified k-fold
    kf = model_selection.StratifiedKFold(n_splits=5)

    # initialize accuracy list
    accuracies = []

    # loop over all folds
    for idx in kf.split(X=x, y=y):
        train_idx, test_idx = idx[0], idx[1]
        xtrain = x[train_idx]
        ytrain = y[train_idx]

        xtest = x[test_idx]
        ytest = y[test_idx]

        # fit model for current fold
        model.fit(xtrain, ytrain)

        #create predictions
        preds = model.predict(xtest)

        # calculate and append accuracy
        fold_accuracy = metrics.accuracy_score(
            ytest,
            preds
        )
        accuracies.append(fold_accuracy)

    # return negative accuracy
    return -1 * np.mean(accuracies)


if __name__ == "__main__":
```

```python
# read the training data
df = pd.read_csv("../input/mobile_train.csv")

# features are all columns without price_range
# note that there is no id column in this dataset
# here we have training features
X = df.drop("price_range", axis=1).values
# and the targets
y = df.price_range.values

# define a parameter space
param_space = [
    # max_depth is an integer between 3 and 10
    space.Integer(3, 15, name="max_depth"),
    # n_estimators is an integer between 50 and 1500
    space.Integer(100, 1500, name="n_estimators"),
    # criterion is a category. here we define list of categories
    space.Categorical(["gini", "entropy"], name="criterion"),
    # you can also have Real numbered space and define a
    # distribution you want to pick it from
    space.Real(0.01, 1, prior="uniform", name="max_features")
]

# make a list of param names
# this has to be same order as the search space
# inside the main function
param_names = [
    "max_depth",
    "n_estimators",
    "criterion",
    "max_features"
]

# by using functools partial, i am creating a
# new function which has same parameters as the
# optimize function except for the fact that
# only one param, i.e. the "params" parameter is
# required. this is how gp_minimize expects the
# optimization function to be. you can get rid of this
# by reading data inside the optimize function or by
# defining the optimize function here.
optimization_function = partial(
    optimize,
    param_names=param_names,
    x=X,
    y=y
)
```

```
# now we call gp_minimize from scikit-optimize
# gp_minimize uses bayesian optimization for
# minimization of the optimization function.
# we need a space of parameters, the function itself,
# the number of calls/iterations we want to have
result = gp_minimize(
    optimization_function,
    dimensions=param_space,
    n_calls=15,
    n_random_starts=10,
    verbose=10
)

# create best params dict and print it
best_params = dict(
    zip(
        param_names,
        result.x
    )
)
print(best_params)
```

Yet again, this produces a lot of output, and the last part of it is shown below.

```
Iteration No: 14 started. Searching for the next optimal point.
Iteration No: 14 ended. Search finished for the next optimal point.
Time taken: 4.7793
Function value obtained: -0.9075
Current minimum: -0.9075
Iteration No: 15 started. Searching for the next optimal point.
Iteration No: 15 ended. Search finished for the next optimal point.
Time taken: 49.4186
Function value obtained: -0.9075
Current minimum: -0.9075
{'max_depth': 12, 'n_estimators': 100, 'criterion': 'entropy',
'max_features': 1.0}
```

It seems like we have managed to crack 0.90 accuracy. That's just amazing!

We can also see (plot) how we achieved convergence by using the following snippet.

```
from skopt.plots import plot_convergence

plot_convergence(result)
```

The convergence plot is shown in figure 2.

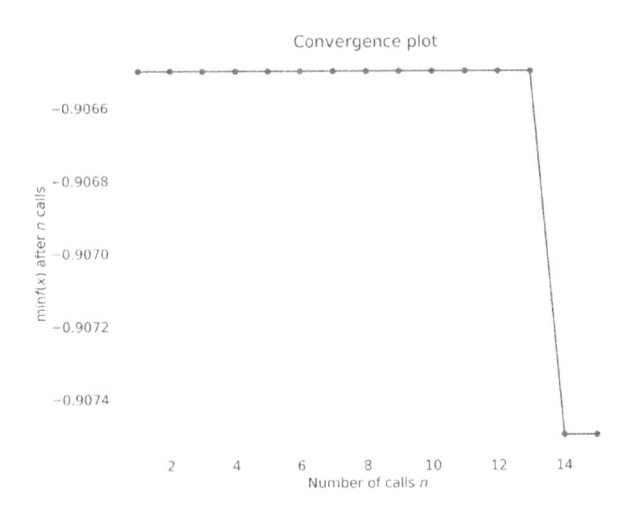

Figure 2: Convergence plot of our random forest parameter optimization

There are many libraries available that offer hyperparameter optimization. scikit-optimize is one such library that you can use. Another useful library for hyperparameter optimization is **hyperopt**. hyperopt uses **Tree-structured Parzen Estimator (TPE)** to find the most optimal parameters. Take a look at the following snippet where I use hyperopt with minimal changes to the previous code.

```
# rf_hyperopt.py
import numpy as np
import pandas as pd

from functools import partial

from sklearn import ensemble
from sklearn import metrics
from sklearn import model_selection

from hyperopt import hp, fmin, tpe, Trials
```

```python
from hyperopt.pyll.base import scope


def optimize(params, x, y):
    """
    The main optimization function.
    This function takes all the arguments from the search space
    and training features and targets. It then initializes
    the models by setting the chosen parameters and runs
    cross-validation and returns a negative accuracy score
    :param params: dict of params from hyperopt
    :param x: training data
    :param y: labels/targets
    :return: negative accuracy after 5 folds
    """

    # initialize model with current parameters
    model = ensemble.RandomForestClassifier(**params)

    # initialize stratified k-fold
    kf = model_selection.StratifiedKFold(n_splits=5)

    .
    .
    .

    # return negative accuracy
    return -1 * np.mean(accuracies)


if __name__ == "__main__":
    # read the training data
    df = pd.read_csv("../input/mobile_train.csv")

    # features are all columns without price_range
    # note that there is no id column in this dataset
    # here we have training features
    X = df.drop("price_range", axis=1).values
    # and the targets
    y = df.price_range.values

    # define a parameter space
    # now we use hyperopt
    param_space = {
        # quniform gives round(uniform(low, high) / q) * q
        # we want int values for depth and estimators
```

```
            "max_depth": scope.int(hp.quniform("max_depth", 1, 15, 1)),
            "n_estimators": scope.int(
                hp.quniform("n_estimators", 100, 1500, 1)
            ),
            # choice chooses from a list of values
            "criterion": hp.choice("criterion", ["gini", "entropy"]),
            # uniform chooses a value between two values
            "max_features": hp.uniform("max_features", 0, 1)
    }

    # partial function
    optimization_function = partial(
        optimize,
        x=X,
        y=y
    )

    # initialize trials to keep logging information
    trials = Trials()

    # run hyperopt
    hopt = fmin(
        fn=optimization_function,
        space=param_space,
        algo=tpe.suggest,
        max_evals=15,
        trials=trials

    )
    print(hopt)
```

As you can see, this is not very different from the previous code. You have to define the parameter space in a different format, and you also need to change the actual optimization part by using *hyperopt* instead of *gp_minimize*. The results are quite good!

```
> python rf_hyperopt.py
100%|████████████████| 15/15 [04:38<00:00, 18.57s/trial, best loss: -0.9095000000000001]
{'criterion': 1, 'max_depth': 11.0, 'max_features': 0.821163568049807, 'n_estimators': 806.0}
```

We get an accuracy which is a little better than before and a set of parameters that we can use. Please note that criterion is 1 in the final result. This implies that choice 1 was selected, i.e., entropy. The ways of tuning hyperparameters described above are the most common, and these will work with almost all models: linear regression, logistic regression, tree-based methods, gradient boosting models such as xgboost, lightgbm, and even neural networks!

Although, these methods exist, to learn, one must start with tuning the hyper-parameters manually, i.e., by hand. Hand tuning will help you learn the basics, for example, in gradient boosting, when you increase the depth, you should reduce the learning rate. It won't be possible to learn this if you use automated tools. Refer to the following table to know what to tune. RS* implies random search should be better.

Once you get better with hand-tuning the parameters, you might not even need any automated hyper-parameter tuning. When you create large models or introduce a lot of features, you also make it susceptible to overfitting the training data. To avoid overfitting, you need to introduce noise in training data features or penalize the cost function. This penalization is called **regularization** and helps with generalizing the model. In linear models, the most common types of regularizations are L1 and L2. L1 is also known as Lasso regression and L2 as Ridge regression. When it comes to neural networks, we use dropouts, the addition of augmentations, noise, etc. to regularize our models. Using hyper-parameter optimization, you can also find the correct penalty to use.

Model	Optimize	Range of values
Linear Regression	- fit_intercept - normalize	- True/False - True/False
Ridge	- alpha - fit_intercept - normalize	- 0.01, 0.1, 1.0, 10, 100 - True/False - True/False
k-neighbors	- n_neighbors - p	- 2, 4, 8, 16 …. - 2, 3
SVM	- C - gamma - class_weight	- 0.001,0.01..10..100..1000 - 'auto', RS* - 'balanced', None
Logistic Regression	- Penalty - C	- l1 or l2 - 0.001, 0.01…..10…100
Lasso	- Alpha - Normalize	- 0.1, 1.0, 10 - True/False
Random Forest	- n_estimators - max_depth - min_samples_split - min_samples_leaf - max features	- 120, 300, 500, 800, 1200 - 5, 8, 15, 25, 30, None - 1, 2, 5, 10, 15, 100 - 1, 2, 5, 10 - log2, sqrt, None
XGBoost	- eta - gamma - max_depth - min_child_weight - subsample - colsample_bytree - lambda - alpha	- 0.01,0.015, 0.025, 0.05, 0.1 - 0.05-0.1,0.3,0.5,0.7,0.9,1.0 - 3, 5, 7, 9, 12, 15, 17, 25 - 1, 3, 5, 7 - 0.6, 0.7, 0.8, 0.9, 1.0 - 0.6, 0.7, 0.8, 0.9, 1.0 - 0.01-0.1, 1.0 , RS* - 0, 0.1, 0.5, 1.0 RS*

Approaching image classification & segmentation

When it comes to images, a lot has been achieved in the last few years. Computer vision is progressing quite fast, and it feels like many problems of computer vision are now much easier to solve. With the advent of pretrained models and cheaper compute, it's now as easy as pie to train a near state-of-the-art model at home for most of the problems related to images. But there are many different types of image problems. You can have the standard classification of images in two or more categories to a challenging problem like self-driving cars. We won't look at self-driving cars in this book, but we will obviously deal with some of the most common image problems.

What are the different approaches that we can apply to images? Image is nothing but a matrix of numbers. The computer cannot see the images as humans do. It only looks at numbers, and that's what the images are. A grayscale image is a two-dimensional matrix with values ranging from 0 to 255. 0 is black, 255 is white and in between you have all shades of grey. Previously, when there was no deep learning (or when deep learning was not popular), people used to look at pixels. Each pixel was a feature. You can do this easily in Python. Just read the grayscale image using OpenCV or Python-PIL, convert to a numpy array and ravel (flatten) the matrix. If you are dealing with RGB images, then you have three matrices instead of one. But the idea remains the same.

```
import numpy as np
import matplotlib.pyplot as plt

# generate random numpy array with values from 0 to 255
# and a size of 256x256
random_image = np.random.randint(0, 256, (256, 256))
# initialize plot
plt.figure(figsize=(7, 7))
# show grayscale image, nb: cmap, vmin and vmax
plt.imshow(random_image, cmap='gray', vmin=0, vmax=255)
plt.show()
```

The code above generates a random matrix using numpy. This matrix consists of values ranging from 0 to 255 (included) and is of size 256x256 (also known as pixels).

Image	Ravelled version of the image
[[251, 130, 37, ..., 234, 194, 18], [207, 31, 174, ..., 148, 215, 27], [78, 237, 167, ..., 154, 24, 26], ..., [134, 200, 9, ..., 143, 41, 220], [111, 21, 204, ..., 131, 15, 176], [237, 120, 199, ..., 253, 6, 153]]	[251, 130, 37, ..., 253, 6, 153]

Figure 1: A 2-D image array (single channel) and its ravelled version

As you can see that the ravelled version is nothing but a vector of size M, where M = N * N. In this case, this vector is of the size 256 * 256 = 65536.

Now, if we go ahead and do it for all the images in our dataset, we have 65536 features for each sample. We can now quickly build a **decision tree model or random forest or SVM-based model** on this data. The models will look at pixel values and would try to separate positive samples from negative samples (in case of a binary classification problem).

All of you must have heard about the cats vs dogs problem. It's a classic one. But let's try something different. If you remember, at the beginning of the chapter on evaluation metrics, I introduced you to a dataset of pneumothorax images. So, let's try building a model to detect if an X-ray image of a lung has pneumothorax or not. That is, a (not so) simple binary classification.

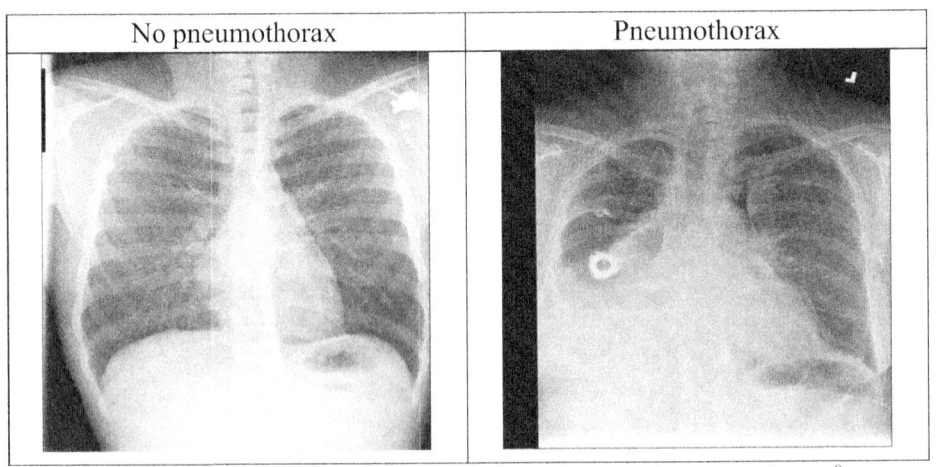

Figure 2: Comparison of non-pneumothorax and pneumothorax x-ray images[8].

---

[8] https://www.kaggle.com/c/siim-acr-pneumothorax-segmentation

In figure 2, you can see a comparison between non-pneumothorax and pneumothorax images. As you must have already noticed, it is quite difficult for a non-expert (like me) to even identify which of these images have pneumothorax.

The original dataset is about detecting where exactly pneumothorax is present, but we have modified the problem to find if the given x-ray image has pneumothorax or not. Don't worry; we will cover the where part in this chapter. The dataset consists of 10675 unique images and 2379 have pneumothorax (note that these numbers are after some cleaning of data and thus do not match original dataset). As a data doctor would say: this is a **classic case of skewed binary classification**. Therefore, we choose the evaluation metric to be AUC and go for a stratified k-fold cross-validation scheme.

You can flatten out the features and try some classical methods like SVM, RF for doing classification, which is perfectly fine, but it won't get you anywhere near state of the art. Also, the images are of size 1024x1024. It's going to take a long time to train a model on this dataset. For what it's worth, let's try building a simple random forest model on this data. Since the images are grayscale, we do not need to do any kind of conversion. We will resize the images to 256x256 to make them smaller and use AUC as a metric as discussed before.

Let's see how this performs.

```
import os

import numpy as np
import pandas as pd

from PIL import Image
from sklearn import ensemble
from sklearn import metrics
from sklearn import model_selection
from tqdm import tqdm


def create_dataset(training_df, image_dir):
    """
    This function takes the training dataframe
    and outputs training array and labels
    :param training_df: dataframe with ImageId, Target columns
    :param image_dir: location of images (folder), string
    :return: X, y (training array with features and labels)
```

```python
"""
# create empty list to store image vectors
images = []
# create empty list to store targets
targets = []
# loop over the dataframe
for index, row in tqdm(
    training_df.iterrows(),
    total=len(training_df),
    desc="processing images"
):
    # get image id
    image_id = row["ImageId"]
    # create image path
    image_path = os.path.join(image_dir, image_id)
    # open image using PIL
    image = Image.open(image_path + ".png")
    # resize image to 256x256. we use bilinear resampling
    image = image.resize((256, 256), resample=Image.BILINEAR)
    # convert image to array
    image = np.array(image)
    # ravel
    image = image.ravel()
    # append images and targets lists
    images.append(image)
    targets.append(int(row["target"]))
# convert list of list of images to numpy array
images = np.array(images)
# print size of this array
print(images.shape)
return images, targets


if __name__ == "__main__":
    csv_path = "/home/abhishek/workspace/siim_png/train.csv"
    image_path = "/home/abhishek/workspace/siim_png/train_png/"

    # read CSV with imageid and target columns
    df = pd.read_csv(csv_path)

    # we create a new column called kfold and fill it with -1
    df["kfold"] = -1

    # the next step is to randomize the rows of the data
    df = df.sample(frac=1).reset_index(drop=True)

    # fetch labels
```

```python
y = df.target.values

# initiate the kfold class from model_selection module
kf = model_selection.StratifiedKFold(n_splits=5)

# fill the new kfold column
for f, (t_, v_) in enumerate(kf.split(X=df, y=y)):
    df.loc[v_, 'kfold'] = f

# we go over the folds created
for fold_ in range(5):
    # temporary dataframes for train and test
    train_df = df[df.kfold != fold_].reset_index(drop=True)
    test_df = df[df.kfold == fold_].reset_index(drop=True)

    # create train dataset
    # you can move this outside to save some computation time
    xtrain, ytrain = create_dataset(train_df, image_path)

    # create test dataset
    # you can move this outside to save some computation time
    xtest, ytest = create_dataset(test_df, image_path)

    # fit random forest without any modification of params
    clf = ensemble.RandomForestClassifier(n_jobs=-1)
    clf.fit(xtrain, ytrain)

    # predict probability of class 1
    preds = clf.predict_proba(xtest)[:, 1]

    # print results
    print(f"FOLD: {fold_}")
    print(f"AUC = {metrics.roc_auc_score(ytest, preds)}")
    print("")
```

This gives a mean AUC of around 0.72.

Which is not bad but hopefully, we can do a lot better. You can use this approach for images, and this is how it was used in good old times. SVM was quite famous for image datasets. Deep Learning has been proved to be the state of the art when solving such problems, hence we could try that next.

I won't go into the history of deep learning and who invented what. Instead, let's take a look at one of the most famous deep learning models **AlexNet** and see what's happening there.

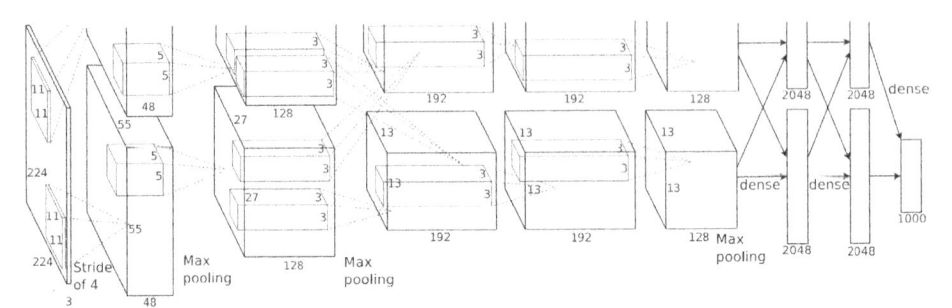

Figure 3: AlexNet architecture[9]. Please note that the input size in this figure is not 224x224 but 227x227

Nowadays, you might say that it is a basic **deep convolutional neural network,** but it is the foundation of many new deep nets (deep neural networks). We see that the network in figure 3 is a convolutional neural network with five convolution layers, two dense layers and an output layer. We see that there is also max pooling. What is it? Let's look at some terms which you will come across when doing deep learning.

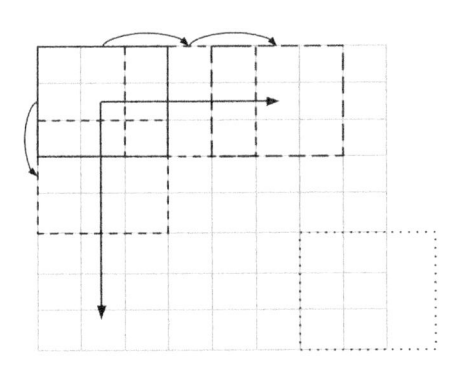

Figure 4: An image of size 8x8 with a filter of size 3x3 and stride of 2.

Figure 4 introduces two new terms: filter and strides. **Filters** are nothing but two-dimensional matrices which are initialized by a given function. "**He initialization**"

---

[9] A. Krizhevsky, I. Sutskever, and G. Hinton. Imagenet classification with deep convolutional neural networks. In NIPS, 2012

which is also known "**Kaiming normal initialization**" is a good choice for convolutional neural networks. It is because most modern networks use **ReLU (Rectified Linear Units)** activation function and proper initialization is required to avoid the problem of **vanishing gradients** (when gradients approach zero and weights of network do not change). This filter is convolved with the image. Convolution is nothing but a summation of elementwise multiplication (cross-correlation) between the filter and the pixels it is currently overlapping in a given image. You can read more about convolution in any high school mathematics textbook. We start convolution of this filter from the top left corner of the image, and we move it horizontally. If we move it by 1 pixel, the stride is 1. If we move it by 2 pixels, the stride is 2. And that's what **stride** is.

Stride is a useful concept even in natural language processing, e.g. in question and answering systems when you have to filter answer from a large text corpus. When we are exhausted horizontally, we move the filter by the same stride downwards vertically, starting from left again. Figure 4 also shows a filter going outside the image. In these cases, it's not possible to calculate the convolution. So, we skip it. If you don't want to skip it, you will need to **pad the image**. It must also be noted that convolution will decrease the size of the image. Padding is also a way to keep the size of the image the same. In figure 4, A 3x3 filter is moving horizontally and vertically, and every time it moves, it skips two columns and two rows (i.e. pixels) respectively. Since it skips two pixels, stride = 2. And resulting image size is $[(8-3)/2] + 1 = 3.5$. We take the floor of 3.5, so its 3x3. You can do it by hand by moving the filters on a pen and paper.

Originally, this image is 6x6. We pad this image with a 0 pixel on each side to make it 8x8

3x3 filter is convolved with 8x8 image with a stride of 1

Resulting image is of the same size as original image, i.e. 6x6.

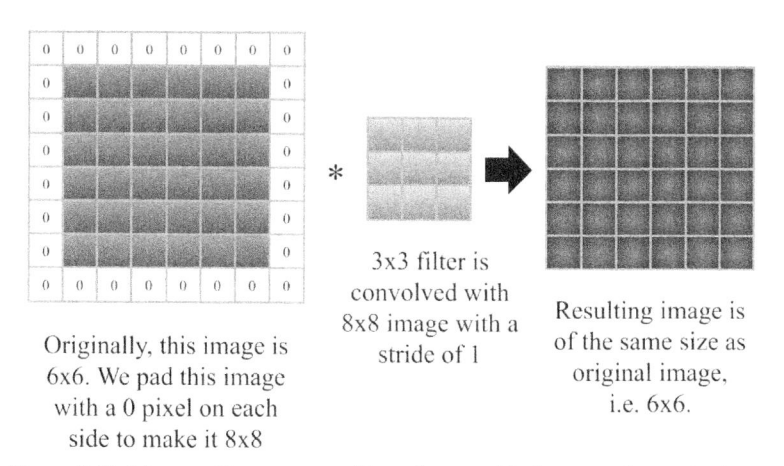

Figure 5: Padding enables us to provide an image with the same size as the input

We see the effect of padding in figure 5. Now, we have a 3x3 filter which is moving with a stride of 1. Size of the original image is 6x6, and we have added padding of 1. The **padding** of 1 means increasing the size of the image by adding zero pixels on each side once. In this case, the resulting image will be of the same size as the input image, i.e. 6x6. Another relevant term that you might come across when dealing with deep neural networks is **dilation,** as shown in figure 6.

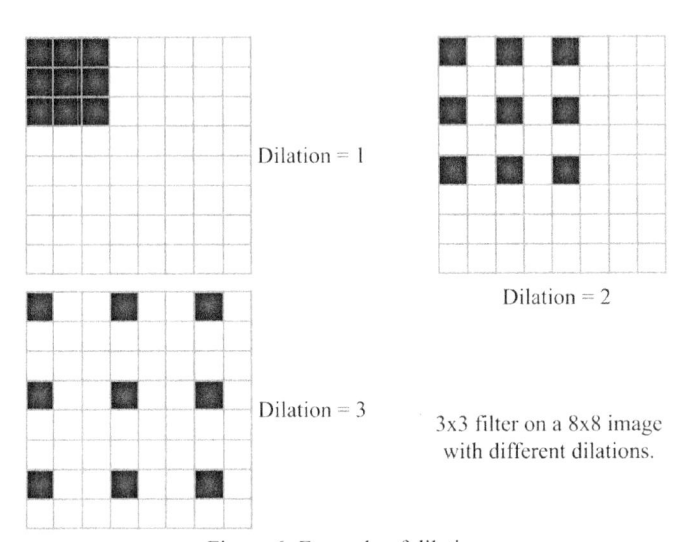

Dilation = 1

Dilation = 2

Dilation = 3

3x3 filter on a 8x8 image with different dilations.

Figure 6: Example of dilation

In **dilation**, we expand the filter by N-1, where N is the value of dilation rate or simply known as dilation. In this kind of kernel with dilation, you skip some pixels in each convolution. This is particularly effective in segmentation tasks. Please note that we have only talked about 2-dimensional convolutions. There are 1-d convolutions too and also in higher dimensions. All work on the same underlying concept.

Next comes max-pooling. **Max pooling** is nothing but a filter which returns max. So, instead of convolution, we are extracting the max value of pixels. Similarly, **average pooling** or **mean-pooling** returns mean of pixels. They are used in the same way as the convolutional kernel. Pooling is faster than convolution and is a way to down-sample the image. Max pooling detects edges and average pooling smoothens the image.

There are way too many concepts in convolutional neural networks and deep learning. The ones that I discussed are some of the basics that will help you get started. Now, we are well prepared to start building our first convolutional neural network in PyTorch. PyTorch provides an intuitive and easy way to implement deep neural networks, and you don't need to care about back-propagation. We define the network in a python class and a forward function that tells PyTorch how the layers are connected to each other. In PyTorch, the image notation is BS, C, H, W, where, BS is the batch size, C channels, H is height and W is the width. Let's see how AlexNet is implemented in PyTorch.

```python
import torch
import torch.nn as nn
import torch.nn.functional as F


class AlexNet(nn.Module):
    def __init__(self):
        super(AlexNet, self).__init__()
        # convolution part
        self.conv1 = nn.Conv2d(
            in_channels=3,
            out_channels=96,
            kernel_size=11,
            stride=4,
            padding=0
        )
        self.pool1 = nn.MaxPool2d(kernel_size=3, stride=2)
        self.conv2 = nn.Conv2d(
            in_channels=96,
            out_channels=256,
            kernel_size=5,
            stride=1,
            padding=2
        )
        self.pool2 = nn.MaxPool2d(kernel_size=3, stride=2)
        self.conv3 = nn.Conv2d(
            in_channels=256,
            out_channels=384,
            kernel_size=3,
            stride=1,
            padding=1
        )
        self.conv4 = nn.Conv2d(in_channels=384,out_channels=384,
            kernel_size=3, stride=1,padding=1)
```

```python
        self.conv5 = nn.Conv2d(in_channels=384, out_channels=256,
            kernel_size=3,
            stride=1,
            padding=1
        )
        self.pool3 = nn.MaxPool2d(kernel_size=3, stride=2)
        # dense part
        self.fc1 = nn.Linear(
            in_features=9216,
            out_features=4096
        )
        self.dropout1 = nn.Dropout(0.5)
        self.fc2 = nn.Linear(
            in_features=4096,
            out_features=4096
        )
        self.dropout2 = nn.Dropout(0.5)
        self.fc3 = nn.Linear(
            in_features=4096,
            out_features=1000
        )
    def forward(self, image):
        # get the batch size, channels, height and width
        # of the input batch of images
        # original size: (bs, 3, 227, 227)
        bs, c, h, w = image.size()
        x = F.relu(self.conv1(image))   # size: (bs, 96, 55, 55)
        x = self.pool1(x)   # size: (bs, 96, 27, 27)
        x = F.relu(self.conv2(x))   # size: (bs, 256, 27, 27)
        x = self.pool2(x)   # size: (bs, 256, 13, 13)
        x = F.relu(self.conv3(x))   # size: (bs, 384, 13, 13)
        x = F.relu(self.conv4(x))   # size: (bs, 384, 13, 13)
        x = F.relu(self.conv5(x))   # size: (bs, 256, 13, 13)
        x = self.pool3(x)   # size: (bs, 256, 6, 6)
        x = x.view(bs, -1)   # size: (bs, 9216)
        x = F.relu(self.fc1(x))   # size: (bs, 4096)
        x = self.dropout1(x)   # size: (bs, 4096)
        # dropout does not change size
        # dropout is used for regularization
        # 0.3 dropout means that only 70% of the nodes
        # of the current layer are used for the next layer
        x = F.relu(self.fc2(x))   # size: (bs, 4096)
        x = self.dropout2(x)   # size: (bs, 4096)
        x = F.relu(self.fc3(x))   # size: (bs, 1000)
        # 1000 is number of classes in ImageNet Dataset
        # softmax is an activation function that converts
        # linear output to probabilities that add up to 1
```

```
# for each sample in the batch
x = torch.softmax(x, axis=1)  # size: (bs, 1000)
return x
```

When you have a 3x227x227 image, and you apply a convolutional filter of size 11x11, it means that you are applying a filter of size 11x11x3 and convolving it with an image of size 227x227x3. So, now, you need to think in 3 dimensions instead of 2. The number of output channels is the number of different convolutional filters of the same size applied to the image individually. So, in the first convolutional layer, the input channels are 3, which is the original input, i.e. the R, G, B channels. PyTorch's *torchvision* offers many different models like AlexNet, and it must be noted that this implementation of AlexNet is not the same as torchvision's. Torchvision's implementation of AlexNet is a modified AlexNet from another paper: *Krizhevsky, A. One weird trick for parallelizing convolutional neural networks. CoRR, abs/1404.5997, 2014.*

You can design your own convolutional neural networks for your task, and many times it is a good idea to start from something on your own. Let's build a network to classify images from our initial dataset of this chapter into categories of having pneumothorax or not. But first, let's prepare some files. The first step would be to create a folds file, i.e. *train.csv* but with a new column *kfold*. We will create five folds. Since I have shown how to do this for different datasets in this book, I will skip this part and leave it an exercise for you. For PyTorch based neural networks, we need to create a dataset class. The objective of the dataset class is to return an item or sample of data. This sample of data should consist of everything you need in order to train or evaluate your model.

```
# dataset.py
import torch

import numpy as np

from PIL import Image
from PIL import ImageFile

# sometimes, you will have images without an ending bit
# this takes care of those kind of (corrupt) images
ImageFile.LOAD_TRUNCATED_IMAGES = True


class ClassificationDataset:
```

```python
"""
A general classification dataset class that you can use for all
kinds of image classification problems. For example,
binary classification, multi-class, multi-label classification
"""
def __init__(
    self,
    image_paths,
    targets,
    resize=None,
    augmentations=None
):
    """
    :param image_paths: list of path to images
    :param targets: numpy array
    :param resize: tuple, e.g. (256, 256), resizes image if not None
    :param augmentations: albumentation augmentations
    """
    self.image_paths = image_paths
    self.targets = targets
    self.resize = resize
    self.augmentations = augmentations

def __len__(self):
    """
    Return the total number of samples in the dataset
    """
    return len(self.image_paths)

def __getitem__(self, item):
    """
    For a given "item" index, return everything we need
    to train a given model
    """
    # use PIL to open the image
    image = Image.open(self.image_paths[item])
    # convert image to RGB, we have single channel images
    image = image.convert("RGB")
    # grab correct targets
    targets = self.targets[item]

    # resize if needed
    if self.resize is not None:
        image = image.resize(
            (self.resize[1], self.resize[0]),
            resample=Image.BILINEAR
        )
```

```python
    # convert image to numpy array
    image = np.array(image)

    # if we have albumentation augmentations
    # add them to the image
    if self.augmentations is not None:
        augmented = self.augmentations(image=image)
        image = augmented["image"]

    # pytorch expects CHW instead of HWC
    image = np.transpose(image, (2, 0, 1)).astype(np.float32)

    # return tensors of image and targets
    # take a look at the types!
    # for regression tasks,
    # dtype of targets will change to torch.float
    return {
        "image": torch.tensor(image, dtype=torch.float),
        "targets": torch.tensor(targets, dtype=torch.long),
    }
```

Now we need *engine.py*. *engine.py* has training and evaluation functions. Let's see how *engine.py* looks like.

```python
# engine.py
import torch
import torch.nn as nn

from tqdm import tqdm


def train(data_loader, model, optimizer, device):
    """
    This function does training for one epoch
    :param data_loader: this is the pytorch dataloader
    :param model: pytorch model
    :param optimizer: optimizer, for e.g. adam, sgd, etc
    :param device: cuda/cpu
    """

    # put the model in train mode
    model.train()

    # go over every batch of data in data loader
    for data in data_loader:
```

```python
            # remember, we have image and targets
            # in our dataset class
            inputs = data["image"]
            targets = data["targets"]

            # move inputs/targets to cuda/cpu device
            inputs = inputs.to(device, dtype=torch.float)
            targets = targets.to(device, dtype=torch.float)

            # zero grad the optimizer
            optimizer.zero_grad()
            # do the forward step of model
            outputs = model(inputs)
            # calculate loss
            loss = nn.BCEWithLogitsLoss()(outputs, targets.view(-1, 1))
            # backward step the loss
            loss.backward()
            # step optimizer
            optimizer.step()
            # if you have a scheduler, you either need to
            # step it here or you have to step it after
            # the epoch. here, we are not using any learning
            # rate scheduler


def evaluate(data_loader, model, device):
    """
    This function does evaluation for one epoch
    :param data_loader: this is the pytorch dataloader
    :param model: pytorch model
    :param device: cuda/cpu
    """
    # put model in evaluation mode
    model.eval()

    # init lists to store targets and outputs
    final_targets = []
    final_outputs = []

    # we use no_grad context
    with torch.no_grad():

        for data in data_loader:
            inputs = data["image"]
            targets = data["targets"]
            inputs = inputs.to(device, dtype=torch.float)
            targets = targets.to(device, dtype=torch.float)
```

```
        # do the forward step to generate prediction
        output = model(inputs)

        # convert targets and outputs to lists
        targets = targets.detach().cpu().numpy().tolist()
        output = output.detach().cpu().numpy().tolist()

        # extend the original list
        final_targets.extend(targets)
        final_outputs.extend(output)

    # return final output and final targets
    return final_outputs, final_targets
```

Once we have *engine.py*, we are ready to create a new file: *model.py*. *model.py* will consist of our model. It's a good idea to keep it separate because that allows us to easily experiment with different models and different architectures. A PyTorch library called *pretrainedmodels* has a lot of different model architectures, such as **AlexNet, ResNet, DenseNet**, etc. There are different model architectures which have been trained on large image dataset called ImageNet. We can use them with their weights after training on ImageNet, and we can also use them without these weights. If we train without the ImageNet weights, it means our network is learning everything from scratch. This is what *model.py* looks like.

```
# model.py
import torch.nn as nn
import pretrainedmodels


def get_model(pretrained):
    if pretrained:
        model = pretrainedmodels.__dict__["alexnet"](
            pretrained='imagenet'
        )
    else:
        model = pretrainedmodels.__dict__["alexnet"](
            pretrained=None
        )
    # print the model here to know whats going on.
    model.last_linear = nn.Sequential(
        nn.BatchNorm1d(4096),
        nn.Dropout(p=0.25),
        nn.Linear(in_features=4096, out_features=2048),
```

```
        nn.ReLU(),
        nn.BatchNorm1d(2048, eps=1e-05, momentum=0.1),
        nn.Dropout(p=0.5),
        nn.Linear(in_features=2048, out_features=1),
    )
    return model
```

If you print the final model, you will be able to see what it looks like:

```
AlexNet(
  (avgpool): AdaptiveAvgPool2d(output_size=(6, 6))
  (_features): Sequential(
    (0): Conv2d(3, 64, kernel_size=(11, 11), stride=(4, 4), padding=(2, 2))
    (1): ReLU(inplace=True)
    (2): MaxPool2d(kernel_size=3, stride=2, padding=0, dilation=1, ceil_mode=False)
    (3): Conv2d(64, 192, kernel_size=(5, 5), stride=(1, 1), padding=(2, 2))
    (4): ReLU(inplace=True)
    (5): MaxPool2d(kernel_size=3, stride=2, padding=0, dilation=1, ceil_mode=False)
    (6): Conv2d(192, 384, kernel_size=(3, 3), stride=(1, 1), padding=(1, 1))
    (7): ReLU(inplace=True)
    (8): Conv2d(384, 256, kernel_size=(3, 3), stride=(1, 1), padding=(1, 1))
    (9): ReLU(inplace=True)
    (10): Conv2d(256, 256, kernel_size=(3, 3), stride=(1, 1), padding=(1, 1))
    (11): ReLU(inplace=True)
    (12): MaxPool2d(kernel_size=3, stride=2, padding=0, dilation=1, ceil_mode=False)
  )
  (dropout0): Dropout(p=0.5, inplace=False)
  (linear0): Linear(in_features=9216, out_features=4096, bias=True)
  (relu0): ReLU(inplace=True)
  (dropout1): Dropout(p=0.5, inplace=False)
  (linear1): Linear(in_features=4096, out_features=4096, bias=True)
  (relu1): ReLU(inplace=True)
  (last_linear): Sequential(
    (0): BatchNorm1d(4096, eps=1e-05, momentum=0.1, affine=True, track_running_stats=True)
    (1): Dropout(p=0.25, inplace=False)
    (2): Linear(in_features=4096, out_features=2048, bias=True)
```

```
    (3): ReLU()
    (4): BatchNorm1d(2048, eps=1e-05, momentum=0.1, affine=True,
track_running_stats=True)
    (5): Dropout(p=0.5, inplace=False)
    (6): Linear(in_features=2048, out_features=1, bias=True)
  )
)
```

Now, we have everything, and we can start training. We will do so using *train.py*.

```
# train.py
import os

import pandas as pd
import numpy as np

import albumentations
import torch

from sklearn import metrics
from sklearn.model_selection import train_test_split

import dataset
import engine
from model import get_model


if __name__ == "__main__":
    # location of train.csv and train_png folder
    # with all the png images
    data_path = "/home/abhishek/workspace/siim_png/"

    # cuda/cpu device
    device = "cuda"

    # let's train for 10 epochs
    epochs = 10

    # load the dataframe
    df = pd.read_csv(os.path.join(data_path, "train.csv"))

    # fetch all image ids
    images = df.ImageId.values.tolist()
```

```python
# a list with image locations
images = [
    os.path.join(data_path, "train_png", i + ".png") for i in images
]

# binary targets numpy array
targets = df.target.values

# fetch out model, we will try both pretrained
# and non-pretrained weights
model = get_model(pretrained=True)

# move model to device
model.to(device)

# mean and std values of RGB channels for imagenet dataset
# we use these pre-calculated values when we use weights
# from imagenet.
# when we do not use imagenet weights, we use the mean and
# standard deviation values of the original dataset
# please note that this is a separate calculation
mean = (0.485, 0.456, 0.406)
std = (0.229, 0.224, 0.225)

# albumentations is an image augmentation library
# that allows you to do many different types of image
# augmentations. here, i am using only normalization
# notice always_apply=True. we always want to apply
# normalization
aug = albumentations.Compose(
    [
        albumentations.Normalize(
            mean, std, max_pixel_value=255.0, always_apply=True
        )
    ]
)

# instead of using kfold, i am using train_test_split
# with a fixed random state
train_images, valid_images, train_targets, valid_targets = train_test_split(
    images, targets, stratify=targets, random_state=42
)

# fetch the ClassificationDataset class
train_dataset = dataset.ClassificationDataset(
    image_paths=train_images,
```

```
        targets=train_targets,
        resize=(227, 227),
        augmentations=aug,
    )
    # torch dataloader creates batches of data
    # from classification dataset class
    train_loader = torch.utils.data.DataLoader(
        train_dataset, batch_size=16, shuffle=True, num_workers=4
    )

    # same for validation data
    valid_dataset = dataset.ClassificationDataset(
        image_paths=valid_images,
        targets=valid_targets,
        resize=(227, 227),
        augmentations=aug,
    )

    valid_loader = torch.utils.data.DataLoader(
        valid_dataset, batch_size=16, shuffle=False, num_workers=4
    )

    # simple Adam optimizer
    optimizer = torch.optim.Adam(model.parameters(), lr=5e-4)

    # train and print auc score for all epochs
    for epoch in range(epochs):
        engine.train(train_loader, model, optimizer, device=device)
        predictions, valid_targets = engine.evaluate(
            valid_loader, model, device=device
        )
        roc_auc = metrics.roc_auc_score(valid_targets, predictions)
        print(
            f"Epoch={epoch}, Valid ROC AUC={roc_auc}"
        )
```

Let's train it without pretrained weights:

```
Epoch=0, Valid ROC AUC=0.5737161981475328
Epoch=1, Valid ROC AUC=0.5362868001588292
Epoch=2, Valid ROC AUC=0.6163448214387008
Epoch=3, Valid ROC AUC=0.6119219143780944
Epoch=4, Valid ROC AUC=0.6229718888519726
Epoch=5, Valid ROC AUC=0.5983014999635341
```

```
Epoch=6, Valid ROC AUC=0.5523236874306134
Epoch=7, Valid ROC AUC=0.4717721611306046
Epoch=8, Valid ROC AUC=0.6473408263980617
Epoch=9, Valid ROC AUC=0.6639862888260415
```

This AUC is around 0.66 which is even lower than our random forest model. What happens when we use pretrained weights?

```
Epoch=0, Valid ROC AUC=0.5730387429803165
Epoch=1, Valid ROC AUC=0.5319813942934937
Epoch=2, Valid ROC AUC=0.627111577514323
Epoch=3, Valid ROC AUC=0.6819736959393209
Epoch=4, Valid ROC AUC=0.5747117168950512
Epoch=5, Valid ROC AUC=0.5994619255609669
Epoch=6, Valid ROC AUC=0.5080889443530546
Epoch=7, Valid ROC AUC=0.6323792776512727
Epoch=8, Valid ROC AUC=0.6685753182661686
Epoch=9, Valid ROC AUC=0.6861802387300147
```

The AUC is much better now. However, it is still lower. The good thing about pretrained models is that we can try many different models easily. Let's try **resnet18 with pretrained weights**.

```python
# model.py
import torch.nn as nn
import pretrainedmodels


def get_model(pretrained):
    if pretrained:
        model = pretrainedmodels.__dict__["resnet18"](
            pretrained='imagenet'
        )
    else:
        model = pretrainedmodels.__dict__["resnet18"](
            pretrained=None
        )
    # print the model here to know whats going on.
    model.last_linear = nn.Sequential(
        nn.BatchNorm1d(512),
        nn.Dropout(p=0.25),
        nn.Linear(in_features=512, out_features=2048),
```

```
    nn.ReLU(),
    nn.BatchNorm1d(2048, eps=1e-05, momentum=0.1),
    nn.Dropout(p=0.5),
    nn.Linear(in_features=2048, out_features=1),
)
return model
```

When trying this model, I also changed the image size to 512x512 and added a step learning rate scheduler which multiplies the learning rate by 0.5 after every 3 epochs.

```
Epoch=0, Valid ROC AUC=0.5988225569880796
Epoch=1, Valid ROC AUC=0.730349343208836
Epoch=2, Valid ROC AUC=0.5870943169939142
Epoch=3, Valid ROC AUC=0.5775864444138311
Epoch=4, Valid ROC AUC=0.7330502499939224
Epoch=5, Valid ROC AUC=0.7500336296524395
Epoch=6, Valid ROC AUC=0.7563722113724951
Epoch=7, Valid ROC AUC=0.7987463837994215
Epoch=8, Valid ROC AUC=0.798505708937384
Epoch=9, Valid ROC AUC=0.8025477500546988
```

This model seems to perform the best. However, you might be able to tune the different parameters and image size in AlexNet to get a better score. Using augmentations will improve the score further. Optimising deep neural networks is difficult but not impossible. Choose Adam optimizer, use a low learning rate, reduce learning rate on a plateau of validation loss, try some augmentations, try preprocessing the images (e.g. cropping if needed, this can also be considered pre-processing), change the batch size, etc. There's a lot that you can do to optimize your deep neural network.

ResNet is an architecture much more complicated compared to AlexNet. ResNet stands for Residual Neural Network and was introduced by K. He, X. Zhang, S. Ren and J. Sun in the paper, deep residual learning for image recognition, in 2015. ResNet consists of **residual blocks** that transfer the knowledge from one layer to further layers by skipping some layers in between. These kinds of connections of layers are known as **skip-connections** since we are skipping one or more layers. Skip-connections help with the vanishing gradient issue by propagating the gradients to further layers. This allows us to train very large convolutional neural networks without loss of performance. Usually, the training loss increases at a given point if we are using a large neural network, but that can be prevented by using skip-connections. This can be better understood by figure 7.

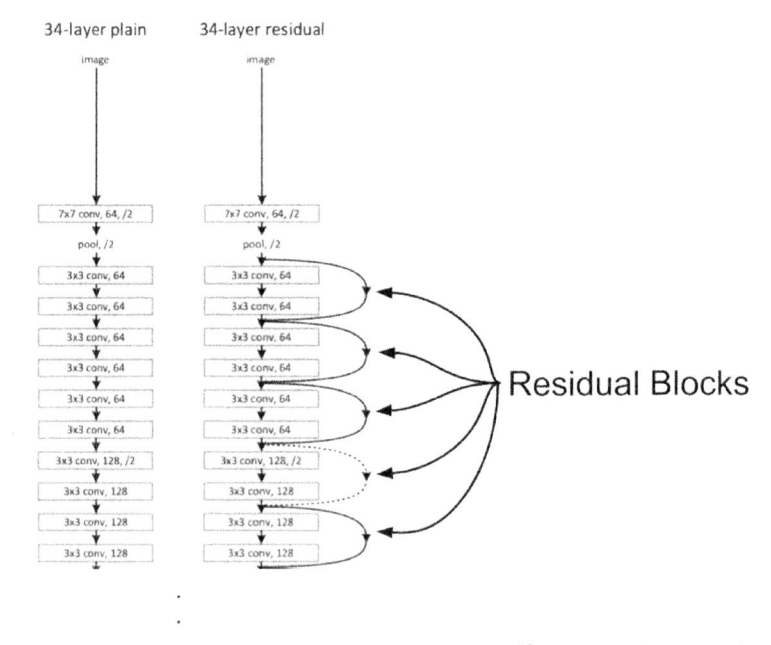

Figure 7: Comparison of simple convnet and residual convnet[10]. See the skip connections. Please note that the final layers are omitted in this figure.

A residual block is quite simple to understand. You take the output from a layer, skip some layers and add that output to a layer further in the network. The dotted lines mean that the input shape needs to be adjusted as max-pooling is being used and use of max-pooling changes the size of the output.

ResNet comes in many different variations: 18, 34, 50, 101 and 152 layers and all of them are available with weights pre-trained on ImageNet dataset. These days pretrained models work for (almost) everything but make sure that you start with smaller models, for example, begin with resnet-18 rather than resnet-50. Some other ImageNet pre-trained models include:

- Inception
- DenseNet (different variations)

---

[10] K. He, X. Zhang, S. Ren and J. Sun, Deep residual learning for image recognition, 2015

- NASNet
- PNASNet
- VGG
- Xception
- ResNeXt
- EfficientNet, etc.

A majority of the pre-trained state-of-the-art models can be found in *pytorch-pretrainedmodels* repository on GitHub: *https://github.com/Cadene/pretrained-models.pytorch*. It is out of the scope of this chapter (and this book) to discuss these models in details. Since we are only looking at applications, let's see how a pre-trained model like this can be used for a segmentation task.

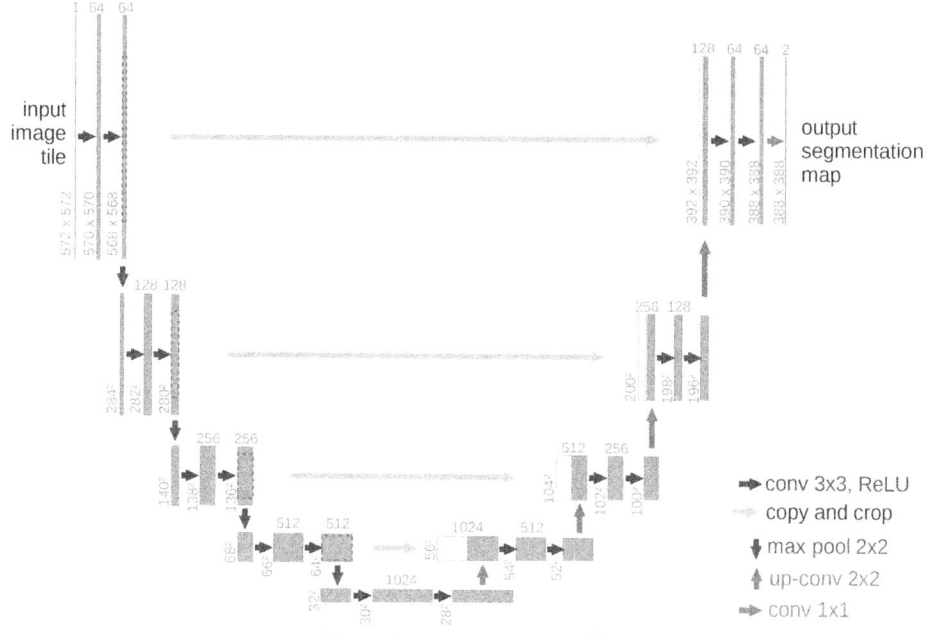

Figure 8: U-Net architecture[11].

Segmentation is a task which is quite popular in computer vision. In a segmentation task, we try to remove/extract foreground from background. Foreground and

---

[11] O. Ronneberger, P. Fischer and T. Brox. U-Net: Convolutional networks for biomedical image segmentation. In MICCAI, 2015

background can have different definitions. We can also say that it is a pixel-wise classification task in which your job is to assign a class to each pixel in a given image. The pneumothorax dataset that we are working on is, in fact, a segmentation task. In this task, given the chest radiographic images, we are required to segment pneumothorax. The most popular model used for segmentation tasks is **U-Net**. The structure is represented in figure 8.

U-Nets have two parts: encoder and decoder. The encoder is the same as any convnet you have seen till now. The decoder is a bit different. Decoder consists of up-convolutional layers. In up-convolutions (**transposed convolutions**), we use filters that when applied to a small image, creates a larger image. In PyTorch, you can use *ConvTranspose2d* for this operation. It must be noted that up-convolution is not the same as up-sampling. Up-sampling is an easy process in which we apply a function to an image to resize it. In up-convolution, we *learn* the filters. We take some parts of the encoder as inputs to some of the decoders. This is important for the up-convolutional layers.

Let's see how this U-Net is implemented.

```
# simple_unet.py
import torch
import torch.nn as nn
from torch.nn import functional as F


def double_conv(in_channels, out_channels):
    """
    This function applies two convolutional layers
    each followed by a ReLU activation function
    :param in_channels: number of input channels
    :param out_channels: number of output channels
    :return: a down-conv layer
    """
    conv = nn.Sequential(
        nn.Conv2d(in_channels, out_channels, kernel_size=3),
        nn.ReLU(inplace=True),
        nn.Conv2d(out_channels, out_channels, kernel_size=3),
        nn.ReLU(inplace=True)
    )
    return conv


def crop_tensor(tensor, target_tensor):
```

```python
    """
    Center crops a tensor to size of a given target tensor size
    Please note that this function is applicable only to
    this implementation of unet. There are a few assumptions
    in this implementation that might not be applicable to all
    networks and all other use-cases.
    Both tensors are of shape (bs, c, h, w)
    :param tensor: a tensor that needs to be cropped
    :param target_tensor: target tensor of smaller size
    :return: cropped tensor
    """
    target_size = target_tensor.size()[2]
    tensor_size = tensor.size()[2]
    delta = tensor_size - target_size
    delta = delta // 2
    return tensor[
        :,
        :,
        delta:tensor_size - delta,
        delta:tensor_size - delta
    ]


class UNet(nn.Module):
    def __init__(self):
        super(UNet, self).__init__()

        # we need only one max_pool as it is not learned
        self.max_pool_2x2 = nn.MaxPool2d(kernel_size=2, stride=2)

        self.down_conv_1 = double_conv(1, 64)
        self.down_conv_2 = double_conv(64, 128)
        self.down_conv_3 = double_conv(128, 256)
        self.down_conv_4 = double_conv(256, 512)
        self.down_conv_5 = double_conv(512, 1024)

        self.up_trans_1 = nn.ConvTranspose2d(
            in_channels=1024,
            out_channels=512,
            kernel_size=2,
            stride=2
        )
        self.up_conv_1 = double_conv(1024, 512)

        self.up_trans_2 = nn.ConvTranspose2d(
            in_channels=512,
            out_channels=256,
```

```python
            kernel_size=2,
            stride=2
        )
        self.up_conv_2 = double_conv(512, 256)

        self.up_trans_3 = nn.ConvTranspose2d(
            in_channels=256,
            out_channels=128,
            kernel_size=2,
            stride=2
        )
        self.up_conv_3 = double_conv(256, 128)

        self.up_trans_4 = nn.ConvTranspose2d(
            in_channels=128,
            out_channels=64,
            kernel_size=2,
            stride=2
        )
        self.up_conv_4 = double_conv(128, 64)

        self.out = nn.Conv2d(
            in_channels=64,
            out_channels=2,
            kernel_size=1
        )

    def forward(self, image):
        # encoder
        x1 = self.down_conv_1(image)
        x2 = self.max_pool_2x2(x1)
        x3 = self.down_conv_2(x2)
        x4 = self.max_pool_2x2(x3)
        x5 = self.down_conv_3(x4)
        x6 = self.max_pool_2x2(x5)
        x7 = self.down_conv_4(x6)
        x8 = self.max_pool_2x2(x7)
        x9 = self.down_conv_5(x8)

        # decoder
        x = self.up_trans_1(x9)
        y = crop_tensor(x7, x)
        x = self.up_conv_1(torch.cat([x, y], axis=1))
        x = self.up_trans_2(x)
        y = crop_tensor(x5, x)
        x = self.up_conv_2(torch.cat([x, y], axis=1))
        x = self.up_trans_3(x)
```

```
        y = crop_tensor(x3, x)
        x = self.up_conv_3(torch.cat([x, y], axis=1))
        x = self.up_trans_4(x)
        y = crop_tensor(x1, x)
        x = self.up_conv_4(torch.cat([x, y], axis=1))

        # output layer
        out = self.out(x)

        return out

if __name__ == "__main__":
    image = torch.rand((1, 1, 572, 572))
    model = UNet()
    print(model(image))
```

Please note that the implementation of U-Net that I have shown above is the original implementation of the U-Net paper. There are many variations that can be found on the internet. Some prefer to use bilinear sampling instead of transposed convolutions for up-sampling, but that's not the real implementation of the paper. It might, however, perform better. In the original implementation shown above, there is a single channel image with two channels in the output: one for foreground and one for the background. As you can see, this can be customized for any number of classes and any number of input channels very easily. The input image size is different than output image size in this implementation as we are using convolutions without padding.

We see that the encoder part of the U-Net is a nothing but a simple convolutional network. We can, thus, replace this with any network such as ResNet. The replacement can also be done with pretrained weights. Thus, we can use a ResNet based encoder which is pretrained on ImageNet and a generic decoder. In place of ResNet, many different network architectures can be used. *Segmentation Models Pytorch*[12] *by Pavel Yakubovskiy* is an implementation of many such variations where an encoder can be replaced by a pretrained model. Let's apply a ResNet based U-Net for pneumothorax detection problem.

Most of the problems like this should have two inputs: the original image and a mask. In the case of multiple objects, there will be multiple masks. In our pneumothorax dataset, we are provided with RLE instead. RLE stands for run-

---

[12] https://github.com/qubvel/segmentation_models.pytorch

length encoding and is a way to represent binary masks to save space. Going deep into RLE is beyond the scope of this chapter. So, let's assume that we have an input image and corresponding mask. Let's first design a dataset class which outputs image and mask images. Please note that we will create these scripts in such a way that they can be applied to almost any segmentation problem. The training dataset is a CSV file consisting only of image ids which are also filenames.

```python
# dataset.py
import os
import glob
import torch

import numpy as np
import pandas as pd

from PIL import Image, ImageFile

from tqdm import tqdm
from collections import defaultdict
from torchvision import transforms

from albumentations import (
    Compose,
    OneOf,
    RandomBrightnessContrast,
    RandomGamma,
    ShiftScaleRotate,
)

ImageFile.LOAD_TRUNCATED_IMAGES = True


class SIIMDataset(torch.utils.data.Dataset):
    def __init__(
        self,
        image_ids,
        transform=True,
        preprocessing_fn=None
    ):
        """
        Dataset class for segmentation problem
        :param image_ids: ids of the images, list
        :param transform: True/False, no transform in validation
        :param preprocessing_fn: a function for preprocessing image
        """
```

```python
        # we create a empty dictionary to store iamge
        # and mask paths
        self.data = defaultdict(dict)

        # for augmentations
        self.transform = transform

        # preprocessing function to normalize
        # images
        self.preprocessing_fn = preprocessing_fn

        # albumentation augmentations
        # we have shift, scale & rotate
        # applied with 80% probability
        # and then one of gamma and brightness/contrast
        # is applied to the image
        # albumentation takes care of which augmentation
        # is applied to image and mask
        self.aug = Compose(
            [
                ShiftScaleRotate(
                    shift_limit=0.0625,
                    scale_limit=0.1,
                    rotate_limit=10, p=0.8
                ),
                OneOf(
                    [
                        RandomGamma(
                            gamma_limit=(90, 110)
                        ),
                        RandomBrightnessContrast(
                            brightness_limit=0.1,
                            contrast_limit=0.1
                        ),
                    ],
                    p=0.5,
                ),
            ]
        )
        # going over all image_ids to store
        # image and mask paths
        for imgid in image_ids:
            files = glob.glob(os.path.join(TRAIN_PATH, imgid, "*.png"))
            self.data[counter] = {
                "img_path": os.path.join(
                    TRAIN_PATH, imgid + ".png"
```

```
            ),
            "mask_path": os.path.join(
                TRAIN_PATH, imgid + "_mask.png"
            ),
        }

def __len__(self):
    # return length of dataset
    return len(self.data)

def __getitem__(self, item):
    # for a given item index,
    # return image and mask tensors
    # read image and mask paths
    img_path = self.data[item]["img_path"]
    mask_path = self.data[item]["mask_path"]

    # read image and convert to RGB
    img = Image.open(img_path)
    img = img.convert("RGB")

    # PIL image to numpy array
    img = np.array(img)

    # read mask image
    mask = Image.open(mask_path)

    # convert to binary float matrix
    mask = (mask >= 1).astype("float32")

    # if this is training data, apply transforms
    if self.transform is True:
        augmented = self.aug(image=img, mask=mask)
        img = augmented["image"]
        mask = augmented["mask"]

    # preprocess the image using provided
    # preprocessing tensors. this is basically
    # image normalization
    img = self.preprocessing_fn(img)

    # return image and mask tensors
    return {
        "image": transforms.ToTensor()(img),
        "mask": transforms.ToTensor()(mask).float(),
    }
```

Once, we have the dataset class; we can create a training function.

```python
# train.py
import os
import sys
import torch

import numpy as np
import pandas as pd
import segmentation_models_pytorch as smp
import torch.nn as nn
import torch.optim as optim

from apex import amp
from collections import OrderedDict
from sklearn import model_selection
from tqdm import tqdm
from torch.optim import lr_scheduler

from dataset import SIIMDataset

# training csv file path
TRAINING_CSV = "../input/train_pneumothorax.csv"

# training and test batch sizes
TRAINING_BATCH_SIZE = 16
TEST_BATCH_SIZE = 4

# number of epochs
EPOCHS = 10

# define the encoder for U-Net
# check: https://github.com/qubvel/segmentation_models.pytorch
# for all supported encoders
ENCODER = "resnet18"

# we use imagenet pretrained weights for the encoder
ENCODER_WEIGHTS = "imagenet"

# train on gpu
DEVICE = "cuda"

def train(dataset, data_loader, model, criterion, optimizer):
    """
    training function that trains for one epoch
    :param dataset: dataset class (SIIMDataset)
```

```
:param data_loader: torch dataset loader
:param model: model
:param criterion: loss function
:param optimizer: adam, sgd, etc.
"""
# put the model in train mode
model.train()

# calculate number of batches
num_batches = int(len(dataset) / data_loader.batch_size)

# init tqdm to track progress
tk0 = tqdm(data_loader, total=num_batches)

# loop over all batches
for d in tk0:
    # fetch input images and masks
    # from dataset batch
    inputs = d["image"]
    targets = d["mask"]

    # move images and masks to cpu/gpu device
    inputs = inputs.to(DEVICE, dtype=torch.float)
    targets = targets.to(DEVICE, dtype=torch.float)

    # zero grad the optimizer
    optimizer.zero_grad()

    # forward step of model
    outputs = model(inputs)

    # calculate loss
    loss = criterion(outputs, targets)

    # backward loss is calculated on a scaled loss
    # context since we are using mixed precision training
    # if you are not using mixed precision training,
    # you can use loss.backward() and delete the following
    # two lines of code
    with amp.scale_loss(loss, optimizer) as scaled_loss:
        scaled_loss.backward()

    # step the optimizer
    optimizer.step()

# close tqdm
tk0.close()
```

```python
def evaluate(dataset, data_loader, model):
    """
    evaluation function to calculate loss on validation
    set for one epoch
    :param dataset: dataset class (SIIMDataset)
    :param data_loader: torch dataset loader
    :param model: model
    """
    # put model in eval mode
    model.eval()
    # init final_loss to 0
    final_loss = 0
    # calculate number of batches and init tqdm
    num_batches = int(len(dataset) / data_loader.batch_size)
    tk0 = tqdm(data_loader, total=num_batches)

    # we need no_grad context of torch. this save memory
    with torch.no_grad():
        for d in tk0:
            inputs = d["image"]
            targets = d["mask"]
            inputs = inputs.to(DEVICE, dtype=torch.float)
            targets = targets.to(DEVICE, dtype=torch.float)
            output = model(inputs)
            loss = criterion(output, targets)
            # add loss to final loss
            final_loss += loss
    # close tqdm
    tk0.close()
    # return average loss over all batches
    return final_loss / num_batches


if __name__ == "__main__":

    # read the training csv file
    df = pd.read_csv(TRAINING_CSV)

    # split data into training and validation
    df_train, df_valid = model_selection.train_test_split(
        df, random_state=42, test_size=0.1
    )

    # training and validation images lists/arrays
    training_images = df_train.image_id.values
    validation_images = df_valid.image_id.values
```

```python
# fetch unet model from segmentation models
# with specified encoder architecture
model = smp.Unet(
    encoder_name=ENCODER,
    encoder_weights=ENCODER_WEIGHTS,
    classes=1,
    activation=None,
)
# segmentation model provides you with a preprocessing
# function that can be used for normalizing images
# normalization is only applied on images and not masks
prep_fn = smp.encoders.get_preprocessing_fn(
    ENCODER,
    ENCODER_WEIGHTS
)

# send model to device
model.to(DEVICE)
# init training dataset
# transform is True for training data
train_dataset = SIIMDataset(
    training_images,
    transform=True,
    preprocessing_fn=prep_fn,
)

# wrap training dataset in torch's dataloader
train_loader = torch.utils.data.DataLoader(
    train_dataset,
    batch_size=TRAINING_BATCH_SIZE,
    shuffle=True,
    num_workers=12
)

# init validation dataset
# augmentations is disabled
valid_dataset = SIIMDataset(
    validation_images,
    transform=False,
    preprocessing_fn=prep_fn,
)

# wrap validation dataset in torch's dataloader
valid_loader = torch.utils.data.DataLoader(
    valid_dataset,
    batch_size=TEST_BATCH_SIZE,
    shuffle=True,
```

```python
    num_workers=4
)

# NOTE: define the criterion here
# this is left as an excercise
# code won't work without defining this
# criterion = ......

# we will use Adam optimizer for faster convergence
optimizer = torch.optim.Adam(model.parameters(), lr=1e-3)
# reduce learning rate when we reach a plateau on loss
scheduler = lr_scheduler.ReduceLROnPlateau(
    optimizer, mode="min", patience=3, verbose=True
)
# wrap model and optimizer with NVIDIA's apex
# this is used for mixed precision training
# if you have a GPU that supports mixed precision,
# this is very helpful as it will allow us to fit larger images
# and larger batches
model, optimizer = amp.initialize(
    model, optimizer, opt_level="O1", verbosity=0
)
# if we have more than one GPU, we can use both of them!
if torch.cuda.device_count() > 1:
    print(f"Let's use {torch.cuda.device_count()} GPUs!")
    model = nn.DataParallel(model)

# some logging
print(f"Training batch size: {TRAINING_BATCH_SIZE}")
print(f"Test batch size: {TEST_BATCH_SIZE}")
print(f"Epochs: {EPOCHS}")
print(f"Image size: {IMAGE_SIZE}")
print(f"Number of training images: {len(train_dataset)}")
print(f"Number of validation images: {len(valid_dataset)}")
print(f"Encoder: {ENCODER}")

# loop over all epochs
for epoch in range(EPOCHS):
    print(f"Training Epoch: {epoch}")
    # train for one epoch
    train(
        train_dataset,
        train_loader,
        model,
        criterion,
        optimizer
    )
```

```python
print(f"Validation Epoch: {epoch}")
# calculate validation loss
val_log = evaluate(
    valid_dataset,
    valid_loader,
    model
)
# step the scheduler
scheduler.step(val_log["loss"])
print("\n")
```

In segmentation problems you can use a variety of loss functions, for example, pixel-wise binary cross-entropy, focal loss, dice loss etc. I'm leaving it for the reader to decide the appropriate loss given the evaluation metric. When you train a model like this, you will create a model that tries to predict the location of pneumothorax, as shown in figure 9. In the above code, we used mixed precision training using **NVIDIA apex**. Please note that this is available natively in PyTorch from version 1.6.0+.

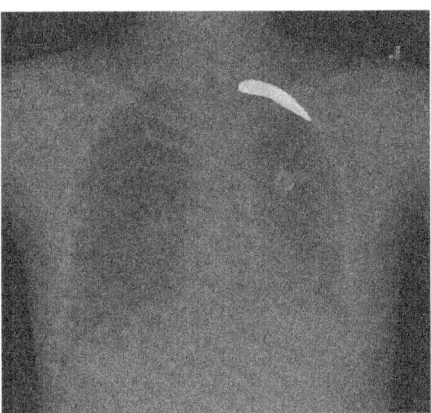

Figure 9: Example of pneumothorax detection from the trained model (might not be correct prediction).

I have included some of the commonly used functions in a python package called Well That's Fantastic Machine Learning (WTFML). Let's see how this helps us to build a multi-class classification model for plant images from the plant pathology challenge of FGVC 2020[13].

---

[13] Ranjita Thapa, Noah Snavely, Serge Belongie, Awais Khan. The Plant Pathology 2020 challenge dataset to classify foliar disease of apples. ArXiv e-prints

```python
import os

import pandas as pd
import numpy as np

import albumentations
import argparse
import torch
import torchvision
import torch.nn as nn
import torch.nn.functional as F

from sklearn import metrics
from sklearn.model_selection import train_test_split

from wtfml.engine import Engine
from wtfml.data_loaders.image import ClassificationDataLoader


class DenseCrossEntropy(nn.Module):
    # Taken from:
    # https://www.kaggle.com/pestipeti/plant-pathology-2020-pytorch
    def __init__(self):
        super(DenseCrossEntropy, self).__init__()

    def forward(self, logits, labels):
        logits = logits.float()
        labels = labels.float()

        logprobs = F.log_softmax(logits, dim=-1)

        loss = -labels * logprobs
        loss = loss.sum(-1)

        return loss.mean()


class Model(nn.Module):
    def __init__(self):
        super().__init__()
        self.base_model = torchvision.models.resnet18(pretrained=True)
        in_features = self.base_model.fc.in_features
        self.out = nn.Linear(in_features, 4)

    def forward(self, image, targets=None):
        batch_size, C, H, W = image.shape
```

```python
        x = self.base_model.conv1(image)
        x = self.base_model.bn1(x)
        x = self.base_model.relu(x)
        x = self.base_model.maxpool(x)

        x = self.base_model.layer1(x)
        x = self.base_model.layer2(x)
        x = self.base_model.layer3(x)
        x = self.base_model.layer4(x)

        x = F.adaptive_avg_pool2d(x, 1).reshape(batch_size, -1)
        x = self.out(x)

        loss = None
        if targets is not None:
            loss = DenseCrossEntropy()(x, targets.type_as(x))

        return x, loss


if __name__ == "__main__":
    parser = argparse.ArgumentParser()
    parser.add_argument(
        "--data_path", type=str,
    )
    parser.add_argument(
        "--device", type=str,
    )
    parser.add_argument(
        "--epochs", type=int,
    )
    args = parser.parse_args()

    df = pd.read_csv(os.path.join(args.data_path, "train.csv"))
    images = df.image_id.values.tolist()
    images = [
        os.path.join(args.data_path, "images", i + ".jpg")
        for i in images
    ]
    targets = df[["healthy", "multiple_diseases", "rust", "scab"]].values

    model = Model()
    model.to(args.device)

    mean = (0.485, 0.456, 0.406)
    std = (0.229, 0.224, 0.225)
```

```python
aug = albumentations.Compose(
    [
        albumentations.Normalize(
            mean,
            std,
            max_pixel_value=255.0,
            always_apply=True
        )
    ]
)
(
    train_images, valid_images,
    train_targets, valid_targets
) = train_test_split(images, targets)

train_loader = ClassificationDataLoader(
    image_paths=train_images,
    targets=train_targets,
    resize=(128, 128),
    augmentations=aug,
).fetch(
    batch_size=16,
    num_workers=4,
    drop_last=False,
    shuffle=True,
    tpu=False
)

valid_loader = ClassificationDataLoader(
    image_paths=valid_images,
    targets=valid_targets,
    resize=(128, 128),
    augmentations=aug,
).fetch(
    batch_size=16,
    num_workers=4,
    drop_last=False,
    shuffle=False,
    tpu=False
)

optimizer = torch.optim.Adam(model.parameters(), lr=5e-4)
scheduler = torch.optim.lr_scheduler.StepLR(
    optimizer, step_size=15, gamma=0.6
)
```

```python
    for epoch in range(args.epochs):
        train_loss = Engine.train(
            train_loader, model, optimizer, device=args.device
        )
        valid_loss = Engine.evaluate(
            valid_loader, model, device=args.device
        )
        print(
            f"{epoch}, Train Loss={train_loss} Valid Loss={valid_loss}"
        )
```

Once you have the data[14], you can run the script using:

```
> python plant.py --data_path ../../plant_pathology --device cuda --epochs 2
100%|████████████| 86/86 [00:12<00:00, 6.73it/s, loss=0.723]
100%|████████████| 29/29 [00:04<00:00, 6.62it/s, loss=0.433]
0, Train Loss=0.7228777609592261 Valid Loss=0.4327834551704341
100%|████████████| 86/86 [00:12<00:00, 6.74it/s, loss=0.271]
100%|████████████| 29/29 [00:04<00:00, 6.63it/s, loss=0.568]
1, Train Loss=0.2708700496790021 Valid Loss=0.56841839541649
```

As you can see, how this makes our life simple and code easy to read and understand. PyTorch without any wrappers work best. There is a lot more in images than just classification, and if I start writing about all of them, I'll have to write another book. So, I have decided to do that instead: *Approaching (Almost) Any Image Problem*.

---

[14] https://www.kaggle.com/c/plant-pathology-2020-fgvc7

Approaching text classification/regression

Text problems are my favourite. In general, these problems are also known as **Natural Language Processing (NLP)** problems. NLP problems are also like images in the sense that, it's quite different. You need to create pipelines you have never created before for tabular problems. You need to understand the business case to build a good model. By the way, that is true for anything in machine learning. Building models will take you to a certain level, but to improve and contribute to a business you are building the model for, you must understand how it impacts the business. Let's not get too philosophical here.

There are many different types of NLP problems, and the most common type is the classification of strings. Many times, it is seen that people are doing well with tabular data or with images, but when it comes to text, they don't even have a clue where to start from. Text data is no different than other types of datasets. For computers, everything is numbers.

Let's say we start with a fundamental task of sentiment classification. We will try to classify sentiment from movie reviews. So, you have a text, and there is a sentiment associated with it. How will you approach this kind of problem? Apply a deep neural network right, or maybe muppets can come and save you? No, absolutely wrong. You start with the basics. Let's see what this data looks like first.

We start with **IMDB movie review dataset**[15] that consists of 25000 reviews for positive sentiment and 25000 reviews for negative sentiment.

The concepts that I will discuss here can be applied to almost any text classification dataset.

This dataset is quite easy to understand. One review maps to one target variable. Note that I wrote review instead of sentence. A review is a bunch of sentences. So, until now you must have seen classifying only a single sentence, but in this problem, we will be classifying multiple sentences. In simple words, it means that not only

---

[15] Maas, Andrew L, Daly, Raymond E, Pham, Peter T, Huang, Dan, Ng, Andrew Y, and Potts, Christopher. Learning word vectors for sentiment analysis. In Proceedings of the 49th Annual Meeting of the Association for Computational Linguistics: Human Language Technologies-Volume 1, pp. 142–150. Association for Computational Linguistics, 2011.

one sentence contributes to the sentiment, but the sentiment score is a combination of score from multiple sentences. A snapshot of the data is presented in figure 1.

	review	sentiment
0	One of the other reviewers has mentioned that ...	positive
1	A wonderful little production. The...	positive
2	I thought this was a wonderful way to spend ti...	positive
3	Basically there's a family where a little boy ...	negative
4	Petter Mattei's "Love in the Time of Money" is...	positive

Figure 1. Snapshot of IMDB movie review dataset.

How would you start with such a problem?

A simple way would be just to create two handmade lists of words. One list will contain all the positive words you can imagine, for example, good, awesome, nice, etc. and another list will include all the negative words, such as bad, evil, etc. Let's leave examples of bad words else I'll have to make this book available only for 18+. Once you have these lists, you do not even need a model to make a prediction. These lists are also known as sentiment lexicons. A bunch of them for different languages are available on the internet.

You can have a simple counter that counts the number of positive and negative words in the sentence. If the number of positive words is higher, it is a positive sentiment, and if the number of negative words is higher, it is a sentence with a negative sentiment. If none of them are present in the sentence, you can say that the sentence has a neutral sentiment. This is one of the oldest ways, and some people still use it. It does not require much code either.

```
def find_sentiment(sentence, pos, neg):
    """
    This function returns sentiment of sentence
    :param sentence: sentence, a string
    :param pos: set of positive words
    :param neg: set of negative words
    :return: returns positive, negative or neutral sentiment
    """

    # split sentence by a space
```

```python
# "this is a sentence!" becomes:
# ["this", "is" "a", "sentence!"]
# note that im splitting on all whitespaces
# if you want to split by space use .split(" ")
sentence = sentence.split()

# make sentence into a set
sentence = set(sentence)

# check number of common words with positive
num_common_pos = len(sentence.intersection(pos))

# check number of common words with negative
num_common_neg = len(sentence.intersection(neg))

# make conditions and return
# see how return used eliminates if else
if num_common_pos > num_common_neg:
    return "positive"
if num_common_pos < num_common_neg:
    return "negative"
return "neutral"
```

However, this kind of approach does not take a lot into consideration. And as you can see that our *split()* is also not perfect. If you use *split()*, a sentence like:

"hi, how are you?"

gets split into

["hi,", "how", "are", "you?"]

This is not ideal, because you see the comma and question mark, they are not split. It is therefore not recommended to use this method if you don't have a pre-processing that handles these special characters before the split. Splitting a string into a list of words is known as **tokenization**. One of the most popular tokenization comes from **NLTK (Natural Language Tool Kit)**.

```
In [X]: from nltk.tokenize import word_tokenize

In [X]: sentence = "hi, how are you?"
```

```
In [X]: sentence.split()
Out[X]: ['hi,', 'how', 'are', 'you?']

In [X]: word_tokenize(sentence)
Out[X]: ['hi', ',', 'how', 'are', 'you', '?']
```

As you can see, using NLTK's word tokenize, the same sentence is split in a much better manner. Comparing using a list of words will also work much better now! This is what we will apply to our first model to detect sentiment.

One of the basic models that you should always try with a classification problem in NLP is **bag of words**. In bag of words, we create a huge sparse matrix that stores counts of all the words in our corpus (corpus = all the documents = all the sentences). For this, we will use *CountVectorizer* from scikit-learn. Let's see how it works.

```
from sklearn.feature_extraction.text import CountVectorizer

# create a corpus of sentences
corpus = [
    "hello, how are you?",
    "im getting bored at home. And you? What do you think?",
    "did you know about counts",
    "let's see if this works!",
    "YES!!!!"
]

# initialize CountVectorizer
ctv = CountVectorizer()

# fit the vectorizer on corpus
ctv.fit(corpus)

corpus_transformed = ctv.transform(corpus)
```

If we print *corpus_transformed*, we get something like the following:

```
(0, 2)     1
(0, 9)     1
(0, 11)    1
(0, 22)    1
```

```
  (1, 1)     1
  (1, 3)     1
  (1, 4)     1
  (1, 7)     1
  (1, 8)     1
  (1, 10)    1
  (1, 13)    1
  (1, 17)    1
  (1, 19)    1
  (1, 22)    2
  (2, 0)     1
  (2, 5)     1
  (2, 6)     1
  (2, 14)    1
  (2, 22)    1
  (3, 12)    1
  (3, 15)    1
  (3, 16)    1
  (3, 18)    1
  (3, 20)    1
  (4, 21)    1
```

We have already seen this representation in previous chapters. It is the sparse representation. So, our corpus is now a sparse matrix, where, for first sample, we have four elements, for sample 2 we have ten elements, and so on, for sample 3 we have five elements and so on. We also see that these elements have a count associated with them. Some are seen twice, some are seen only once. For example, in sample 2 (row 1), we see that column 22 has a value of two. Why is that? And what is column 22?

The way *CountVectorizer* works is it first tokenizes the sentence and then assigns a value to each token. So, each token is represented by a unique index. These unique indices are the columns that we see. The CountVectorizer stores this information.

```
print(ctv.vocabulary_)
{'hello': 9, 'how': 11, 'are': 2, 'you': 22, 'im': 13, 'getting': 8,
'bored': 4, 'at': 3, 'home': 10, 'and': 1, 'what': 19, 'do': 7, 'think':
17, 'did': 6, 'know': 14, 'about': 0, 'counts': 5, 'let': 15, 'see': 16,
'if': 12, 'this': 18, 'works': 20, 'yes': 21}
```

We see that index 22 belongs to "you" and in the second sentence, we have used "you" twice. Thus, the count is 2. I hope it's clear now what is bag of words. But we are missing some special characters. Sometimes those special characters can be useful too. For example, "?" denotes a question in most sentences. Let's integrate *word_tokenize* from scikit-learn in *CountVectorizer* and see what happens.

```python
from sklearn.feature_extraction.text import CountVectorizer
from nltk.tokenize import word_tokenize


# create a corpus of sentences
corpus = [
    "hello, how are you?",
    "im getting bored at home. And you? What do you think?",
    "did you know about counts",
    "let's see if this works!",
    "YES!!!!"
]

# initialize CountVectorizer with word_tokenize from nltk
# as the tokenizer
ctv = CountVectorizer(tokenizer=word_tokenize, token_pattern=None)

# fit the vectorizer on corpus
ctv.fit(corpus)

corpus_transformed = ctv.transform(corpus)
print(ctv.vocabulary_)
```

This changes our vocabulary to:

```
{'hello': 14, ',': 2, 'how': 16, 'are': 7, 'you': 27, '?': 4, 'im': 18,
'getting': 13, 'bored': 9, 'at': 8, 'home': 15, '.': 3, 'and': 6, 'what':
24, 'do': 12, 'think': 22, 'did': 11, 'know': 19, 'about': 5, 'counts':
10, 'let': 20, "'s": 1, 'see': 21, 'if': 17, 'this': 23, 'works': 25,
'!': 0, 'yes': 26}
```

Now, we have more words in the vocabulary. Thus, we can now create a sparse matrix by using all the sentences in IMDB dataset and can build a model. The ratio to positive and negative samples in this dataset is 1:1, and thus, we can use accuracy as the metric. We will use StratifiedKFold and create a single script to train five folds. Which model to use you ask? Which is the fastest model for high dimensional sparse data? Logistic regression. We will use logistic regression for this dataset to start with and to create our first actual benchmark.

Let's see how this is done.

```python
# import what we need
import pandas as pd

from nltk.tokenize import word_tokenize
from sklearn import linear_model
from sklearn import metrics
from sklearn import model_selection
from sklearn.feature_extraction.text import CountVectorizer


if __name__ == "__main__":
    # read the training data
    df = pd.read_csv("../input/imdb.csv")

    # map positive to 1 and negative to 0
    df.sentiment = df.sentiment.apply(
        lambda x: 1 if x == "positive" else 0
    )

    # we create a new column called kfold and fill it with -1
    df["kfold"] = -1

    # the next step is to randomize the rows of the data
    df = df.sample(frac=1).reset_index(drop=True)

    # fetch labels
    y = df.sentiment.values

    # initiate the kfold class from model_selection module
    kf = model_selection.StratifiedKFold(n_splits=5)

    # fill the new kfold column
    for f, (t_, v_) in enumerate(kf.split(X=df, y=y)):
        df.loc[v_, 'kfold'] = f

    # we go over the folds created
    for fold_ in range(5):
        # temporary dataframes for train and test
        train_df = df[df.kfold != fold_].reset_index(drop=True)
```

```python
    test_df = df[df.kfold == fold_].reset_index(drop=True)

    # initialize CountVectorizer with NLTK's word_tokenize
    # function as tokenizer
    count_vec = CountVectorizer(
        tokenizer=word_tokenize,
        token_pattern=None
    )

    # fit count_vec on training data reviews
    count_vec.fit(train_df.review)

    # transform training and validation data reviews
    xtrain = count_vec.transform(train_df.review)
    xtest = count_vec.transform(test_df.review)

    # initialize logistic regression model
    model = linear_model.LogisticRegression()

    # fit the model on training data reviews and sentiment
    model.fit(xtrain, train_df.sentiment)

    # make predictions on test data
    # threshold for predictions is 0.5
    preds = model.predict(xtest)

    # calculate accuracy
    accuracy = metrics.accuracy_score(test_df.sentiment, preds)

    print(f"Fold: {fold_}")
    print(f"Accuracy = {accuracy}")
    print("")
```

This piece of code takes time to run but should give you the following output:

```
❯ python ctv_logres.py
Fold: 0
Accuracy = 0.8903

Fold: 1
Accuracy = 0.897

Fold: 2
Accuracy = 0.891
```

```
Fold: 3
Accuracy = 0.8914

Fold: 4
Accuracy = 0.8931
```

Wow, we are already at 89% accuracy, and all we did was use bag of words with logistic regression! This is super amazing! However, this model took a lot of time to train, let's see if we can improve the time by using naïve bayes classifier. Naïve bayes classifier is quite popular in NLP tasks as the sparse matrices are huge and naïve bayes is a simple model. To use this model, we need to change one import and the line with the model. Let's see how this model performs. We will use *MultinomialNB* from scikit-learn.

```
# import what we need
import pandas as pd

from nltk.tokenize import word_tokenize
from sklearn import naive_bayes
from sklearn import metrics
from sklearn import model_selection
from sklearn.feature_extraction.text import CountVectorizer
.
.
.
.
        # initialize naive bayes model
        model = naive_bayes.MultinomialNB()

        # fit the model on training data reviews and sentiment
        model.fit(xtrain, train_df.sentiment)
.
.
.
```

Results are as follows:

```
> python ctv_nb.py
Fold: 0
Accuracy = 0.8444
```

```
Fold: 1
Accuracy = 0.8499

Fold: 2
Accuracy = 0.8422

Fold: 3
Accuracy = 0.8443

Fold: 4
Accuracy = 0.8455
```

We see that this score is low. But the *naïve bayes model is superfast*.

Another method in NLP that most of the people these days tend to ignore or don't care to know about is called **TF-IDF**. TF is term frequencies, and IDF is inverse document frequency. It might seem difficult from these terms, but things will become apparent with the formulae for TF and IDF.

$$TF(t) = \frac{\text{Number of times a term } t \text{ appears in a document}}{\text{Total number of terms in the document}}$$

$$IDF(t) = LOG\left(\frac{\text{Total number of documents}}{\text{Number of documents with term } t \text{ in it}}\right)$$

And TF-IDF for a term t is defined as:

$$TF\text{-}IDF(t) = TF(t) * IDF(t)$$

Similar to *CountVectorizer* in scikit-learn, we have *TfidfVectorizer*. Let's try using it the same way we used *CountVectorizer*.

```
from sklearn.feature_extraction.text import TfidfVectorizer
from nltk.tokenize import word_tokenize

# create a corpus of sentences
corpus = [
```

```
    "hello, how are you?",
    "im getting bored at home. And you? What do you think?",
    "did you know about counts",
    "let's see if this works!",
    "YES!!!!"
]

# initialize TfidfVectorizer with word_tokenize from nltk
# as the tokenizer
tfv = TfidfVectorizer(tokenizer=word_tokenize, token_pattern=None)

# fit the vectorizer on corpus
tfv.fit(corpus)

corpus_transformed = tfv.transform(corpus)
print(corpus_transformed)
```

This gives the following output:

(0, 27)	0.2965698850220162
(0, 16)	0.4428321995085722
(0, 14)	0.4428321995085722
(0, 7)	0.4428321995085722
(0, 4)	0.35727423026525224
(0, 2)	0.4428321995085722
(1, 27)	0.35299699146792735
(1, 24)	0.2635440111190765
(1, 22)	0.2635440111190765
(1, 18)	0.2635440111190765
(1, 15)	0.2635440111190765
(1, 13)	0.2635440111190765
(1, 12)	0.2635440111190765
(1, 9)	0.2635440111190765
(1, 8)	0.2635440111190765
(1, 6)	0.2635440111190765
(1, 4)	0.42525129752567803
(1, 3)	0.2635440111190765
(2, 27)	0.31752680284846835
(2, 19)	0.4741246485558491
(2, 11)	0.4741246485558491
(2, 10)	0.4741246485558491
(2, 5)	0.4741246485558491
(3, 25)	0.38775666010579296
(3, 23)	0.38775666010579296
(3, 21)	0.38775666010579296

```
(3, 20)      0.38775666010579296
(3, 17)      0.38775666010579296
(3, 1)       0.38775666010579296
(3, 0)       0.3128396318588854
(4, 26)      0.2959842226518677
(4, 0)       0.9551928286692534
```

We see that instead of integer values, this time we get floats. Replacing *CountVectorizer* with *TfidfVectorizer* is also a piece of cake. Scikit-learn also offers *TfidfTransformer*. If you have count values, you can use *TfidfTransformer* and get the same behaviour as *TfidfVectorizer*.

```
# import what we need
import pandas as pd

from nltk.tokenize import word_tokenize
from sklearn import linear_model
from sklearn import metrics
from sklearn import model_selection
from sklearn.feature_extraction.text import TfidfVectorizer
.
.
.
    # we go over the folds created
    for fold_ in range(5):
        # temporary dataframes for train and test
        train_df = df[df.kfold != fold_].reset_index(drop=True)
        test_df = df[df.kfold == fold_].reset_index(drop=True)

        # initialize TfidfVectorizer with NLTK's word_tokenize
        # function as tokenizer
        tfidf_vec = TfidfVectorizer(
            tokenizer=word_tokenize,
            token_pattern=None
        )

        # fit tfidf_vec on training data reviews
        tfidf_vec.fit(train_df.review)

        # transform training and validation data reviews
        xtrain = tfidf_vec.transform(train_df.review)
        xtest = tfidf_vec.transform(test_df.review)

        # initialize logistic regression model
```

```
model = linear_model.LogisticRegression()

# fit the model on training data reviews and sentiment
model.fit(xtrain, train_df.sentiment)

# make predictions on test data
# threshold for predictions is 0.5
preds = model.predict(xtest)

# calculate accuracy
accuracy = metrics.accuracy_score(test_df.sentiment, preds)

print(f"Fold: {fold_}")
print(f"Accuracy = {accuracy}")
print("")
```

It would be interesting to see how TF-IDF performs with our old logistic regression model on the sentiment dataset.

```
❯ python tfv_logres.py
Fold: 0
Accuracy = 0.8976

Fold: 1
Accuracy = 0.8998

Fold: 2
Accuracy = 0.8948

Fold: 3
Accuracy = 0.8912

Fold: 4
Accuracy = 0.8995
```

We see that these scores are a bit higher than *CountVectorizer,* and thus, it becomes the new benchmark that we would want to beat.

Another interesting concept in NLP is n-grams. **N-grams** are combinations of words in order. N-grams are easy to create. You just need to take care of the order. To make things even more comfortable, we can use n-gram implementation from NLTK.

```
from nltk import ngrams
from nltk.tokenize import word_tokenize

# let's see 3 grams
N = 3
# input sentence
sentence = "hi, how are you?"
# tokenized sentence
tokenized_sentence = word_tokenize(sentence)
# generate n_grams
n_grams = list(ngrams(tokenized_sentence, N))
print(n_grams)
```

Which gives:

```
[('hi', ',', 'how'),
 (',', 'how', 'are'),
 ('how', 'are', 'you'),
 ('are', 'you', '?')]
```

Similarly, we can also create 2-grams, or 4-grams, etc. Now, these n-grams become a part of our vocab, and when we calculate counts or tf-idf, we consider one n-gram as one entirely new token. So, in a way, we are incorporating context to some extent. Both *CountVectorizer* and *TfidfVectorizer* implementations of scikit-learn offers n-grams by *ngram_range* parameter, which has a minimum and maximum limit. By default, this is (1, 1). When we change it to (1, 3), we are looking at unigrams, bigrams and trigrams. The code change is minimal. Since we had the best result till now with tf-idf, let's see if including n-grams up to trigrams improves the model.

The only change required is in the initialization of *TfidfVectorizer*.

```
    tfidf_vec = TfidfVectorizer(
        tokenizer=word_tokenize,
        token_pattern=None,
        ngram_range=(1, 3)
    )
```

Let's see if we get any kind of improvements.

```
> python tfv_logres_trigram.py
Fold: 0
Accuracy = 0.8931

Fold: 1
Accuracy = 0.8941

Fold: 2
Accuracy = 0.897

Fold: 3
Accuracy = 0.8922

Fold: 4
Accuracy = 0.8847
```

This looks okay, but we do not see any improvements. Maybe we can get improvements by using only up to bigrams. I'm not showing that part here. Probably you can try to do it on your own.

There are a lot more things in the basics of NLP. One term that you must be aware of is stemming. Another is lemmatization. **Stemming and lemmatization** reduce a word to its smallest form. In the case of stemming, the processed word is called the stemmed word, and in the case of lemmatization, it is known as the lemma. It must be noted that lemmatization is more aggressive than stemming and stemming is more popular and widely used. Both stemming and lemmatization come from linguistics. And you need to have an in-depth knowledge of a given language if you plan to make a stemmer or lemmatizer for that language. Going into too much detail of these would mean adding one more chapter in this book. Both stemming and lemmatization can be done easily by using the NLTK package. Let's take a look at some examples for both of them. There are many different types of stemmers and lemmatizers. I will show an example using the most common **Snowball Stemmer** and **WordNet Lemmatizer**.

```
from nltk.stem import WordNetLemmatizer
from nltk.stem.snowball import SnowballStemmer

# initialize lemmatizer
lemmatizer = WordNetLemmatizer()
```

```
# initialize stemmer
stemmer = SnowballStemmer("english")

words = ["fishing", "fishes", "fished"]

for word in words:
    print(f"word={word}")
    print(f"stemmed_word={stemmer.stem(word)}")
    print(f"lemma={lemmatizer.lemmatize(word)}")
    print("")
```

This will print:

```
word=fishing
stemmed_word=fish
lemma=fishing

word=fishes
stemmed_word=fish
lemma=fish

word=fished
stemmed_word=fish
lemma=fished
```

As you can see, stemming and lemmatization are very different from each other. When we do stemming, we are given the smallest form of a word which may or may not be a word in the dictionary for the language the word belongs to. However, in the case of lemmatization, this will be a word. You can now try on your own to add stemming and lemmatizations and see if it improves your result.

One more topic that you should be aware of is topic extraction. Topic extraction can be done using **non-negative matrix factorization (NMF)** or **latent semantic analysis (LSA),** which is also popularly known as singular value decomposition or SVD. These are decomposition techniques that reduce the data to a given number of components. You can fit any of these on sparse matrix obtained from *CountVectorizer* or *TfidfVectorizer*.

Let's apply it on *TfidfVetorizer* that we have used before.

```python
import pandas as pd
from nltk.tokenize import word_tokenize
from sklearn import decomposition
from sklearn.feature_extraction.text import TfidfVectorizer

# create a corpus of sentences
# we read only 10k samples from training data
# for this example
corpus = pd.read_csv("../input/imdb.csv", nrows=10000)
corpus = corpus.review.values

# initialize TfidfVectorizer with word_tokenize from nltk
# as the tokenizer
tfv = TfidfVectorizer(tokenizer=word_tokenize, token_pattern=None)

# fit the vectorizer on corpus
tfv.fit(corpus)

# transform the corpus using tfidf
corpus_transformed = tfv.transform(corpus)

# initialize SVD with 10 components
svd = decomposition.TruncatedSVD(n_components=10)

# fit SVD
corpus_svd = svd.fit(corpus_transformed)

# choose first sample and create a dictionary
# of feature names and their scores from svd
# you can change the sample_index variable to
# get dictionary for any other sample
sample_index = 0
feature_scores = dict(
    zip(
        tfv.get_feature_names(),
        corpus_svd.components_[sample_index]
    )
)

# once we have the dictionary, we can now
# sort it in decreasing order and get the
# top N topics
N = 5
print(sorted(feature_scores, key=feature_scores.get, reverse=True)[:N])
```

You can run it for multiple samples by using a loop.

```
N = 5

for sample_index in range(5):
    feature_scores = dict(
        zip(
            tfv.get_feature_names(),
            corpus_svd.components_[sample_index]
        )
    )
    print(
        sorted(
            feature_scores,
            key=feature_scores.get,
            reverse=True
        )[:N]
    )
```

This gives the following output.

```
['the', ',', '.', 'a', 'and']
['br', '<', '>', '/', '-']
['i', 'movie', '!', 'it', 'was']
[',', '!', '"', '`', 'you']
['!', 'the', '...', '"', '`']
```

You can see that it doesn't make any sense at all. It happens. What can one do? Let's try cleaning and see if it makes any sense.

To clean any text data, especially when it's in pandas dataframe, you can make a function.

```
import re
import string

def clean_text(s):
    """
    This function cleans the text a bit
    :param s: string
```

```
    :return: cleaned string
    """
    # split by all whitespaces
    s = s.split()

    # join tokens by single space
    # why we do this?
    # this will remove all kinds of weird space
    # "hi.   how are you" becomes
    # "hi. how are you"
    s = " ".join(s)

    # remove all punctuations using regex and string module
    s = re.sub(f'[{re.escape(string.punctuation)}]', '', s)

    # you can add more cleaning here if you want
    # and then return the cleaned string
    return s
```

This function will convert a string like "hi, how are you????" to "hi how are you". Let's apply this function to the old SVD code and see if it brings any value to the extracted topics. With pandas, you can use the *apply* function to "apply" the clean-up code to any given column.

```
import pandas as pd
.
corpus = pd.read_csv("../input/imdb.csv", nrows=10000)
corpus.loc[:, "review"] = corpus.review.apply(clean_text)
.
.
```

Note that we have added only one line of code to our main SVD script and that's the beauty of using a function and apply from pandas. The topics generated this time look like the following.

```
['the', 'a', 'and', 'of', 'to']
['i', 'movie', 'it', 'was', 'this']
['the', 'was', 'i', 'were', 'of']
['her', 'was', 'she', 'i', 'he']
['br', 'to', 'they', 'he', 'show']
```

Phew! At least this is better than what we had earlier. But you know what? You can make it even better by **removing stopwords** in your cleaning function. What are stopwords? These are high-frequency words that exist in every language. For example, in the English language, these words are "a", "an", "the", "for", etc. Removing stopwords is not always a wise choice and depends a lot on the business problem. A sentence like "I need a new dog" after removing stopwords will become "need new dog", so we don't know who needs a new dog.

We lose a lot of context information if we remove stopwords all the time. You can find stopwords for many languages in NLTK, and if it's not there, you can find it by a quick search on your favourite search engine.

Let's move to an approach most of us like to use these days: deep learning. But first, we must know what **word embeddings** are. You have seen that till now we converted the tokens into numbers. So, if there are N unique tokens in a given corpus, they can be represented by integers ranging from 0 to N-1. Now we will represent these integer tokens with vectors. This representation of words into vectors is known as word embeddings or word vectors. Google's Word2Vec is one of the oldest approaches to convert words into vectors. We also have **FastText** from Facebook and **GloVe** (Global Vectors for Word Representation) from Stanford. These approaches are quite different from each other.

The basic idea is to build a shallow network that learns the embeddings for words by reconstruction of an input sentence. So, you can train a network to predict a missing word by using all the words around and during this process, the network will learn and update embeddings for all the words involved. This approach is also known as **Continuous Bag of Words or CBoW model**. You can also try to take one word and predict the context words instead. This is called **skip-gram model**. Word2Vec can learn embedding using these two methods.

FastText learns embeddings for character n-grams instead. Just like word n-grams, if we use characters, it is known as character n-grams, and finally, GloVe learns these embeddings by using co-occurrence matrices. So, we can say that all these different types of embeddings are in the end returning a dictionary where the key is a word in the corpus (for example English Wikipedia) and value is a vector of size N (usually 300).

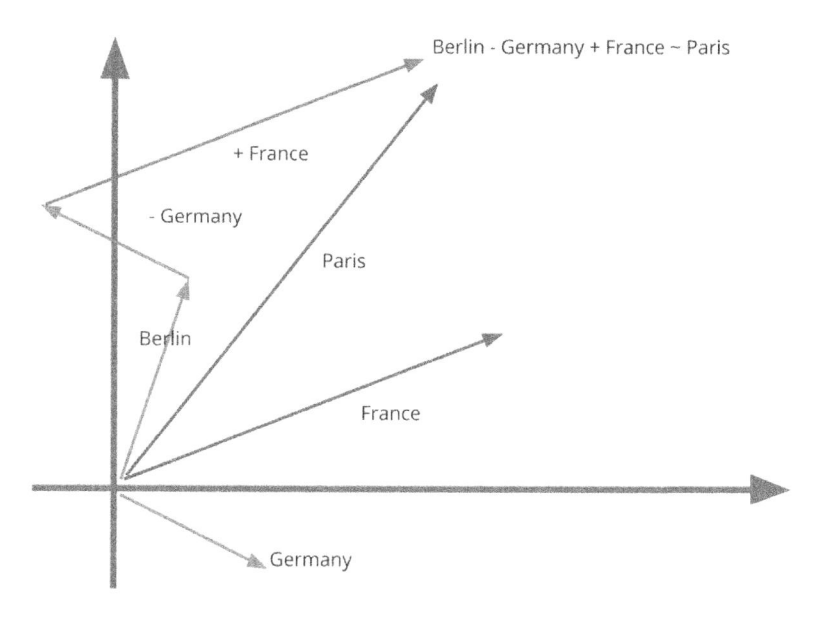

Figure 1: Visualizing word embeddings in two-dimensions.

Figure 1 shows a visualization of word embeddings in two-dimensions. Suppose, we have done it somehow and represented the words in two dimensions. Figure 1 shows that if you subtract the vector for Germany from the vector of Berlin (capital of Germany) and add the vector of France to it, you will get a vector close to the vector for Paris (capital of France). This shows that embeddings also work with analogies. This is not always true, but examples like these are useful for understanding the usefulness of word embeddings. A sentence like "hi, how are you ?" can be represented by a bunch of vectors as follows.

hi	—>	[vector (v1) of size 300]
,	—>	[vector (v2) of size 300]
how	—>	[vector (v3) of size 300]
are	—>	[vector (v4) of size 300]
you	—>	[vector (v5) of size 300]
?	—>	[vector (v6) of size 300]

There are multiple ways to use this information. One of the simplest ways would be to use the embeddings as they are. As you can see in the example above, we have a 1x300 embedding vector for each word. Using this information, we can calculate the embedding for the whole sentence. There are multiple ways to do it. One such method is shown as follows. In this function, we take all the individual word vectors in a given sentence and create a normalized word vector from all word vectors of the tokens. This provides us with a **sentence vector**.

```python
import numpy as np

def sentence_to_vec(s, embedding_dict, stop_words, tokenizer):
    """
    Given a sentence and other information,
    this function returns embedding for the whole sentence
    :param s: sentence, string
    :param embedding_dict: dictionary word:vector
    :param stop_words: list of stop words, if any
    :param tokenizer: a tokenization function
    """
    # convert sentence to string and lowercase it
    words = str(s).lower()

    # tokenize the sentence
    words = tokenizer(words)

    # remove stop word tokens
    words = [w for w in words if not w in stop_words]

    # keep only alpha-numeric tokens
    words = [w for w in words if w.isalpha()]

    # initialize empty list to store embeddings
    M = []
    for w in words:
        # for every word, fetch the embedding from
        # the dictionary and append to list of
        # embeddings
        if w in embedding_dict:
            M.append(embedding_dict[w])

    # if we dont have any vectors, return zeros
    if len(M) == 0:
        return np.zeros(300)

    # convert list of embeddings to array
    M = np.array(M)

    # calculate sum over axis=0
    v = M.sum(axis=0)
```

```
    # return normalized vector
    return v / np.sqrt((v ** 2).sum())
```

We can use this method to convert all our examples to one vector. Can we use fastText vectors to improve the previous results? We have 300 features for every review.

```
# fasttext.py

import io
import numpy as np
import pandas as pd

from nltk.tokenize import word_tokenize
from sklearn import linear_model
from sklearn import metrics
from sklearn import model_selection
from sklearn.feature_extraction.text import TfidfVectorizer

def load_vectors(fname):
    # taken from: https://fasttext.cc/docs/en/english-vectors.html
    fin = io.open(
            fname,
            'r',
            encoding='utf-8',
            newline='\n',
            errors='ignore'
    )
    n, d = map(int, fin.readline().split())
    data = {}
    for line in fin:
        tokens = line.rstrip().split(' ')
        data[tokens[0]] = list(map(float, tokens[1:]))
    return data


def sentence_to_vec(s, embedding_dict, stop_words, tokenizer):
    .
    .
    .
if __name__ == "__main__":
    # read the training data
    df = pd.read_csv("../input/imdb.csv")
```

```python
# map positive to 1 and negative to 0
df.sentiment = df.sentiment.apply(
    lambda x: 1 if x == "positive" else 0
)

# the next step is to randomize the rows of the data
df = df.sample(frac=1).reset_index(drop=True)

# load embeddings into memory
print("Loading embeddings")
embeddings = load_vectors("../input/crawl-300d-2M.vec")

# create sentence embeddings
print("Creating sentence vectors")
vectors = []
for review in df.review.values:
    vectors.append(
        sentence_to_vec(
            s = review,
            embedding_dict = embeddings,
            stop_words = [],
            tokenizer = word_tokenize
        )
    )

vectors = np.array(vectors)

# fetch labels
y = df.sentiment.values

# initiate the kfold class from model_selection module
kf = model_selection.StratifiedKFold(n_splits=5)

# fill the new kfold column
for fold_, (t_, v_) in enumerate(kf.split(X=vectors, y=y)):
    print(f"Training fold: {fold_}")
    # temporary dataframes for train and test
    xtrain = vectors[t_, :]
    ytrain = y[t_]

    xtest = vectors[v_, :]
    ytest = y[v_]

    # initialize logistic regression model
    model = linear_model.LogisticRegression()

    # fit the model on training data reviews and sentiment
```

```
model.fit(xtrain, ytrain)

# make predictions on test data
# threshold for predictions is 0.5
preds = model.predict(xtest)

# calculate accuracy
accuracy = metrics.accuracy_score(ytest, preds)
print(f"Accuracy = {accuracy}")
print("")
```

This gives the following results.

```
> python fasttext.py
Loading embeddings
Creating sentence vectors
Training fold: 0
Accuracy = 0.8619

Training fold: 1
Accuracy = 0.8661

Training fold: 2
Accuracy = 0.8544

Training fold: 3
Accuracy = 0.8624

Training fold: 4
Accuracy = 0.8595
```

Wow! That's quite unexpected. We get excellent results, and all we did was to use the FastText embeddings. Try changing the embeddings to GloVe and see what happens. I'm leaving it as an exercise for you.

When we talk about text data, we must keep one thing in our mind. Text data is very similar to the time series data. Any sample in our reviews is a sequence of tokens at different timestamps which are in increasing order, and each token can be represented as a vector/embedding, as shown in figure 2.

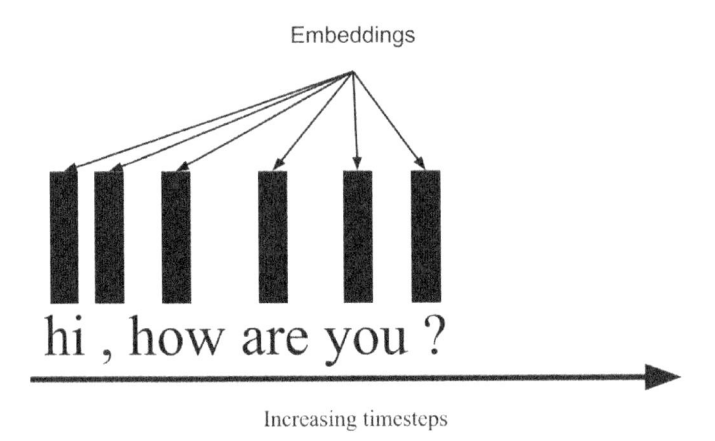

Figure 2: Representing tokens as embeddings and treating it as a time series

This means that we can use models that are widely used for time series data such as **Long Short Term Memory (LSTM)** or **Gated Recurrent Units (GRU)** or even **Convolutional Neural Networks (CNNs)**. Let's see how to train a simple bi-directional LSTM model on this dataset.

First of all, we will create a project. Feel free to name it whatever you want. And then our first step will be splitting the data for cross-validation.

```
# create_folds.py
# import pandas and model_selection module of scikit-learn
import pandas as pd
from sklearn import model_selection

if __name__ == "__main__":
    # Read training data
    df = pd.read_csv("../input/imdb.csv")

    # map positive to 1 and negative to 0
    df.sentiment = df.sentiment.apply(
        lambda x: 1 if x == "positive" else 0
    )

    # we create a new column called kfold and fill it with -1
    df["kfold"] = -1
```

```python
    # the next step is to randomize the rows of the data
    df = df.sample(frac=1).reset_index(drop=True)

    # fetch labels
    y = df.sentiment.values

    # initiate the kfold class from model_selection module
    kf = model_selection.StratifiedKFold(n_splits=5)

    # fill the new kfold column
    for f, (t_, v_) in enumerate(kf.split(X=df, y=y)):
        df.loc[v_, 'kfold'] = f

    # save the new csv with kfold column
    df.to_csv("../input/imdb_folds.csv", index=False)
```

Once we have the dataset divided into folds, we create a simple dataset class in *dataset.py*. Dataset class returns one sample of the training or validation data.

```python
# dataset.py
import torch


class IMDBDataset:
    def __init__(self, reviews, targets):
        """
        :param reviews: this is a numpy array
        :param targets: a vector, numpy array
        """
        self.reviews = reviews
        self.target = targets

    def __len__(self):
        # returns length of the dataset
        return len(self.reviews)

    def __getitem__(self, item):
        # for any given item, which is an int,
        # return review and targets as torch tensor
        # item is the index of the item in concern
        review = self.reviews[item, :]
        target = self.target[item]

        return {
```

```
            "review": torch.tensor(review, dtype=torch.long),
            "target": torch.tensor(target, dtype=torch.float)
        }
```

Once the dataset class is done, we can create *lstm.py* which consists of our LSTM model.

```
# lstm.py

import torch
import torch.nn as nn


class LSTM(nn.Module):
    def __init__(self, embedding_matrix):
        """
        :param embedding_matrix: numpy array with vectors for all words
        """
        super(LSTM, self).__init__()
        # number of words = number of rows in embedding matrix
        num_words = embedding_matrix.shape[0]

        # dimension of embedding is num of columns in the matrix
        embed_dim = embedding_matrix.shape[1]

        # we define an input embedding layer
        self.embedding = nn.Embedding(
            num_embeddings=num_words,
            embedding_dim=embed_dim
        )

        # embedding matrix is used as weights of
        # the embedding layer
        self.embedding.weight = nn.Parameter(
            torch.tensor(
                embedding_matrix,
                dtype=torch.float32
            )
        )

        # we dont want to train the pretrained embeddings
        self.embedding.weight.requires_grad = False

        # a simple bidirectional LSTM with
        # hidden size of 128
```

```python
        self.lstm = nn.LSTM(
            embed_dim,
            128,
            bidirectional=True,
            batch_first=True,
        )

        # output layer which is a linear layer
        # we have only one output
        # input (512) = 128 + 128 for mean and same for max pooling
        self.out = nn.Linear(512, 1)

    def forward(self, x):
        # pass data through embedding layer
        # the input is just the tokens
        x = self.embedding(x)

        # move embedding output to lstm
        x, _ = self.lstm(x)

        # apply mean and max pooling on lstm output
        avg_pool = torch.mean(x, 1)
        max_pool, _ = torch.max(x, 1)

        # concatenate mean and max pooling
        # this is why size is 512
        # 128 for each direction = 256
        # avg_pool = 256 and max_pool = 256
        out = torch.cat((avg_pool, max_pool), 1)

        # pass through the output layer and return the output
        out = self.out(out)

        # return linear output
        return out
```

Now, we create *engine.py* which consists of our training and evaluation functions.

```
# engine.py
import torch
import torch.nn as nn


def train(data_loader, model, optimizer, device):
    """
```

```python
    This is the main training function that trains model
    for one epoch
    :param data_loader: this is the torch dataloader
    :param model: model (lstm model)
    :param optimizer: torch optimizer, e.g. adam, sgd, etc.
    :param device: this can be "cuda" or "cpu"
    """
    # set model to training mode
    model.train()

    # go through batches of data in data loader
    for data in data_loader:
        # fetch review and target from the dict
        reviews = data["review"]
        targets = data["target"]

        # move the data to device that we want to use
        reviews = reviews.to(device, dtype=torch.long)
        targets = targets.to(device, dtype=torch.float)

        # clear the gradients
        optimizer.zero_grad()

        # make predictions from the model
        predictions = model(reviews)

        # calculate the loss
        loss = nn.BCEWithLogitsLoss()(
            predictions,
            targets.view(-1, 1)
        )

        # compute gradient of loss w.r.t.
        # all parameters of the model that are trainable
        loss.backward()

        # single optimization step
        optimizer.step()


def evaluate(data_loader, model, device):
    # initialize empty lists to store predictions
    # and targets
    final_predictions = []
    final_targets = []

    # put the model in eval mode
```

```
        model.eval()

        # disable gradient calculation
        with torch.no_grad():
            for data in data_loader:
                reviews = data["review"]
                targets = data["target"]
                reviews = reviews.to(device, dtype=torch.long)
                targets = targets.to(device, dtype=torch.float)

                # make predictions
                predictions = model(reviews)

                # move predictions and targets to list
                # we need to move predictions and targets to cpu too
                predictions = predictions.cpu().numpy().tolist()
                targets = data["target"].cpu().numpy().tolist()
                final_predictions.extend(predictions)
                final_targets.extend(targets)

        # return final predictions and targets
        return final_predictions, final_targets
```

These functions will help us in *train.py* which is used for training multiple folds.

```
# train.py
import io
import torch

import numpy as np
import pandas as pd

# yes, we use tensorflow
# but not for training the model!
import tensorflow as tf

from sklearn import metrics

import config
import dataset
import engine
import lstm

def load_vectors(fname):
    # taken from: https://fasttext.cc/docs/en/english-vectors.html
```

```python
    fin = io.open(
        fname,
        'r',
        encoding='utf-8',
        newline='\n',
        errors='ignore'
    )
    n, d = map(int, fin.readline().split())
    data = {}
    for line in fin:
        tokens = line.rstrip().split(' ')
        data[tokens[0]] = list(map(float, tokens[1:]))
    return data


def create_embedding_matrix(word_index, embedding_dict):
    """
    This function creates the embedding matrix.
    :param word_index: a dictionary with word:index_value
    :param embedding_dict: a dictionary with word:embedding_vector
    :return: a numpy array with embedding vectors for all known words
    """
    # initialize matrix with zeros
    embedding_matrix = np.zeros((len(word_index) + 1, 300))
    # loop over all the words
    for word, i in word_index.items():
        # if word is found in pre-trained embeddings,
        # update the matrix. if the word is not found,
        # the vector is zeros!
        if word in embedding_dict:
            embedding_matrix[i] = embedding_dict[word]
    # return embedding matrix
    return embedding_matrix


def run(df, fold):
    """
    Run training and validation for a given fold
    and dataset
    :param df: pandas dataframe with kfold column
    :param fold: current fold, int
    """

    # fetch training dataframe
    train_df = df[df.kfold != fold].reset_index(drop=True)

    # fetch validation dataframe
```

```python
    valid_df = df[df.kfold == fold].reset_index(drop=True)

    print("Fitting tokenizer")
    # we use tf.keras for tokenization
    # you can use your own tokenizer and then you can
    # get rid of tensorflow
    tokenizer = tf.keras.preprocessing.text.Tokenizer()
    tokenizer.fit_on_texts(df.review.values.tolist())

    # convert training data to sequences
    # for example : "bad movie" gets converted to
    # [24, 27] where 24 is the index for bad and 27 is the
    # index for movie
    xtrain = tokenizer.texts_to_sequences(train_df.review.values)

    # similarly convert validation data to
    # sequences
    xtest = tokenizer.texts_to_sequences(valid_df.review.values)

    # zero pad the training sequences given the maximum length
    # this padding is done on left hand side
    # if sequence is > MAX_LEN, it is truncated on left hand side too
    xtrain = tf.keras.preprocessing.sequence.pad_sequences(
        xtrain, maxlen=config.MAX_LEN
    )

    # zero pad the validation sequences
    xtest = tf.keras.preprocessing.sequence.pad_sequences(
        xtest, maxlen=config.MAX_LEN
    )

    # initialize dataset class for training
    train_dataset = dataset.IMDBDataset(
        reviews=xtrain,
        targets=train_df.sentiment.values
    )

    # create torch dataloader for training
    # torch dataloader loads the data using dataset
    # class in batches specified by batch size
    train_data_loader = torch.utils.data.DataLoader(
        train_dataset,
        batch_size=config.TRAIN_BATCH_SIZE,
        num_workers=2
    )

    # initialize dataset class for validation
```

```python
valid_dataset = dataset.IMDBDataset(
    reviews=xtest,
    targets=valid_df.sentiment.values
)

# create torch dataloader for validation
valid_data_loader = torch.utils.data.DataLoader(
    valid_dataset,
    batch_size=config.VALID_BATCH_SIZE,
    num_workers=1
)

print("Loading embeddings")
# load embeddings as shown previously
embedding_dict = load_vectors("../input/crawl-300d-2M.vec")
embedding_matrix = create_embedding_matrix(
    tokenizer.word_index, embedding_dict
)

# create torch device, since we use gpu, we are using cuda
device = torch.device("cuda")

# fetch our LSTM model
model = lstm.LSTM(embedding_matrix)

# send model to device
model.to(device)

# initialize Adam optimizer
optimizer = torch.optim.Adam(model.parameters(), lr=1e-3)

print("Training Model")
# set best accuracy to zero
best_accuracy = 0
# set early stopping counter to zero
early_stopping_counter = 0
# train and validate for all epochs
for epoch in range(config.EPOCHS):
    # train one epoch
    engine.train(train_data_loader, model, optimizer, device)
    # validate
    outputs, targets = engine.evaluate(
                        valid_data_loader, model, device
    )

    # use threshold of 0.5
    # please note we are using linear layer and no sigmoid
```

```
            # you should do this 0.5 threshold after sigmoid
            outputs = np.array(outputs) >= 0.5

            # calculate accuracy
            accuracy = metrics.accuracy_score(targets, outputs)
            print(
                f"FOLD:{fold}, Epoch: {epoch}, Accuracy Score = {accuracy}"
            )

            # simple early stopping
            if accuracy > best_accuracy:
                best_accuracy = accuracy
            else:
                early_stopping_counter += 1

            if early_stopping_counter > 2:
                break

if __name__ == "__main__":

    # load data
    df = pd.read_csv("../input/imdb_folds.csv")

    # train for all folds
    run(df, fold=0)
    run(df, fold=1)
    run(df, fold=2)
    run(df, fold=3)
    run(df, fold=4)
```

And finally, we have *config.py*.

```
# config.py
# we define all the configuration here
MAX_LEN = 128
TRAIN_BATCH_SIZE = 16
VALID_BATCH_SIZE = 8
EPOCHS = 10
```

Let's see what this gives us.

```
> python train.py

FOLD:0, Epoch: 3, Accuracy Score = 0.9015
FOLD:1, Epoch: 4, Accuracy Score = 0.9007
FOLD:2, Epoch: 3, Accuracy Score = 0.8924
FOLD:3, Epoch: 2, Accuracy Score = 0.9
FOLD:4, Epoch: 1, Accuracy Score = 0.878
```

This is by far the best score we have obtained. Please note that I have only shown the epochs with best accuracies in each fold.

You must have noticed that we used pre-trained embeddings and a simple bi-directional LSTM. If you want to change the model, you can just change model in lstm.py and keep everything as it is. This kind of code requires minimal changes for experiments and is easily understandable. For example, you can learn the embeddings on your own instead of using pretrained embeddings, you can use some other pretrained embeddings, you can combine multiple pretrained embeddings, you can use GRU, you can use spatial dropout after embedded, you can add a GRU layer after LSTM, you can add two LSTM layers, you can have LSTM-GRU-LSTM config, you can replace LSTM with a convolutional layer, etc. without making many changes to the code. Most of what I mention requires changes only to model class.

When you use pretrained embeddings, try to see for how many words you are not able to find embeddings and why. The more words for which you have pre-trained embeddings, the better are the results. I present to you the following un-commented (!) function that you can use to create embedding matrix for any kind of pre-trained embedding which is in the same format as glove or fastText (some changes might be needed).

```python
def load_embeddings(word_index, embedding_file, vector_length=300):
    """
    A general function to create embedding matrix
    :param word_index: word:index dictionary
    :param embedding_file: path to embeddings file
    :param vector_length: length of vector
    """
    max_features = len(word_index) + 1
    words_to_find = list(word_index.keys())
    more_words_to_find = []
```

```python
for wtf in words_to_find:
    more_words_to_find.append(wtf)
    more_words_to_find.append(str(wtf).capitalize())
more_words_to_find = set(more_words_to_find)

def get_coefs(word, *arr):
    return word, np.asarray(arr, dtype='float32')

embeddings_index = dict(
    get_coefs(*o.strip().split(" "))
    for o in open(embedding_file)
    if o.split(" ")[0]
    in more_words_to_find
    and len(o) > 100
)

embedding_matrix = np.zeros((max_features, vector_length))
for word, i in word_index.items():
    if i >= max_features:
        continue
    embedding_vector = embeddings_index.get(word)
    if embedding_vector is None:
        embedding_vector = embeddings_index.get(
            str(word).capitalize()
        )
    if embedding_vector is None:
        embedding_vector = embeddings_index.get(
            str(word).upper()
        )
    if (embedding_vector is not None
        and len(embedding_vector) == vector_length):
        embedding_matrix[i] = embedding_vector
return embedding_matrix
```

Read and run the function above and see what's happening. The function can also be modified to use stemmed words or lemmatized words. In the end, you want to have the least number of unknown words in your training corpus. One more trick is to learn the embedding layer, i.e., make it trainable and then train the network.

So far, we have built a lot of models for a classification problem. However, it is the era of muppets, and more and more people are moving towards transformer-based models. **Transformer** based networks are able to handle dependencies which are long term in nature. LSTM looks at the next word only when it has seen the previous word. This is not the case with transformers. It can look at all the words in the whole sentence simultaneously. Due to this, one more advantage is that it can easily be parallelized and uses GPUs more efficiently.

Transformers is a very broad topic, and there are too many models: **BERT, RoBERTa, XLNet, XLM-RoBERTa, T5**, etc. I will show you a general approach that you can use for all these models (except T5) for the classification problem that we have been discussing. Please note that these transformers are hungry in terms of computational power needed to train them. Thus, if you do not have a high-end system, it might take much longer to train a model compared to LSTM or TF-IDF based models.

The first thing we do is to create a config file.

```
# config.py
import transformers

# this is the maximum number of tokens in the sentence
MAX_LEN = 512

# batch sizes is small because model is huge!
TRAIN_BATCH_SIZE = 8
VALID_BATCH_SIZE = 4

# let's train for a maximum of 10 epochs
EPOCHS = 10

# define path to BERT model files
BERT_PATH = "../input/bert_base_uncased/"

# this is where you want to save the model
MODEL_PATH = "model.bin"

# training file
TRAINING_FILE = "../input/imdb.csv"

# define the tokenizer
# we use tokenizer and model
# from huggingface's transformers
TOKENIZER = transformers.BertTokenizer.from_pretrained(
    BERT_PATH,
    do_lower_case=True
)
```

The config file here is the only place where we define tokenizer and other parameters we would like to change frequently—this way we can do many experiments without requiring a lot of changes.

Next step is to build a dataset class.

```
# dataset.py
import config
import torch


class BERTDataset:
    def __init__(self, review, target):
        """
        :param review: list or numpy array of strings
        :param targets: list or numpy array which is binary
        """
        self.review = review
        self.target = target
        # we fetch max len and tokenizer from config.py
        self.tokenizer = config.TOKENIZER
        self.max_len = config.MAX_LEN

    def __len__(self):
        # this returns the length of dataset
        return len(self.review)

    def __getitem__(self, item):
        # for a given item index, return a dictionary
        # of inputs
        review = str(self.review[item])
        review = " ".join(review.split())

        # encode_plus comes from hugginface's transformers
        # and exists for all tokenizers they offer
        # it can be used to convert a given string
        # to ids, mask and token type ids which are
        # needed for models like BERT
        # here, review is a string
        inputs = self.tokenizer.encode_plus(
            review,
            None,
            add_special_tokens=True,
            max_length=self.max_len,
            pad_to_max_length=True,
```

```
    )
    # ids are ids of tokens generated
    # after tokenizing reviews
    ids = inputs["input_ids"]
    # mask is 1 where we have input
    # and 0 where we have padding
    mask = inputs["attention_mask"]
    # token type ids behave the same way as
    # mask in this specific case
    # in case of two sentences, this is 0
    # for first sentence and 1 for second sentence
    token_type_ids = inputs["token_type_ids"]

    # now we return everything
    # note that ids, mask and token_type_ids
    # are all long datatypes and targets is float
    return {
        "ids": torch.tensor(
            ids, dtype=torch.long
        ),
        "mask": torch.tensor(
            mask, dtype=torch.long
        ),
        "token_type_ids": torch.tensor(
            token_type_ids, dtype=torch.long
        ),
        "targets": torch.tensor(
            self.target[item], dtype=torch.float
        )
    }
```

And now we come to the heart of the project, i.e. the model.

```
# model.py
import config
import transformers
import torch.nn as nn


class BERTBaseUncased(nn.Module):
    def __init__(self):
        super(BERTBaseUncased, self).__init__()
        # we fetch the model from the BERT_PATH defined in
        # config.py
        self.bert = transformers.BertModel.from_pretrained(
```

```
            config.BERT_PATH
        )
        # add a dropout for regularization
        self.bert_drop = nn.Dropout(0.3)
        # a simple linear layer for output
        # yes, there is only one output
        self.out = nn.Linear(768, 1)

    def forward(self, ids, mask, token_type_ids):
        # BERT in its default settings returns two outputs
        # last hidden state and output of bert pooler layer
        # we use the output of the pooler which is of the size
        # (batch_size, hidden_size)
        # hidden size can be 768 or 1024 depending on
        # if we are using bert base or large respectively
        # in our case, it is 768
        # note that this model is pretty simple
        # you might want to use last hidden state
        # or several hidden states
        _, o2 = self.bert(
            ids,
            attention_mask=mask,
            token_type_ids=token_type_ids
        )
        # pass through dropout layer
        bo = self.bert_drop(o2)
        # pass through linear layer
        output = self.out(bo)
        # return output
        return output
```

This model returns a single output. We can use **binary cross-entropy loss** with logits which first applies **sigmoid** and then calculates the loss. This is done in *engine.py*.

```
# engine.py

import torch
import torch.nn as nn


def loss_fn(outputs, targets):
    """
    This function returns the loss.
```

```
    :param outputs: output from the model (real numbers)
    :param targets: input targets (binary)
    """
    return nn.BCEWithLogitsLoss()(outputs, targets.view(-1, 1))


def train_fn(data_loader, model, optimizer, device, scheduler):
    """
    This is the training function which trains for one epoch
    :param data_loader: it is the torch dataloader object
    :param model: torch model, bert in our case
    :param optimizer: adam, sgd, etc
    :param device: can be cpu or cuda
    :param scheduler: learning rate scheduler
    """
    # put the model in training mode
    model.train()

    # loop over all batches
    for d in data_loader:
        # extract ids, token type ids and mask
        # from current batch
        # also extract targets
        ids = d["ids"]
        token_type_ids = d["token_type_ids"]
        mask = d["mask"]
        targets = d["targets"]

        # move everything to specified device
        ids = ids.to(device, dtype=torch.long)
        token_type_ids = token_type_ids.to(device, dtype=torch.long)
        mask = mask.to(device, dtype=torch.long)
        targets = targets.to(device, dtype=torch.float)

        # zero-grad the optimizer
        optimizer.zero_grad()
        # pass through the model
        outputs = model(
            ids=ids,
            mask=mask,
            token_type_ids=token_type_ids
        )
        # calculate loss
        loss = loss_fn(outputs, targets)
        # backward step the loss
        loss.backward()
        # step optimizer
```

```python
        optimizer.step()
        # step scheduler
        scheduler.step()


def eval_fn(data_loader, model, device):
    """
    this is the validation function that generates
    predictions on validation data
    :param data_loader: it is the torch dataloader object
    :param model: torch model, bert in our case
    :param device: can be cpu or cuda
    :return: output and targets
    """
    # put model in eval mode
    model.eval()
    # initialize empty lists for
    # targets and outputs
    fin_targets = []
    fin_outputs = []
    # use the no_grad scope
    # its very important else you might
    # run out of gpu memory
    with torch.no_grad():
        # this part is same as training function
        # except for the fact that there is no
        # zero_grad of optimizer and there is no loss
        # calculation or scheduler steps.
        for d in data_loader:
            ids = d["ids"]
            token_type_ids = d["token_type_ids"]
            mask = d["mask"]
            targets = d["targets"]

            ids = ids.to(device, dtype=torch.long)
            token_type_ids = token_type_ids.to(device, dtype=torch.long)
            mask = mask.to(device, dtype=torch.long)
            targets = targets.to(device, dtype=torch.float)

            outputs = model(
                ids=ids,
                mask=mask,
                token_type_ids=token_type_ids
            )
            # convert targets to cpu and extend the final list
            targets = targets.cpu().detach()
            fin_targets.extend(targets.numpy().tolist())
```

```
            # convert outputs to cpu and extend the final list
            outputs = torch.sigmoid(outputs).cpu().detach()
            fin_outputs.extend(outputs.numpy().tolist())
    return fin_outputs, fin_targets
```

And finally, we are ready to train. Let's look at the training script!

```
# train.py
import config
import dataset
import engine
import torch
import pandas as pd
import torch.nn as nn
import numpy as np

from model import BERTBaseUncased
from sklearn import model_selection
from sklearn import metrics
from transformers import AdamW
from transformers import get_linear_schedule_with_warmup


def train():
    # this function trains the model

    # read the training file and fill NaN values with "none"
    # you can also choose to drop NaN values in this
    # specific dataset
    dfx = pd.read_csv(config.TRAINING_FILE).fillna("none")

    # sentiment = 1 if its positive
    # else sentiment = 0
    dfx.sentiment = dfx.sentiment.apply(
        lambda x: 1 if x == "positive" else 0
    )

    # we split the data into single training
    # and validation fold
    df_train, df_valid = model_selection.train_test_split(
        dfx,
        test_size=0.1,
        random_state=42,
        stratify=dfx.sentiment.values
```

```python
)

# reset index
df_train = df_train.reset_index(drop=True)
df_valid = df_valid.reset_index(drop=True)

# initialize BERTDataset from dataset.py
# for training dataset
train_dataset = dataset.BERTDataset(
    review=df_train.review.values,
    target=df_train.sentiment.values
)

# create training dataloader
train_data_loader = torch.utils.data.DataLoader(
    train_dataset,
    batch_size=config.TRAIN_BATCH_SIZE,
    num_workers=4
)

# initialize BERTDataset from dataset.py
# for validation dataset
valid_dataset = dataset.BERTDataset(
    review=df_valid.review.values,
    target=df_valid.sentiment.values
)

# create validation data loader
valid_data_loader = torch.utils.data.DataLoader(
    valid_dataset,
    batch_size=config.VALID_BATCH_SIZE,
    num_workers=1
)

# initialize the cuda device
# use cpu if you dont have GPU
device = torch.device("cuda")
# load model and send it to the device
model = BERTBaseUncased()
model.to(device)

# create parameters we want to optimize
# we generally dont use any decay for bias
# and weight layers
param_optimizer = list(model.named_parameters())
no_decay = ["bias", "LayerNorm.bias", "LayerNorm.weight"]
optimizer_parameters = [
```

```python
    {
        "params": [
            p for n, p in param_optimizer if
            not any(nd in n for nd in no_decay)
        ],
        "weight_decay": 0.001,
    },
    {
        "params": [
            p for n, p in param_optimizer if
            any(nd in n for nd in no_decay)
        ],
        "weight_decay": 0.0,
    },
]

# calculate the number of training steps
# this is used by scheduler
num_train_steps = int(
    len(df_train) / config.TRAIN_BATCH_SIZE * config.EPOCHS
)

# AdamW optimizer
# AdamW is the most widely used optimizer
# for transformer based networks
optimizer = AdamW(optimizer_parameters, lr=3e-5)

# fetch a scheduler
# you can also try using reduce lr on plateau
scheduler = get_linear_schedule_with_warmup(
    optimizer,
    num_warmup_steps=0,
    num_training_steps=num_train_steps
)

# if you have multiple GPUs
# model model to DataParallel
# to use multiple GPUs
model = nn.DataParallel(model)

# start training the epochs
best_accuracy = 0
for epoch in range(config.EPOCHS):
    engine.train_fn(
        train_data_loader, model, optimizer, device, scheduler
    )
    outputs, targets = engine.eval_fn(
```

```
            valid_data_loader, model, device
        )
        outputs = np.array(outputs) >= 0.5
        accuracy = metrics.accuracy_score(targets, outputs)
        print(f"Accuracy Score = {accuracy}")
        if accuracy > best_accuracy:
            torch.save(model.state_dict(), config.MODEL_PATH)
            best_accuracy = accuracy


if __name__ == "__main__":
    train()
```

It might look like a lot at first, but it isn't once you understand the individual components. You can easily change it to any other transformer model you want to use just by changing a few lines of code.

This model gives an accuracy of 93%! Whoa! That's much better than any other model. But is it worth it?

We were able to achieve 90% using LSTMs, and they are much simpler, easier to train and faster when it comes to inference. We could improve that model probably by a percent by using different data processing or by tuning the parameters such as layers, nodes, dropout, learning rate, changing the optimizer, etc. Then we will have ~2% benefit from BERT. BERT, on the other hand, took much longer to train, has a lot of parameters and is also slow when it comes to inference. In the end, you should look at your business and choose wisely. Don't choose BERT only because it's "cool".

It must be noted that the only task we discussed here is classification but changing it to regression, multi-label or multi-class will require only a couple of lines of code changes. For example, the same problem in multi-class classification setting will have multiple outputs and Cross-Entropy loss. Everything else should remain the same. Natural language processing is huge, and we discussed only a small fraction of it. Apparently, this is a huge fraction as most of the industrial models are classification or regression models. If I start writing in detail about everything I might end up writing a few hundred pages, and that's why I have decided to include everything in a separate book: *Approaching (Almost) Any NLP Problem*!

Approaching ensembling and stacking

When we hear these two words, the first thing that comes to our mind is that it's all about online/offline machine learning competitions. This used to be the case a few years ago, but now with the advancements in computing power and cheaper virtual instances, people have started using ensemble models even in industries. For example, it's very easy to deploy multiple neural networks and serve them in real-time with a response time of less than 500ms. Sometimes, a huge neural network or a large model can also be replaced by a few other models which are small in size, perform similar to the large model and are twice as fast. If this is the case, which model(s) will you choose? I, personally, would prefer multiple small models, which are faster and give the same performance as a much larger and slower model. Please remember that smaller models are also easier and faster to tune.

Ensembling is nothing but a combination of different models. The models can be combined by their predictions/probabilities. The simplest way to combine models would be just to do an average.

Ensemble Probabilities = (M1_proba + M2_proba + ... + Mn_Proba) / n

This is simple and yet the most effective way of combining models. In simple averaging, the weights are equal to all models. One thing that you should keep in mind for any method of combining is that you should always combine predictions/probabilities of models which are different from each other. In simple words, the combination of models which are not highly correlated works better than the combination of models which are very correlated with each other.

If you do not have probabilities, you can combine predictions too. The most simple way of doing this is to take a **vote**. Suppose we are doing a multi-class classification with three classes: 0, 1 and 2.

[0, 0, 1] : Highest voted class: 0

[0, 1, 2] : Highest voted class: None (Choose one randomly)

[2, 2, 2] : Highest voted class: 2

The following simple functions can accomplish these simple operations.

```
import numpy as np


def mean_predictions(probas):
    """
    Create mean predictions
    :param probas: 2-d array of probability values
    :return: mean probability
    """
    return np.mean(probas, axis=1)


def max_voting(preds):
    """
    Create mean predictions
    :param probas: 2-d array of prediction values
    :return: max voted predictions
    """
    idxs = np.argmax(preds, axis=1)
    return np.take_along_axis(preds, idxs[:, None], axis=1)
```

Please note that *probas* have a single probability (i.e. binary classification, usually class 1) in each column. Each column is thus a new model. Similarly, for *preds*, each column is a prediction from different models. Both these functions assume a 2-dimensional numpy array. You can modify it according to your requirements. For example, you might have a 2-d array of probabilities for each model. In that case, the function will change a bit. Another way of combining multiple models is by **ranks of their probabilities**. This type of combination works quite good when the concerned metric is the area under curve as AUC is all about ranking samples.

```
def rank_mean(probas):
    """
    Create mean predictions using ranks
    :param probas: 2-d array of probability values
    :return: mean ranks
    """
    ranked = []
    for i in range(probas.shape[1]):
        rank_data = stats.rankdata(probas[:, i])
        ranked.append(rank_data)
```

```
ranked = np.column_stack(ranked)
return np.mean(ranked, axis=1)
```

Please note that in scipy's *rankdata*, ranks start at 1.

Why do these kinds of ensembles work? Let's look at figure 1.

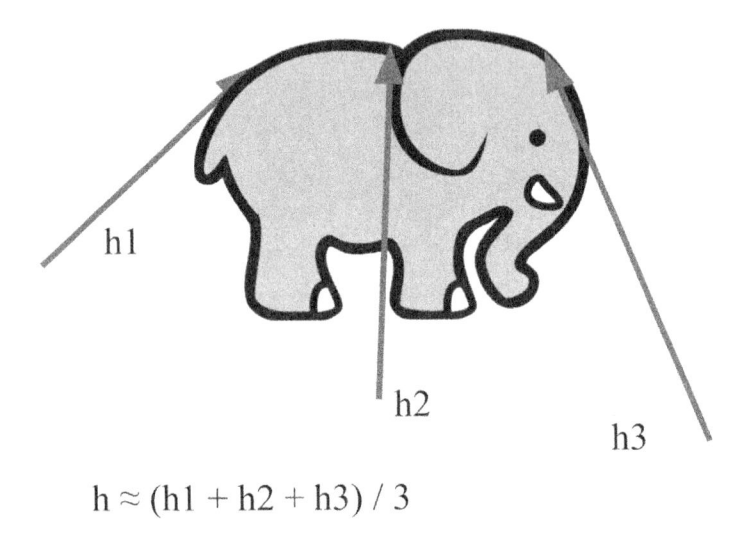

$$h \approx (h1 + h2 + h3) / 3$$

Figure 1: Three people guessing the height of an elephant

Figure 1 shows that if three people are guessing the height of an elephant, the original height will be very close to the average of the three guesses. Let's assume these people can guess very close to the original height of the elephant. Close estimate means an error, but this error can be minimized when we average the three predictions. This is the main idea behind the averaging of multiple models.

Probabilities can also be combined by weights.

Final Probabilities = w1*M1_proba + w2*M2_proba + ... + wn*Mn_proba

Where *(w1 + w2 + w3 + ... + wn) = 1.0*
For example, if you have a random forest model that gives very high AUC and a logistic regression model with a little lower AUC, you can combine them with 70%

for random forest and 30% for logistic regression. So, how did I come up with these numbers? Let's add another model, let's say now we also have an xgboost model that gives an AUC higher than random forest. Now I will combine them with a ratio of 3:2:1 for xgboost : random forest : logistic regression. Easy right? Arriving at these numbers is a piece of cake. Let's see how.

Assume that we have three monkeys with three knobs with values that range between 0 and 1. These monkeys turn the knobs, and we calculate the AUC score at each value they turn the knob to. Eventually, the monkeys will find a combination that gives the best AUC. Yes, it is a random search! Before doing these kinds of searches, you must remember the two most important rules of ensembling.

The first rule of ensembling is that you always create folds before starting with ensembling.

The second rule of ensembling is that you always create folds before starting with ensembling.

YES. These are the two most important rules, and no, there is no mistake in what I wrote. The first step is to create folds. For simplicity, let's say we divide the data into two parts: fold 1 and fold 2. Please note that this is only done for simplicity in explaining. In a real-world scenario, you should create more folds.

Now, we train our random forest model, logistic regression model and our xgboost model on fold 1 and make predictions on fold 2. After this, we train the models from scratch on fold 2 and make predictions on fold 1. Thus, we have created predictions for all of the training data. Now to combine these models, we take fold 1 and all the predictions for fold 1 and create an optimization function that tries to find the best weights so as to minimize error or maximize AUC against the targets for fold 2. So, we are kind of training an optimization model on fold 1 with the predicted probabilities for the three models and evaluating it on fold 2. Let's first look at a class we can use to **find the best weights of multiple models to optimize for AUC** (or any kind of prediction-metric combination in general).

```
import numpy as np

from functools import partial
from scipy.optimize import fmin
from sklearn import metrics
```

```python
class OptimizeAUC:
    """
    Class for optimizing AUC.
    This class is all you need to find best weights for
    any model and for any metric and for any types of predictions.
    With very small changes, this class can be used for optimization of
    weights in ensemble models of _any_ type of predictions
    """
    def __init__(self):
        self.coef_ = 0

    def _auc(self, coef, X, y):
        """
        This functions calulates and returns AUC.
        :param coef: coef list, of the same length as number of models
        :param X: predictions, in this case a 2d array
        :param y: targets, in our case binary 1d array
        """
        # multiply coefficients with every column of the array
        # with predictions.
        # this means: element 1 of coef is multiplied by column 1
        # of the prediction array, element 2 of coef is multiplied
        # by column 2 of the prediction array and so on!
        x_coef = X * coef

        # create predictions by taking row wise sum
        predictions = np.sum(x_coef, axis=1)

        # calculate auc score
        auc_score = metrics.roc_auc_score(y, predictions)

        # return negative auc
        return -1.0 * auc_score

    def fit(self, X, y):
        # remember partial from hyperparameter optimization chapter?
        loss_partial = partial(self._auc, X=X, y=y)

        # dirichlet distribution. you can use any distribution you want
        # to initialize the coefficients
        # we want the coefficients to sum to 1
        initial_coef = np.random.dirichlet(np.ones(X.shape[1]), size=1)

        # use scipy fmin to minimize the loss function, in our case auc
        self.coef_ = fmin(loss_partial, initial_coef, disp=True)

    def predict(self, X):
```

```
            # this is similar to _auc function
            x_coef = X * self.coef_
            predictions = np.sum(x_coef, axis=1)
            return predictions
```

Let's see how to use this and compare it with simple averaging.

```
import xgboost as xgb
from sklearn.datasets import make_classification
from sklearn import ensemble
from sklearn import linear_model
from sklearn import metrics
from sklearn import model_selection


# make a binary classification dataset with 10k samples
# and 25 features
X, y = make_classification(n_samples=10000, n_features=25)

# split into two folds (for this example)
xfold1, xfold2, yfold1, yfold2 = model_selection.train_test_split(
    X,
    y,
    test_size=0.5,
    stratify=y
)

# fit models on fold 1 and make predictions on fold 2
# we have 3 models:
# logistic regression, random forest and xgboost
logreg = linear_model.LogisticRegression()
rf = ensemble.RandomForestClassifier()
xgbc = xgb.XGBClassifier()

# fit all models on fold 1 data
logreg.fit(xfold1, yfold1)
rf.fit(xfold1, yfold1)
xgbc.fit(xfold1, yfold1)

# predict all models on fold 2
# take probability for class 1
pred_logreg = logreg.predict_proba(xfold2)[:, 1]
pred_rf = rf.predict_proba(xfold2)[:, 1]
pred_xgbc = xgbc.predict_proba(xfold2)[:, 1]
```

```python
# create an average of all predictions
# that is the simplest ensemble
avg_pred = (pred_logreg + pred_rf + pred_xgbc) / 3

# a 2d array of all predictions
fold2_preds = np.column_stack((
    pred_logreg,
    pred_rf,
    pred_xgbc,
    avg_pred
))

# calculate and store individual AUC values
aucs_fold2 = []
for i in range(fold2_preds.shape[1]):
    auc = metrics.roc_auc_score(yfold2, fold2_preds[:, i])
    aucs_fold2.append(auc)

print(f"Fold-2: LR AUC = {aucs_fold2[0]}")
print(f"Fold-2: RF AUC = {aucs_fold2[1]}")
print(f"Fold-2: XGB AUC = {aucs_fold2[2]}")
print(f"Fold-2: Average Pred AUC = {aucs_fold2[3]}")

# now we repeat the same for the other fold
# this is not the ideal way, if you ever have to repeat code,
# create a function!
# fit models on fold 2 and make predictions on fold 1
logreg = linear_model.LogisticRegression()
rf = ensemble.RandomForestClassifier()
xgbc = xgb.XGBClassifier()

logreg.fit(xfold2, yfold2)
rf.fit(xfold2, yfold2)
xgbc.fit(xfold2, yfold2)

pred_logreg = logreg.predict_proba(xfold1)[:, 1]
pred_rf = rf.predict_proba(xfold1)[:, 1]
pred_xgbc = xgbc.predict_proba(xfold1)[:, 1]
avg_pred = (pred_logreg + pred_rf + pred_xgbc) / 3

fold1_preds = np.column_stack((
    pred_logreg,
    pred_rf,
    pred_xgbc,
    avg_pred
))
```

```
aucs_fold1 = []
for i in range(fold1_preds.shape[1]):
    auc = metrics.roc_auc_score(yfold1, fold1_preds[:, i])
    aucs_fold1.append(auc)

print(f"Fold-1: LR AUC = {aucs_fold1[0]}")
print(f"Fold-1: RF AUC = {aucs_fold1[1]}")
print(f"Fold-1: XGB AUC = {aucs_fold1[2]}")
print(f"Fold-1: Average prediction AUC = {aucs_fold1[3]}")

# find optimal weights using the optimizer
opt = OptimizeAUC()
# dont forget to remove the average column
opt.fit(fold1_preds[:, :-1], yfold1)
opt_preds_fold2 = opt.predict(fold2_preds[:, :-1])
auc = metrics.roc_auc_score(yfold2, opt_preds_fold2)
print(f"Optimized AUC, Fold 2 = {auc}")
print(f"Coefficients = {opt.coef_}")

opt = OptimizeAUC()
opt.fit(fold2_preds[:, :-1], yfold2)
opt_preds_fold1 = opt.predict(fold1_preds[:, :-1])
auc = metrics.roc_auc_score(yfold1, opt_preds_fold1)
print(f"Optimized AUC, Fold 1 = {auc}")
print(f"Coefficients = {opt.coef_}")
```

Let's look at the output.

```
> python auc_opt.py
Fold-2: LR AUC = 0.9145446769443348
Fold-2: RF AUC = 0.9269918948683287
Fold-2: XGB AUC = 0.9302436595508696
Fold-2: Average Pred AUC = 0.927701495890154

Fold-1: LR AUC = 0.9050872233256017
Fold-1: RF AUC = 0.9179382818311258
Fold-1: XGB AUC = 0.9195837242005629
Fold-1: Average prediction AUC = 0.9189669233123695

Optimization terminated successfully.
         Current function value: -0.920643
         Iterations: 50
         Function evaluations: 109
Optimized AUC, Fold 2 = 0.9305386199756128
Coefficients = [-0.00188194  0.19328336  0.35891836]
```

```
Optimization terminated successfully.
         Current function value: -0.931232
         Iterations: 56
         Function evaluations: 113
Optimized AUC, Fold 1 = 0.9192523637234037
Coefficients = [-0.15655124  0.22393151  0.58711366]
```

We see that average is better but using the optimizer to find the threshold is even better! Sometimes, the average is the best choice. As you can see, the coefficients do not add up to 1.0, but that's okay as we are dealing with AUC and AUC cares only about ranks.

Even random forest is an ensemble model. Random forest is just a combination of many simple decision trees. Random forest comes in a category of ensemble models which is popularly known as **bagging**. In bagging, we create small subsets of data and train multiple simple models. The final result is obtained by a combination of predictions, such as average, of all such small models.

And the xgboost model that we used is also an ensemble model. All gradient **boosting** models are ensemble models and come under the umbrella name: boosting. Boosting models work similar to bagging models, except for the fact that consecutive models in boosting are trained on error residuals and tend to minimize the errors of preceding models. This way, boosting models can learn the data perfectly and are thus susceptible to overfitting.

What we saw in the code snippets till now considers only one column. This is not always the case, and there will be many times when you have to deal with multiple columns for predictions. For example, you might have a problem where you are predicting one class out of multiple classes, i.e., multi-class classification problem. For a multi-class classification problem, you can easily choose the voting approach. But voting might not always be the best approach. If you want to combine the probabilities, you will have a two-dimensional array instead of a vector as we had previously when we were optimizing for AUC. With multiple classes, you can try optimizing for log-loss instead (or some other business-relevant metric). To combine, you can use a list of numpy arrays instead of a numpy array in the fit function (X) and subsequently, you would also need to change the optimizer and the predict function. I'm going to leave it as an exercise for you.

And now we can move to the next interesting topic which is quite popular and is known as **stacking**. Figure 2 shows how you can stack models.

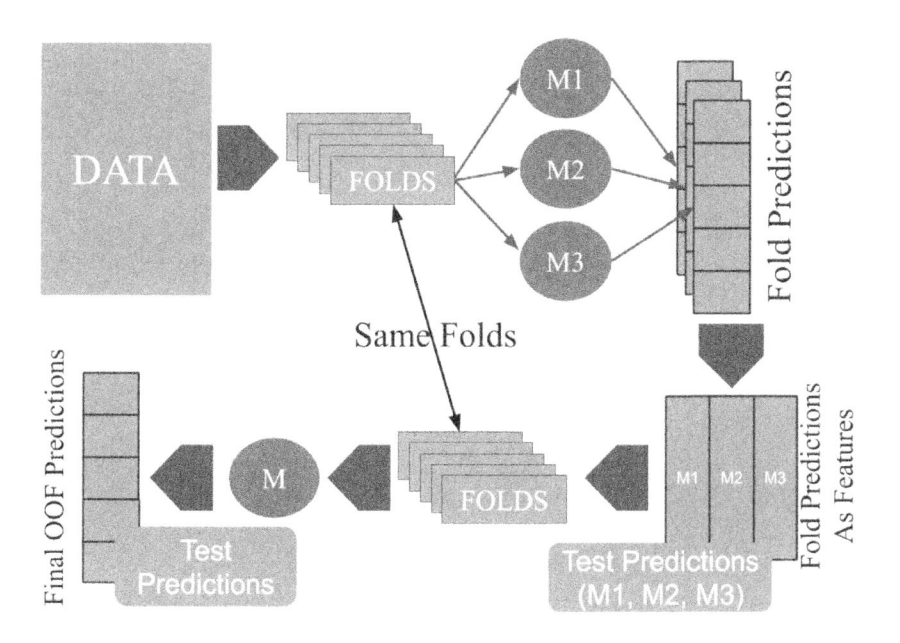

Figure 2: Stacking

Stacking is not rocket science. It's straightforward. If you have correct cross-validation and keep the folds same throughout the journey of your modelling task, nothing should overfit.

Let me describe the idea to you in simple points.

- Divide the training data into folds.
- Train a bunch of models: M1, M2.....Mn.
- Create full training predictions (using out of fold training) and test predictions using all these models.
- Till here it is Level – 1 (L1).
- Use the fold predictions from these models as features to another model. This is now a Level – 2 (L2) model.
- Use the same folds as before to train this L2 model.
- Now create OOF (out of fold) predictions on the training set and the test set.
- Now you have L2 predictions for training data and also the final test set predictions.

You can keep repeating the L1 part and can create as many levels as you want.

Sometimes, you will also come across a term called **blending**. If you do, don't worry about it much. It is nothing but stacking with a holdout set instead of multiple folds.

It must be noted that what I have described in this chapter can be applied to any kind of problem: classification, regression, multi-label classification, etc.

Approaching reproducible code & model serving

We have now reached a stage where we should be able to distribute our models/training code to others so that they can use it. You can distribute or share the code with others in a floppy disk, but that's not ideal. Is it? May be many years ago, it was ideal but not anymore. The preferred way of sharing code and collaborating with others is by using a source code management system. Git is one of the most popular source code management systems. So, let's say you have learned git and formatted the code properly, have written proper documentation and have open-sourced your project. Is that enough? No. It's not. It's because you wrote code on your computer and that might not work on someone else's computer because of many different reasons. So, it would be nice if when you distribute the code, you could replicate your computer and others can too when they install your software or run your code. To do this, the most popular way these days is to use **Docker Containers**. To use docker containers, you need to install docker.

Let's install docker using the following commands.

```
$ sudo apt install docker.io
$ sudo systemctl start docker
$ sudo systemctl enable docker

$ sudo groupadd docker
$ sudo usermod -aG docker $USER
```

These commands work in Ubuntu 18.04. The best thing about docker is that it can be installed on any machine: Linux, Windows, OSX. So, it doesn't matter which machine you have if you work inside the docker container all the time!

Docker containers can be considered as small virtual machines. You can create a container for your code, and then everyone will be able to use it and access it. Let's see how we can create containers that can be used for training a model. We will use the BERT model that we trained in the natural language processing chapter and try to containerize the training code.

First and foremost, you need a file with requirements for your python project. Requirements are contained in a file called *requirements.txt*. The filename is the standard. The file consists of all the python libraries that you are using in your project. That is the python libraries that can be downloaded via PyPI (pip). For training our BERT model to detect positive/negative sentiment, we use torch, transformers, tqdm, scikit-learn, pandas and numpy. Let's write them in *requirements.txt*. You can just write the names, or you can also include the version. It's always the best to include version, and that's what you should do. When you include version, it makes sure that others have the same version as yours and not the latest version as the latest version might change something and if that's the case, model won't be trained the same way as was done by you.

The following snippet shows *requirements.txt*.

```
# requirements.txt
pandas==1.0.4
scikit-learn==0.22.1
torch==1.5.0
transformers==2.11.0
```

Now, we will create a **docker file** called *Dockerfile*. No extension. There are several elements to *Dockerfile*. Let's take a look.

```
# Dockerfile
# First of all, we include where we are getting the image
# from. Image can be thought of as an operating system.
# You can do "FROM ubuntu:18.04"
# this will start from a clean ubuntu 18.04 image.
# All images are downloaded from dockerhub
# Here are we grabbing image from nvidia's repo
# they created a docker image using ubuntu 18.04
# and installed cuda 10.1 and cudnn7 in it. Thus, we don't have to
# install it. Makes our life easy.
FROM nvidia/cuda:10.1-cudnn7-runtime-ubuntu18.04

# this is the same apt-get command that you are used to
# except the fact that, we have -y argument. Its because
# when we build this container, we cannot press Y when asked for
RUN apt-get update && apt-get install -y \
    git \
    curl \
    ca-certificates \
    python3 \
```

```
    python3-pip \
    sudo \
    && rm -rf /var/lib/apt/lists/*

# We add a new user called "abhishek"
# this can be anything. Anything you want it
# to be. Usually, we don't use our own name,
# you can use "user" or "ubuntu"
RUN useradd -m abhishek

# make our user own its own home directory
RUN chown -R abhishek:abhishek /home/abhishek/

# copy all files from this direrctory to a
# directory called app inside the home of abhishek
# and abhishek owns it.
COPY --chown=abhishek *.* /home/abhishek/app/

# change to user abhishek
USER abhishek
RUN mkdir /home/abhishek/data/

# Now we install all the requirements
# after moving to the app directory
# PLEASE NOTE that ubuntu 18.04 image
# has python 3.6.9 and not python 3.7.6
# you can also install conda python here and use that
# however, to simplify it, I will be using python 3.6.9
# inside the docker container!!!!
RUN cd /home/abhishek/app/ && pip3 install -r requirements.txt
# install mkl. its needed for transformers
RUN pip3 install mkl

# when we log into the docker container,
# we will go inside this directory automatically
WORKDIR /home/abhishek/app
```

Once we have created the docker file, we need to build it. Building the docker container is a very simple command.

```
docker build -f Dockerfile -t bert:train .
```

This command builds a container from the provided *Dockerfile*. The name of the docker container is *bert:train*. This produces the following output:

```
> docker build -f Dockerfile -t bert:train .
Sending build context to Docker daemon  19.97kB
Step 1/7 : FROM nvidia/cuda:10.1-cudnn7-ubuntu18.04
 ---> 3b55548ae91f
Step 2/7 : RUN apt-get update && apt-get install -y  git  curl   ca-certificates    python3 python3-pip    sudo    && rm -rf /var/lib/apt/lists/*
.
.
.
.
Removing intermediate container 8f6975dd08ba
 ---> d1802ac9f1b4
Step 7/7 : WORKDIR /home/abhishek/app
 ---> Running in 257ff09502ed
Removing intermediate container 257ff09502ed
 ---> e5f6eb4cddd7
Successfully built e5f6eb4cddd7
Successfully tagged bert:train
```

Please note that I have removed many lines from the output. Now, you can log into the container using the following command.

```
$ docker run -ti bert:train /bin/bash
```

You need to remember that whatever you do in this shell will be lost once you exit the shell. And you can run the training inside the docker container using:

```
$ docker run -ti bert:train python3 train.py
```

Which gives the following output:

```
Traceback (most recent call last):
  File "train.py", line 2, in <module>
    import config
  File "/home/abhishek/app/config.py", line 28, in <module>
    do_lower_case=True
  File "/usr/local/lib/python3.6/dist-
packages/transformers/tokenization_utils.py", line 393, in
from_pretrained
    return cls._from_pretrained(*inputs, **kwargs)
  File "/usr/local/lib/python3.6/dist-
packages/transformers/tokenization_utils.py", line 496, in
_from_pretrained
    list(cls.vocab_files_names.values()),
OSError: Model name '../input/bert_base_uncased/' was not found in
tokenizers model name list (bert-base-uncased, bert-large-uncased, bert-
base-cased, bert-large-cased, bert-base-multilingual-uncased, bert-base-
multilingual-cased, bert-base-chinese, bert-base-german-cased, bert-
large-uncased-whole-word-masking, bert-large-cased-whole-word-masking,
bert-large-uncased-whole-word-masking-finetuned-squad, bert-large-cased-
whole-word-masking-finetuned-squad, bert-base-cased-finetuned-mrpc, bert-
base-german-dbmdz-cased, bert-base-german-dbmdz-uncased, bert-base-
finnish-cased-v1, bert-base-finnish-uncased-v1, bert-base-dutch-cased).
We assumed '../input/bert_base_uncased/' was a path, a model identifier,
or url to a directory containing vocabulary files named ['vocab.txt'] but
couldn't find such vocabulary files at this path or url.
```

Oops, it's an error!

And why would I print an error in a book?

Because it's very important to understand this error. This error says that the code was unable to find the directory "../input/bert_base_cased". Why does this happen? We were able to train without docker, and we can see that the directory and all the files exist. It happens because docker is like a virtual machine! *It has its own filesystem and the files from your local machine are not shared to the docker container*. If you want to use a path from your local machine and want to modify it too, you would need to mount it to the docker container when running it. When we look at this folder path, we know that it is one level up in a folder called input. Let's change the *config.py* file a bit!

```python
# config.py
import os
import transformers

# fetch home directory
# in our docker container, it is
# /home/abhishek
HOME_DIR = os.path.expanduser("~")

# this is the maximum number of tokens in the sentence
MAX_LEN = 512

# batch sizes is low because model is huge!
TRAIN_BATCH_SIZE = 8
VALID_BATCH_SIZE = 4

# let's train for a maximum of 10 epochs
EPOCHS = 10

# define path to BERT model files
# Now we assume that all the data is stored inside
# /home/abhishek/data
BERT_PATH = os.path.join(HOME_DIR, "data", "bert_base_uncased")

# this is where you want to save the model
MODEL_PATH = os.path.join(HOME_DIR, "data", "model.bin")

# training file
TRAINING_FILE = os.path.join(HOME_DIR, "data", "imdb.csv")

TOKENIZER = transformers.BertTokenizer.from_pretrained(
    BERT_PATH,
    do_lower_case=True
)
```

Now, the code assumes everything to be inside a folder called *data* inside the home directory.

Note that any change in the python scripts, means that the docker container needs to be rebuilt! So, we rebuild the container and rerun the docker command but this time with a twist. However, this won't work either if we do not have the NVIDIA docker runtimes. Don't worry. It's just a docker container again, and you need to do it only once. To install the NVIDIA docker runtime, you can run the following commands in Ubuntu 18.04.

```
# taken from: https://github.com/NVIDIA/nvidia-docker/
# Add the package repositories
distribution=$(. /etc/os-release;echo $ID$VERSION_ID)
curl -s -L https://nvidia.github.io/nvidia-docker/gpgkey | sudo apt-key add -
curl -s -L https://nvidia.github.io/nvidia-docker/$distribution/nvidia-docker.list | sudo tee /etc/apt/sources.list.d/nvidia-docker.list

sudo apt-get update && sudo apt-get install -y nvidia-container-toolkit
sudo systemctl restart docker
```

Now we can build our container again and start the training process:

```
$ docker run --gpus 1 -v
/home/abhishek/workspace/approaching_almost/input/:/home/abhishek/data/ -ti bert:train python3 train.py
```

Where *–gpus 1* says that we use 1 GPU inside the docker container and -v is mounting a volume. So, we are mounting our local directory, */home/abhishek/workspace/approaching_almost/input/* to */home/abhishek/data/* in the docker container. This step is going to take a while, but when it's done, you will have *model.bin* inside the local folder.

So, with some very simple changes, you have now "dockerized" your training code. You can now take this code and train on (almost) any system you want.

The next part is "serving" this model that we have trained to the end-user. Suppose, you want to extract sentiment from a stream of incoming tweets. To do this kind of task, you must create an API that can be used to input the sentence and in turns returns an output with sentiment probabilities. The most common way of building an API using Python is with **Flask**, which is a micro web service framework.

```
# api.py
import config
import flask
```

```python
import time
import torch
import torch.nn as nn
from flask import Flask
from flask import request
from model import BERTBaseUncased

app = Flask(__name__)

# init model to None
MODEL = None

# choose device
# please note that we are using cuda device
# you can also use cpu!
DEVICE = "cuda"


def sentence_prediction(sentence):
    """
    A prediction function that takes an input sentence
    and returns the probability for it being associated
    to a positive sentiment
    """
    # fetch the tokenizer and max len of tokens from config.py
    tokenizer = config.TOKENIZER
    max_len = config.MAX_LEN

    # the processing is same as it was done for training
    review = str(sentence)
    review = " ".join(review.split())

    # encode the sentence into ids,
    # truncate to max length &
    # add CLS and SEP tokens
    inputs = tokenizer.encode_plus(
        review,
        None,
        add_special_tokens=True,
        max_length=max_len
    )

    # fetch input ids, mask & token type ids
    ids = inputs["input_ids"]
    mask = inputs["attention_mask"]
    token_type_ids = inputs["token_type_ids"]
```

```python
    # add padding if needed
    padding_length = max_len - len(ids)
    ids = ids + ([0] * padding_length)
    mask = mask + ([0] * padding_length)
    token_type_ids = token_type_ids + ([0] * padding_length)

    # convert all the inputs to torch tensors
    # we use unsqueeze(0) since we have only one sample
    # this makes the batch size 1
    ids = torch.tensor(ids, dtype=torch.long).unsqueeze(0)
    mask = torch.tensor(mask, dtype=torch.long).unsqueeze(0)
    token_type_ids = torch.tensor(token_type_ids,
                                    dtype=torch.long).unsqueeze(0)

    # send everything to device
    ids = ids.to(DEVICE, dtype=torch.long)
    token_type_ids = token_type_ids.to(DEVICE, dtype=torch.long)
    mask = mask.to(DEVICE, dtype=torch.long)

    # use the model to make predictions
    outputs = MODEL(ids=ids, mask=mask, token_type_ids=token_type_ids)
    # take sigmoid of prediction and return the output
    outputs = torch.sigmoid(outputs).cpu().detach().numpy()
    return outputs[0][0]


@app.route("/predict", methods=["GET"])
def predict():
    # this is our endpoint!
    # this endpoint can be accessed by http://HOST:PORT/predict
    # the endpoint needs sa sentence and can only use GET
    # POST request is not allowed
    sentence = request.args.get("sentence")

    # keep track of time
    start_time = time.time()

    # make prediction
    positive_prediction = sentence_prediction(sentence)

    # negative = 1 - positive
    negative_prediction = 1 - positive_prediction

    # create return dictionary
    response = {}
    response["response"] = {
        "positive": str(positive_prediction),
```

```
        "negative": str(negative_prediction),
        "sentence": str(sentence),
        "time_taken": str(time.time() - start_time),
    }
    # we use jsonify from flask for dictionaries
    return flask.jsonify(response)

if __name__ == "__main__":
    # init the model
    MODEL = BERTBaseUncased()

    # load the dictionary
    MODEL.load_state_dict(torch.load(
        config.MODEL_PATH, map_location=torch.device(DEVICE)
    ))

    # send model to device
    MODEL.to(DEVICE)

    # put model in eval mode
    MODEL.eval()

    # start the application
    # 0.0.0.0 means that this endpoint can be
    # accessed from all computers in a network
    app.run(host="0.0.0.0")
```

And you start the API by running the command "*python api.py*". The API will start on localhost on port 5000.

A sample **cURL request** and its response is shown as follows.

```
❯ curl
$'http://192.168.86.48:5000/predict?sentence=this%20is%20the%20best%20boo
k%20ever'

{"response":{"negative":"0.0032927393913269043","positive":"0.99670726","
sentence":"this is the best book
ever","time_taken":"0.029126882553100586"}}
```

As you can see that we got a high probability for positive sentiment for the provided input sentence. You can also access the results by visiting *http://127.0.0.1:5000/predict?sentence=this%20book%20is%20too%20complicated%20for%20me* in your favourite browser. This will return a JSON again.

```
{
    response: {
        negative: "0.8646619468927383",
        positive: "0.13533805",
        sentence: "this book is too complicated for me",
        time_taken: "0.03852701187133789"
        }
}
```

Now, we have created a simple API that we can use to serve a small number of users. Why small? Because this API will serve only one request at a time. Let's use CPU and make it work for many parallel requests using **gunicorn** which is a python WSGI HTTP server for UNIX. Gunicorn can create multiple processes for the API, and thus, we can serve many customers at once. You can install gunicorn by using "*pip install gunicorn*".

To convert the code compatible with gunicorn, we need to remove init main and move everything out of it to the global scope. Also, we are now using CPU instead of the GPU. See the modified code as follows.

```
# api.py
import config
import flask
import time
import torch
import torch.nn as nn
from flask import Flask
from flask import request
from model import BERTBaseUncased

app = Flask(__name__)

# now we use cpu!
DEVICE = "cpu"

# init the model
```

```python
MODEL = BERTBaseUncased()

# load the dictionary
MODEL.load_state_dict(torch.load(
    config.MODEL_PATH, map_location=torch.device(DEVICE)
    ))

# send model to device
MODEL.to(DEVICE)

# put model in eval mode
MODEL.eval()


def sentence_prediction(sentence):
    """
    A prediction function that takes an input sentence
    and returns the probability for it being associated
    to a positive sentiment
    """
    .
    .
    .
    return outputs[0][0]


@app.route("/predict", methods=["GET"])
def predict():
    # this is our endpoint!
    .
    .
    .
    return flask.jsonify(response)
```

And we run this API using the following command.

```
$ gunicorn api:app --bind 0.0.0.0:5000 --workers 4
```

This means we are running our flask *app* with 4 workers on a provided IP address and port. Since there are 4 workers, we are now serving 4 simultaneous requests. Please note that now our endpoint uses CPU and thus, it does not need a GPU machine and can run on any standard server/VM. Still, we have one problem, we have done everything in our local machine, so we must dockerize it. Take a look at the following uncommented Dockerfile which can be used to deploy this API.

Notice the difference between the old Dockerfile for training and this one. There are not many differences.

```
# CPU Dockerfile
FROM ubuntu:18.04

RUN apt-get update && apt-get install -y \
    git \
    curl \
    ca-certificates \
    python3 \
    python3-pip \
    sudo \
    && rm -rf /var/lib/apt/lists/*

RUN useradd -m abhishek

RUN chown -R abhishek:abhishek /home/abhishek/

COPY --chown=abhishek *.* /home/abhishek/app/

USER abhishek
RUN mkdir /home/abhishek/data/

RUN cd /home/abhishek/app/ && pip3 install -r requirements.txt
RUN pip3 install mkl

WORKDIR /home/abhishek/app
```

Let's build a new docker container.

```
$ docker build -f Dockerfile -t bert:api .
```

When the docker container is built, we can now run the API directly by using the following command.

```
$ docker run -p 5000:5000 -v
/home/abhishek/workspace/approaching_almost/input/:/home/abhishek/data/ -
ti bert:api /home/abhishek/.local/bin/gunicorn api:app --bind
0.0.0.0:5000 --workers 4
```

Please note that we expose port 5000 from the container to 5000 outside the container. This can also be done in a nice way if you use docker-compose. Docker compose is a tool that can allow you to run different services from different or the same containers at the same time. You can install docker-compose using "*pip install docker-compose*" and then run "*docker-compose up*" after building the container. To use docker-compose, you need a docker-compose.yml file.

```
# docker-compose.yml
# specify a version of the compose
version: '3.7'

# you can add multiple services
services:
  # specify service name. we call our service: api
  api:
    # specify image name
    image: bert:api
    # the command that you would like to run inside the container
    command: /home/abhishek/.local/bin/gunicorn api:app --bind 0.0.0.0:5000 --workers 4
    # mount the volume
    volumes:
      -
/home/abhishek/workspace/approaching_almost/input/:/home/abhishek/data/
    # this ensures that our ports from container will be
    # exposed as it is
    network_mode: host
```

Now you can rerun the API just by using the command mentioned above, and it will work the same way as before. Congratulations! Now you have managed to dockerized the prediction API too, and it is ready for deployment anywhere you want. In this chapter, we learned docker, building APIs using flask, serving API using **gunicorn and docker and docker-compose**. There is a lot more to docker than we have seen here, but this should give you a start. Rest can be learned as you progress. We have also skipped on many tools like kubernetes, bean-stalk, sagemaker, heroku and many others that people use these days for deploying models in production. "What am I going to write? Click on modify docker container in figure X"? It's not feasible and advisable to describe these in a book, so I will be using a different medium complimenting this part of the book. Remember that once you have dockerized your application, deploying using any of these technologies/platforms is a piece of cake. Always remember to make your code and model usable and well-documented for others so that anyone can use what you have developed without asking you several times. This will save you time, and it will also save their time. Good, open-source, re-usable code also looks good in your portfolio. ☺

Notes

Notes

Notes

Printed in Great Britain
by Amazon